*Sometimes play can disrupt how people see the world.*

—Jackson Fackler at 8 years old

*A historically panoramic examination of human playfulness as a naturally healthy and politically subversive force.…Siegel's thesis is philosophically provocative and original.…combines intellectual rigor with a bracing optimism—he believes the history of disruptive playfulness provides empirical reasons to believe in its sociopolitical power.*

—*Kirkus Reviews*

*Somebody once said, "The beginnings of wisdom is a firm grasp of the obvious." That's what came to mind as I learned about Shepherd Siegel's* Disruptive Play, *an in-depth look at the power of play. Or maybe this work should be viewed, not as an historical review, but more as a DIY on play as an antidote to domination. Check it out, you might just see the forest.*

—Daniel Barrett,
Co-Creator and founder of *Navigation 101*,
a high school guidance and counseling program

*Shepherd Siegel is looking at play in a very serious way. This book may tell us more about how to break down limitations and open creativity than all the gobbledygook self-help tomes of the past decade.*

—Tom Long,
*The Detroit News*

*From the anti-war art of dada to the wit, wisdom and shenanigans of Lisa and Bart Simpson, Dr. Siegel reminds us that the play of art is always a play against power. This book is a timely and irresistible story about what play is and why artistically, politically and culturally, we should play more.*

—Dr. Michael Vicente Perez,
Assistant Professor of Anthropology,
*The University of Memphis*

*I was in a better mood after I finished reading about the possibilities of play. I remembered there was a way to approach life that was based around joy and pleasure, rather than fear and drudgery. And that's a good thing!*

—Alex Marshall,
author of *How Cities Work,*
*The Surprising Design of Market Economies*
and *Beneath the Metropolis;*
columnist for *Governing* magazine

# DISRUPTIVE
# PLAY

## THE TRICKSTER IN POLITICS AND CULTURE

SHEPHERD SIEGEL, PhD

WAKDJUNKAGA PRESS ✵ SEATTLE

Printed in the United States of America

First Printing, 2018

ISBN 978-1-7322948-4-4

Wakdjunkaga Press
2316 – 41ˢᵗ Ave SW
Seattle, WA 98116-2060

Cover by Pete Garceau.
Copyediting by Kathy Burge.
Interior Book Design by Ampersand Book Interiors.
Photo by Laura Totten.

WWW.SHEPHERDSIEGEL.COM

Print: $21.95
Ebook: $9.99

*For the Rroses and The Bugs*

# Acknowledgements

THERE IS A FEAST, a banquet of people to thank, all apologies now for the ones I may have left out! *Disruptive Play* is infused with the wisdom and joy shared by so many friends. So thank you for supporting me, challenging me, turning me on to new sources, and digging the project. First of all, of all people, Ruth Weinstein, resonant friend, bountiful supporter, and dutiful reader of the entire manuscript...in order! And Carla Janes-Heneghan, the same. The stalwart West Seattle Writers Group: Paul, Paula, Linda, Lynn, Pam, Ann, Art. The professionals: Shepherdess Beth Jusino, Chris Matthias, Kathy Burge, Pete Garceau, Laura Totten, Colleen Sheehan, Katie Mulligan. The Play Scholars, Tony Perone and Thomas Henricks and all the folks at The Association for the Study of Play. Roger Shattuck. Brian Garrett. Marian Donly, Alison Reilly, Laurie Garrett, Dan Barrett, Marla Barrett, Alex Marshall, Alan Armstrong, Sandi Armstrong, Victoria McGilvray, Atticus George-Andrijeski, Bill Scheinman, Carla Bradshaw, Dan Eisenberg, Todd Snider, Dan Beederman, Ron Pomerantz, Jane Weed-Pomerantz, Dean Smith, Dina Cherin, Ed Dennis, Erik Sackstein, Hannah Chavez, Colby Cronn, Bob Huven, Kirsten McCory, Kim Reed, Jane Chadsey, Janice Roach, Matt Siegel, Deborah Caul, Nathan Siegel, Adah Siegel, Syvia Siegel, Albert B.

Siegel, Jared Mitchell, Jeremy Carey, Kate Mageau, Elizabeth Pew, Kevin Halloran, Kirsten Halloran, Laurie Garrett, Linda Jurca, Mark Lindquist, Michael Perez, Joaquin Perez, Shan-e-Zahra Alavi, Mike Arenson, Fatima Bahloul, Stan Barnes, Natalie Siegel, Natalie Zilverberg, Paul 'Pazzo' Mehling, Tom Long, Tammy Massey-Long, Phil Moser, Ruth Moser, Shira Firestone, Tom Edminster, Patrick Sand, Tracy Record, John Littel, ....and the rest o' ya's.

# Disruptive Play:
## THE TRICKSTER IN POLITICS AND CULTURE

# Contents

# The Difference between Playing and Playing Games

# Play as Politics . . .
# It's Not a Game

*Play is the exultation of the possible.*

*Martin Buber*

*Twickster! You're the wabbit!*

*Elmer Fudd*

I REMEMBER the first time I saw *American Beauty*.[1] In this Sam Mendes film, Ricky Fitts is the kid who compulsively videotapes everything around him and invites the teenage girl next door into his antiseptic neat white electric-light teenage suburban bedroom. He asks her if she would like to see "the most beautiful thing I've ever filmed." She agrees. In his minutes-long clip, wind plays with a plastic shopping bag, tossing it back and forth on the sidewalk, always staying in range of the camera. "It's just minutes away from snowing, and there's this electricity in the air," he says. "This bag was just dancing with me, like a little kid begging me to play with it."

He talks about the beauty of it, that the wind is able to catch this bag and show its nature as it plays with the flimsy, filmy piece of discarded plastic. I reacted along with the girl—this somewhat scary, voyeuristic weirdo is perhaps only silly. But as I viewed the video, I

---

[1] *American Beauty*, dir. Sam Mendes (Los Angeles, CA: Paramount Pictures, 1999), film.

found myself taken with it. It is beautiful how the wind plays with the bag. And I was taken with him, fascinated. I discovered that what once was quirky now connects. That I was more like him than I realized. His strangeness came home to me; I saw that it was a sensitive response to the universe. Fitts then describes himself as someone who finds unbearable beauty in the world, more than he can possibly take.

Play is just such an unbearably beautiful energy. Play is that force, beyond culture, found in all life forms, that gives rise to creation. Even the weather, a lingering gust of wind traced by a plastic bag, embodies the elemental form of play. Play can be found in the simplest of life forms, working its way up the evolutionary ladder, from the wind and the elements, to the smallest microorganisms, through reptiles, birds, and mammals, until it finds the baby human, the highest form of life that plays without effort.

Play embraces irrationality—patterns beyond our normal comprehension. But play is problematic as an activity introduced during the struggle to survive, to be healthy, and to create a just and environmentally friendly society. It seems to get in the way of these important tasks.

Humans strive mightily towards progress and measure that progress not by whether we play but by how well we establish order and predictability. And my proposition is that playfulness is a disorderly and unpredictable core activity, and necessary to spiritual and societal growth. As we play, we enter into the larger patterns of the universe. What could be more natural? Yet we insist on forcing a rational world inimical to play onto a universe repeatedly shown to be irrational.

One of the world's most playful artists, Marcel Duchamp, once said that "There is absolutely no chance for a word ever to express anything. As soon as we start putting our thoughts into words and sentences, everything goes wrong.[2]

Play is such a difficult subject to freeze in prose, and I've been haunted by the idea that this narrative will accomplish the oppo-

---

[2] Calvin Tomkins, *Duchamp, A Biography* (New York: Owl, 1997), 65.

site of its intention. By attempting to put play, an irrational activity, into the rational fictions of words, I fear that naming this magic will dispel it. But I hope for the opposite, to invoke more, better, truer play, to help life live humans.

---

Webster couldn't get to it easily; the dictionary has over forty definitions for *play*. So what do I mean by play?

*Original play* is what happens when one or more beings get together to have fun and experience belonging and acceptance. Nobody gets hurt. All animals, including humans, do it, but humans are best at it during the first few years of life.

You can see it in the pretend-fighting of dogs, where the dance of "I am going to bite you" is observed and then suspended immediately before any harm is possible. You can see it in dolphins,[3] that "it has been observed by many scientists that [dolphins] are pranksters, that they have a sense of humor... Play seems to be their default state."[4]

You can see it in infants and toddlers. If you get down on the ground with a child under the age of four and roll around without clutching, tickling or hitting, you can have great fun without it ever becoming an actual game or without any moral lessons attached to the cavorting. After just a few minutes, you will emerge from the experience body and soul refreshed.

Original players know that they are playing and observe the rules of an imagined reality, though those rules are flexible and can be changed by mutual agreement. Players are spontaneously creative, and they play, irrationally, with no internal moral objective and no external judgment. They have no goals, winners, losers, or products. Their play has meaning but not purpose. The energy of play is ancient and predates culture but doesn't rule it.

---

[3] Marta Zaraska, "The Play's the Thing," *Discover*, June 2017, 55-59.

[4] Susan Casey, "People and Dolphins: It's a Mutual Fascination" (speech, Seattle Public Central Library, Seattle, WA, August 17, 2015).

And all life forms play, from amoebas to kangaroos. The trouble starts with the big-shot life form, humans. Humans play. Up until about age three, we engage in *original play*.

Then along comes parents. Parents have often stopped playing, repeating a pattern learned from their parents. That is, when kids are about three or four, parents make a fateful decision: they get into their kids' business by trying to teach them lessons when the kids simply want to play. They encourage them to use their play to pretend that they are grownups. They have the kids start playing games and sports that have winners and losers. Practice and skills and moral lessons are introduced into play, which then becomes games with rules, and then games with histories, so that they can keep score and resume play where they left off. So that one kid could compete better than another, so that there can be rankings. And we end up with something quite different from original play. We end up with *cultural play*, which is in many ways original play's opposite.

Society needs the things that arise from cultural play: people with skills and competence and morals and, God save us, purpose. But cultural play, based upon accumulated skills, ranking, contest, etc., has gotten all out of proportion. Not too long ago, two "hockey fathers" got in a fight over their sons' playing, and one killed the other—over a game! Sadly, we are afflicting many of our young children with obsessive achievement goals in cultural play arenas, goals that are stifling opportunities to experience the world of meaning—without purpose, winning, or losing—that original play brings.

Basically, you leave original play when you enter contest.

Now while the connection between most adults and original play is frayed, it is nonetheless there, and it is renewable. The closest many adults come is through their explorations of what Diane Ackerman calls *deep play*.[5] This is the play that adult humans do in their own adult human way. This is that "sharpening the saw" type stuff, it's the

---

[5] Diane Ackerman, *Deep Play* (New York: Random House, 1999).

creative function expressed, it is adults being in the "flow" experience. Like hiking and gardening and painting and flying planes and creating great food. It's cool, but it is usually cultivated solo, alone.

*Disruptive Play: The Trickster in Politics and Culture* is a collection of stories, ideas, and profiles about players and tricksters, bringers of visions for a society that plays more and fights less. If we take our cue from these characters, we'll find that the mature adult can also connect with play and bring more joy, awareness, and fun into the intimidating reality we call civilized life. But be warned, to introduce play into the not-play arenas that dominate our worlds of politics and commerce is a dangerous game, and as these stories will show, the path to the Play Society is a bloody one.

---

I can tell you how play became such an important inspiration to me. Like all children, I was less aware of the world at large. My world was home, grandma's, my friends' homes, my neighborhood playground—protected environments. By adolescence, life's most idealistic stage, I became old enough to be aware of a world of multiple communities, cultures, races, beliefs, values, and so forth, yet cynicism and fear had not yet cut down my curiosity and optimism.

Before high school there is too little worldly awareness to connect the dots and see play as the bringer of social possibility; after, too much of a demanding world intimidates the idea. So while in that pivotal high school moment, I decided that I wanted to be a high school teacher. This sprang from a desire to help students make the most of the joys of that age—adolescence—and to keep alive the possibilities of that age—the Sixties.

High school in the Bay Area in the late Sixties was a time of breathtaking possibility, an electrifying mix of liberation politics, psychedelic drugs, rock and roll, new spiritual movements, an artistic renaissance, and a militant civil rights movement. All of a sudden, the natural tendency of rebellious teens to want to play and fight the power and fight the not-play world had huge peer support and the support of a national and international movement. The normal abnormalities of adolescence became less a phase and more a revolutionary ethos, one that validated the urges to play hard and constantly. So we reveled in the joyous blasts of the time, and we jettisoned the nuclear family for the Woodstock Nation. We were a generation of fearless and wildly idealistic youths whose chaotic midadolescence coincided with an idealistic, historic moment.

Our ragtag high school troupe would make a daily practice of pranks, everything from playing Jimi Hendrix over the school's public-address system to completely shutting the school down when we demonstrated. We overthrew student government, declaring that the high school would be governed through a consensus, town hall approach. We played around . . . a lot.

It didn't feel so much like a decision as it did an organic development . . . to become not necessarily pacifists but antiwar,[6] and to prankishly engage all aspects of the establishment that we associated with the Vietnam War. And something we learned is that one of the most powerful weapons against the blood and stupidity of war is the refusal to take its rationales seriously, to be playful in spite of war's tragedies. Because you cannot fight and play at the same time. And thus, the idea of approaching life as a place for play made its indelible mark.

## Invitations to Play

So can you come out and play? That is the earthshaking challenge.

This amazing energy that thrives among animals and infants, what happens to it when culture and adulthood get ahold of it? What if adults could play and bring that creative, ebullient energy into the

---

[6] The very word *antiwar* suggests conflict, the conflict to stop conflict.

everyday world? What might our society look like? What if that same energy displayed by the wind, by romping dolphins, lion cubs, and butterflies were allowed to claim a bigger place and a greater moment in our lives?

While play is universal across life forms and can enrich and fulfill our lives, it is controversial to consider an expansion of play's role. The normal functioning of our society depends upon separating play from the so-called real world. Imagine the harsh consequences of presenting a case to the Supreme Court dressed as a clown. Or throwing a pie at the richest man in the world. Or pretending to accidentally kill an elderly woman in a wheelchair while she's accepting a humanitarian award (yes, Sacha Baron Cohen really did this).

We haven't yet found the way to release those life-giving waters for fear of the chaos they might create. History is dotted with intermittent attempts: tricksters and pranksters with the nerve and the boldness to be silly in a way that pulls down the pants of the social order and rips at its fabric just to see what might emerge. For example, in the first of four sections, "The Difference Between Playing and Playing Games," I share an overview of trickster gods like Loki, Èṣù-Elegba, and Raven; of America's quintessential trickster, Bugs Bunny; and of seventeenth-century European fairy tales. I offer a first taste of play's assault on the seriousness of society, and how the prevailing order dealt with such mischief-makers. But not all play is the play of tricksters. I also share a story of two young men with developmental disabilities, Arturo and Remus, for whom play has a meaning that overshadows the meaningfulness of work, and they teach us that expressions of playfulness can pop up almost anywhere.

In *Magical Child,* Joseph Chilton Pearce says that people with intellectual disabilities better retain special inborn talents like ESP, that the disability protects them from acculturation that atrophies those faculties. He quotes Jean Piaget:

[For the child] play cannot be opposed to reality, because in both cases belief is arbitrary and pretty much destitute of logical reasons. Play is a reality which the child is disposed to believe in when by himself, just as reality is a game at which he is willing to play with the adult and anyone else who believes in it. . . . Thus we have to say of the child's play that it constitutes an autonomous reality, but with the understanding that the "true" reality to which it is opposed is considerably less "true" for the child than for us.[7]

## All The Stories Combine and Melt into a Unifying Dream

The idea of childhood is a relatively new one. As recently as two hundred years ago, children were thought of as "little adults." Many died quite young, and parents tended to look to their children as their future providers right from the very start; they were a nuisance to be indulged in until such time.[8]

Raising a child with the conscious intention to instead enhance their lives—conceived by Jean-Jacques Rousseau[9] in the eighteenth century but not widely practiced until the early twentieth—begat a new awareness and a trend towards understanding, protecting, and nurturing the child state of play. The baby boomer children were that trend's greatest beneficiaries. Thus, countercultural politics in the Sixties embraced an unprecedented sense of play as integral to political, spiritual, and human progress.

Liberation politics, for all its intellectual markings, is basically a reach back to recapture some of that innocence of the child's play and introduce it into the political arena. The hippie and civil rights ethos attempted to sustain connection to nature's absence of prejudice and develop a utopian view from that perspective. As naïve as that sounds, this Rousseau's sense of justice, of idealized play and naturalism, has informed key environmental, human rights, health,

---

[7] Joseph Chilton Pearce, *Magical Child* (New York: Plume, 1977), 131, 144.

[8] Lloyd deMause, ed., *The History of Childhood* (London: Jason Aronson, 1995).

[9] Jean-Jacques Rousseau, *Emile or On Education*, trans. Allan Bloom (New York: Basic Books 1979).

and other movements and legal decisions since. It is alive and well in Greenpeace, Black Lives Matter, Occupy, the ACLU, and Anonymous, and among some entrepreneurial "disrupters."

What do we most need to say about nature, if play is all about a direct connection to it? In his book *Flow*, Mihaly Csikszentmihalyi talks about the indifference of a chaotic universe and the distance between its patterns and ours. He describes how it appears so hostile to us, that its purpose is not one of providing happiness to humans:

> It is not that that universe is random in an abstract mathematical sense. The motions of the stars, the transformations of energy that occur in it might be predicted and explained well enough. But natural processes do not take human desires into account. They are deaf and blind to our needs, and thus they are random in contrast with the order we attempt to establish through our goals.[10]

Play means being open to randomness and irrationality—patterns beyond our normal comprehension. To the extent that safe environments can be obtained, humans can experiment with longer and greater intervals of playing. Play complements the flow of the universe, chaotic and unpredictable as it seems. Building bridges between our rational selves and nature's irrationality has characterized much human endeavor.

Béla Bartók's approach to composition provides an apt metaphor. He composed music that connects to patterns taken from nature. The Fibonacci series, a mathematical sequence obtained when adding the previous number to derive the following one (1, 2, 3, 5, 8, 13, 21, 34, etc.), is found in spiral growth patterns like cells, conch shells, and galaxies. Bartók replicated this series by expanding musical themes and phrases in the same ratios, two measures followed by three, five, eight, and so forth.[11] By deliberately using the same patterns found in nature, the music would connect to those forces and patterns and,

---

[10] Mihaly Csikszentmihalyi, *Flow* (New York: Harper Perennial, 1991), 8-14.

[11] Béla Bartók, *Music for Strings, Percussion and Celesta* (1937).

in turn, connect the listener. And this musical example provides a microcosm of a three-part cycle thousands of years in the making.[12]

The first part is one of being in a state that is connected to the universe at large but is nevertheless highly dangerous and threatening. We are victims running from random forces—the prehistory of the cave dwellers and hunters who struggled against harsh climates and competed with feline, canine, and other carnivorous predators.

Secondly, we developed the capacity to create safety and, subsequently, society and lofty goals. But the rush to accumulate security and wealth embraced a rationality that served us well in learning how to dominate the planet, yet compromised and suppressed our spiritual connection to the environment and the universe. This second phase is history, where people, like in our example from Bartók, discover patterns and adapt to them.

The third phase creates expanding opportunities to surrender rationality and reconnect with the universe, but from a place of safety from the elements, poverty, conflict, and ill health and done through the unfettered engagement of play and flow—the imminent next phase of evolution that this book augurs.[13] The effect Bartók seeks to impart through his compositions.

Like Bartók's composition, *flow* can be defined as a microcosmic completion of this entire cycle, wherein one travels to an irrational unconscious where an adverse situation or challenge is successfully met. And here the applications of the second phase—the disciplined development of a skill through rational means—are ultimately transcended by a determination to achieve the third: reconnecting to the universe from a position of greater consciousness, safety, and presence. One's preoccupation with the mastery of a skill is ultimately subsumed to the feelings of exultation and unself-consciousness as one attains flow. Examples range from climbing a mountain to

---

[12] Csikszentmihalyi, *Flow*, 8-14.

[13] Barring environmental catastrophes that would hurl us back to the first one.

playing the violin to performing a difficult surgery. And play plays a role in this cycle.

Such progress creates opportunities for play to be let out of the box of prevailing rational orderliness and to work its magic.

This discussion of play requires an assumption that cannot be casually made, nor can its enormity be ignored. It would be irresponsible to gloss over the fact that a great many people still struggle to survive, and we are still some distance from universal safety and lack of want. For some, the persistent struggle is yet connected to playfulness in the face of adversity. Many others suffer material lack, the ravages of war, and medical tragedy in a cold and lonely world. And many survive at a subsistence level. It almost goes without saying that humanity has yet to create any kind of lasting peace.

The hopefulness of this book rests on the premise that, despite the hardships that continue for so many in this world, our political and economic systems could become functional to the point where peace and environmental balance are obtained, and the basic material needs of food, clothing, shelter, and health care are universally available. There is evidence both to support and challenge this supposition, and serious debate in other forums. But in the event that the material future of humanity is a positive one, we will need this book.

The chief beneficiaries of material comfort—the wealthy and middle class—do not show strong enough signs of being able to put that comfort to its greatest possible use: spiritual advancement. Play is the thing that leads all of us to a coexistence rich in connection and beyond material and health needs. Once those needs have been met, the greatest remaining problem will be one of establishing and maintaining societies of trust. Play, as we shall see, absolutely requires trust in order to thrive, even to exist. Herbert Marcuse saw the dangers of an individualism that corrodes trust and the bonds that hold families and communities together. Marcuse saw the liberating potential of a society that breaks through and past the struggles of meeting material need:

> The technological processes of mechanization and standardization might release individual energy into a yet uncharted realm of freedom beyond necessity. The very structure of human existence would be altered; the individual would be liberated from the work world's imposing upon him alien needs and alien possibilities. The individual would be free to exert autonomy over a life that would be his own. If the productive apparatus could be organized and directed toward the satisfaction of the vital needs, its control might well be centralized; such control would not prevent individual autonomy, but render it possible.[14]

What would the Play Society look like? This is the hardest question to answer. The rapid consolidation of capital and accompanying income disparities, coupled with the onslaught of technological inventions, make it almost impossible to comment or predict. Will technology liberate or enslave us? The evidence thus far indicates that, under current arrangements, trust, community, and human connection—the building of a virtuous and genuinely happy, loving society—are not on the horizon. We are in an age of grossly uneven prosperity, too many put their personal wealth ahead of helping others. It will take a conscious, deliberate, and sustained effort to ensure that a materially affluent future is also one that nurtures humanity and life. Answering the question—Why do all living things except adult humans play?—initiates that quest. The stories that follow of people who play offer an answer. But here is the quick reply: because to play in public is a dangerous political act.

## Original and Cultural Play

Once we understand the nature of play, we can enter into an investigation of what play becomes as the child grows out of infancy. My intention is to trace play's natural and cultural development to the

---

[14] Herbert Marcuse, *One-Dimensional Man: Studies in the Ideology of Advanced Industrial Society* (Boston: Beacon Press, 1964), 2.

point where the two diverge and to highlight examples that suggest the possibilities of a Play Society.

One defining feature of original play is that it creates a true sense of belonging and love among people.[15] Cultural play, paradoxical and based upon contest, ranking, and ego-centeredness, creates the separation between people and "un-belonging."[16] A single individual is a combination of original play and cultural play, as are social groups, communities, nations, and cultures. Cultural play, contest, is the basis of our adult society and its institutions—government, business, family, and custom—and it dominates Americans' lives to the point where many children and adults are uncomfortable in the noncompetitive setting.[17]

There is perhaps no more heartfelt account of the truth and bankruptcy of a life so dominated by contest and competition, by cultural play, than Francis Coppola's *Godfather* trilogy. A biography of American success, of Michael Corleone's rise to power leading a Mafia family, *The Godfather* is a parable of escalating competition. In it, Corleone watches helplessly as the core joys of his life evaporate. Corleone's role as *don* demands that he compete and, like a prize fighter, remain undefeated. The demands of such deadly competition ruin the intimacy of his marriage. To keep his web of power secure, he must kill his own brother—and kill again and again to protect his gains. The responsibility of overseeing, growing, and securing power robs Corleone—robs all of us—of the most inexpensive gift of all, the simple enjoyment of life. Many of us become our own Michael Corleone; his Mafia family was just a more spectacular version of

---

[15] O. Fred Donaldson, *Playing by Heart: The Vision and Practice of Belonging* (Nevada City, CA: Touch the Future, 1993), 129-133.

[16] Ironically, our society's conventional means of giving citizens a sense of belonging is work, sometimes considered opposite of play. Our work environments are, in fact, organized around "not-play" behaviors, though a person's "life work" frequently embraces play behaviors.

[17] Barbara Mahany, "Jam-packed calendars: Are children doing too much too soon?" *Chicago Tribune*, September 17, 1999; Andrew Ferguson, "Inside the Crazy Culture of Kids Sports," *Time Magazine*, July 12, 1999, 50-59.

the work ethic, as mutated into capitalist competition, run amok. Further testament appears in *The Big Short*, another film about the bankruptcy of financial success:

> So let me be honest. Making money is not like I thought it would be. This business kills the part of life that is essential. The part that has nothing to do with business. For the past two years, my insides have felt like they're eating themselves. All the people I respected won't talk to me anymore except through lawyers.[18]

## Disruptive Play

*Disruptive Play: The Trickster in Politics and Culture* recounts past efforts and tees up a future that rebalances cultural and original play. Its insights can be applied to an individual, group, or vision of a society where playing achieves greater value and acceptance. And the lantern held high to illuminate such a transformation is *disruptive play*.

The introduction of play disrupts the normal functioning of society. You cannot play and not play at the same time. People sent to the margins—because of their class, race, gender, sexual orientation, disability, eccentricities, or rebel spirit—are the ones freed to explore playfulness. Postindustrial society looks over its shoulder to the underclass, to street-level artists and bohemians, to those deep in the throes of social or environmental adversity for artistic inspiration and the path to a spiritual connection. Their stories outline a repertoire of playfulness moves that challenge a not-play world.

The second section of the book, "The Sin of Sins," delves into the first of two modern historic eras when adults made play the thing and were audacious and disruptive about it. As the twentieth century dawned, the art scene in Paris exploded and filled the world with the playfulness of the child as it posited café society. Taking advantage of the freer latitude created by the Impressionists, the insubordinate ethos of dada—an international movement erupting in Zurich, Berlin,

---

[18] *The Big Short*, dir. Adam McKay (Los Angeles, CA: Paramount Pictures, 2015), film. Dialogue quoted was spoken by Christian Bale's character, Dr. Michael Burry.

New York, Hanover, Cologne, Barcelona, and Paris—challenged the sense and seriousness of art, existence, and the madness of war. For one brief moment, art broke free of commerce. Its energies were wholly immersed in its unself-conscious impact on society, making its "artness" secondary to its political impact, but being anti-ideological, i.e., being play, it was not propaganda.

The most common device used by such disruptive players is the prank, an opening in the mundane, a looking-glass doorway that utilizes the absurd to make a point and change a mind. Pranks are miniature acts of public theater or performance art. With one gesture, a prankster can demonstrate action's ability to convey an idea and change the world.

Less than forty years later, the Beats had their moment and made it their business to live playfully...and made a lasting statement. They represented the next test: what if we did more than talk about it and constellated our lives around play instead of work and career. Their playfulness was sheltered and obscured by the shade of cool, but underneath was the vulnerability of play. And the Beats were midwife to a hippie generation unafraid to declare utopian ideals, question all seriousness, and be playful. The third section, "History Doesn't Repeat Itself, But It Does Rhyme," recounts this era, from the Beats to Abbie Hoffman, from psychedelic rock to Andy Kaufman. It was play's most famous moment.[19]

Play is like an elusive sprite dancing around the edges of Western history. It's nearly impossible to pin down or trace as a cultural movement. And while play is all around us and allotted more credence today than a court jester, playfulness is still marginalized, more the seasoning than the essence of twenty-first-century mainstream culture.

Yet out of the jumble that was the Sixties emerged a critical case example, a glimpse of utopian possibility. That effort played itself out

---

[19] In 1967, we saw the ultimate prank, when thousands of demonstrators ringed the Pentagon with the intention of levitating it ten inches off the ground (*The New York Times*, October 21, 1967, 28.). Is it a coincidence that Pearce believes that one of the powers of a developing childhood allowed to connect to the earth, sustain their "earth-bond", without cultural interference is telekinesis?

within a resistant mainstream that seemed to prevail but was nonetheless deeply affected. In fact, David Brooks asserted that believers of the bohemian values of the Sixties who also prospered in the Eighties comprise the current ruling class in the United States, the bourgeois bohemians,[20] though they have been overshadowed since by technocratic quasi-hipster millennials.

Whenever and wherever it pops up, *disruptive play*—resistance to contest-based society and a public affirmation of the natural play element that pervades all life—is the inspiration for this book.

## Disruptive Play is a Revolutionary Act

And an essential one. If the Corleone family makes the case for what is wrong with a life bereft of play, then its likely counterpart is *The Simpsons,* America's everyman family that succumbs to the irresistibility of play on a weekly basis. Playfulness confounds their every effort to be serious and provides us a reflection of ourselves perhaps truer than the nightmare of Mafia power struggles. The fourth and final section, "Presently in the Past," brings us close to the present day. Subversive pranksterism, while not cohering as a movement at this time, nonetheless, has numerous champions and multifarious manifestations. From that ancient form, television, come *The Simpsons,* to a more modern form, the Internet, which brings us Anonymous.

We trace this trail of the trickster archetype from the real world to the cyber one. Yet play is, if not originally tactile, best expressed in person, and so the Yes Men, Banksy, and Burning Man offer the most visceral inspiration. In the final chapter, amorality's value is made more transparent, as is the distinction between trickster-like tactics that distract us from an agenda that, paradoxically, serves to further bind the trickster. Authentic and liberating tricksterism, whose only agenda is fun, behaves differently in a liberating environment, like the carnival. Ultimately, I propose carnival as social model, the Play

---

[20] David Brooks, *Bobos in Paradise: The New Upper Class and How They Got There* (New York: Simon & Schuster, 2000).

Society a happy future based upon a regained past. This future cannot be predicted, but there are signals.

## Why Is This Important Now? Why Here in the US?

European cultures of the eighteenth century held together through religion, tradition, monarchies, and a conservatism that assimilated historical events, providing a semblance of security and continuity. Catholicism and the Church of England did not rule nations but exerted considerable influence. In non-Western cultures, from America's indigenous peoples to African tribal societies, spiritual beliefs often determined social order.

But the philosophical foundations of the new country, the United States, removed that regulator by separating religion and state, creating a deliberate structural instability and thus more possibilities to innovate, stumble, and grow wild. And there is an American disposition—from westward expansion to Beat wanderlust, from rock and roll to the great American novel, from space exploration to mind expansion, from entrepreneurs to anticommerce artists and communitarians—to fervently explore, define, and redefine where the old weird America is and what new weird characters can be fashioned and still be called American. Does this kind of radical expression stimulate possibilities for social transformation? Does it cast a light on liberation? Or is it simply a footnote to a trudging rationality?

Individuals such as Alfred Jarry, Marcel Duchamp, Abbie Hoffman, Andy Kaufman, and Banksy burn bright trickster enlightenment, offering us worthy biographies and bountiful repertoire of play. But notions of a Play Society compel us to turn to the collective. Carnivals and parades and spontaneous communities can be forms of disruptive play that, albeit contained, offer a glimpse—challenging the traditions and political structures that stifle or deflect and drawing attention to the traditions that encourage it.[21] Some of the broadly

---

[21] Peter Stallybrass and Allon White, *The Politics and Poetics of Transgression* (Ithaca, NY: Cornell University Press, 1986), 1-44.

celebrated traditions of play, where commerce is diminished and the spirit of connection and play is heightened, hint at how to play more and where it might lead us.

Noncommercial celebration art based on Carnaval and Mardis Gras traditions, the Sabbath, the Potlatch, Burning Man, May Day and Maypole, rock and roll, and the play of young children are all viable traditions of play impatiently waiting to embrace and enrich our daily lives.

What is the potential for bringing more playfulness into the mainstream? In the concluding chapter, I will summarize the case for disruptive play and dare to predict a happy and fun future for our bumbling but lovable human race.

Welcome to this journey, the fun begins on the next page with an introduction to just a few of the tricksters and fools who have illumined history and our collective imaginations.

# ONE

# Tricksters and Fools

*Myths . . . known by the name of The Trickster . . .
belong to the oldest expressions of mankind. Few
other myths have persisted with their fundamental
content unchanged. The Trickster myth is found . . .
among the simplest aboriginal tribes and among
the complex. We encounter it among the ancient
Greeks, the Chinese, the Japanese and in the
Semitic world. Many of the Trickster's traits were
perpetuated in the figure of the mediaeval jester,
and have survived right up to the present day. . . .
In what must be regarded as its earliest and most
archaic form, as found among the North American Indians, Trickster is at one and the same time
creator and destroyer, giver and negator, he who
dupes others and who is always duped himself. He
wills nothing consciously. . . . He is constrained to
behave as he does from impulses over which he
has no control. He knows neither good nor evil yet
he is responsible for both. He possesses no values,
moral or social, is at the mercy of his passions
and appetites, yet through his actions all values
come into being. But not only he, so our myth tells
us, possesses these traits. So, likewise, do . . . the
animals, the various supernatural beings and mon-
sters, and man.*

— *Paul Radin*[1]

---

[1]  Paul Radin, *The Trickster: A Study in American Indian Mythology* (New York: Schocken, 1956),
xxiii–xxiv.

VIRTUALLY ALL FOLKLORES feature a trickster, and there are at least sixty-nine documented oral traditions.[2] A full list would be endless, and Lewis Hyde states, "If trickster is the boundary-crossing figure, then there will be some sort of representative wherever humans invent boundaries, which is to say, everywhere."[3] The status of such a character may range from The Fool who unlocks the ability to transform the social order only to renounce it to the master storyteller and powerful deity. In all cases, the disruptive nature of this character who personifies play calls the rational order of society into question and presents opportunities to transcend it. The more we learn, understand, and accept the Trickster into our collective psyche and our political reality, the more we can embrace such irrationality, the more our society can develop and grow.

In other words, Bugs Bunny. Universal and familiar Bugs Bunny is the most direct route to understanding the Trickster personality. The Trickster, like Bugs, is compulsively at play, and the rapid plot shifts, gender-bending, unresolved situations, and moral ambiguities found in Bugs Bunny cartoons and Trickster myths correspond to and define play in its most elemental form, where the ruling principle is the lack of one.

As Radin states in the opening quote and as his seminal study and retelling of the Winnebago Trickster myth reveals, the Trickster can in one episode be the master manipulator with wily schemes; in the very next, be tricked by others; and in the next, the victim of his own self-inflicted wounds. One Trickster tale may read like a fable with a morality lesson, while the next one is unmoored and adrift in the amoral sea of irrationality.

Like play, Trickster tales are without inhibition and venture as deeply into the irrational as our storytelling skills can carry us. We

---

[2] On June 16, 2016, I conducted a search within Wikipedia on the term "trickster." My results netted sixty-nine different entries referring to tricksters of different cultures.

[3] Lewis Hyde, *Trickster Makes This World* (New York: Farrar, Straus and Giroux, 1998), 356.

will later see how this Trickster personality shows up in the Western world of the nineteenth and twentieth centuries, but this chapter delves into earlier folk tales and mythologies and makes some initial comparisons to Western notions of the Trickster and Fool archetypes.

## Wakdjunkaga, The Winnebago Trickster

The Winnebago, or Ho-Chungra, tribe emerged in northwestern Kentucky in roughly 500 BC. From 500 AD and for about a thousand years, they lived in what is now Wisconsin. They are the stewards of the Wakdjunkaga Cycle, considered the oldest surviving Trickster mythology.[4] The etymology of Wakdjunkaga is unknown and does not appear in any other North American tribes. Some of Wakdjunkaga's stories do show up across the continent, and some are unique to the Winnebago. The story cycle sets the template of all trickster tales, the movement from an undifferentiated and amoral psyche to individuation, self-awareness, and the beginnings of order and values.[5]

It begins with Wakdjunkaga appearing as chief and announcing to the tribe that he is ready to go on the warpath. In the traditional way, a feast is prepared for him and his warriors. He gladly eats, and then breaks with convention and rules and slips away to have sex with a woman while others are left to wonder where he's gone and why he does not gather the tribe and get on the warpath. He is discovered, and everyone goes home, accepting yet confused. He's able to repeat this trick three more times, feasting on deer and bear along the way, frustrating the tribe a little bit more each time. Eating food is a First Pleasure. Wakdjunkaga's ravenous appetite and willingness to deceive in the interest of getting a free feast and forbidden sex is a consistent trickster characteristic, repeated in the Raven tales of the native Northwest tribes and in the Yoruba mythology of West Africa.

---

[4]  Radin, *The Trickster*, xxiii-xxiv.

[5]  Radin, 132-169.

By the fourth time, the angry and exasperated tribe still goes along with the customary feast, expecting the same prankster ending. This time, though, Trickster chief does lead many of the tribe on the warpath, but he makes such a mockery of it, flaunting yet more traditions and talking to his arrows, that eventually the rest of the tribe turns back. Wakdjunkaga is left to wander this world alone.

Wakdjunkaga's wily ways continue as he uses figures made of hay to draw a buffalo into a clearing where he is able to kill him. Such a smart guy. But since all of this killing is done with his right arm, his left arm gets jealous and attacks the right, and a brawl of self-mutilation ensues. Such a foolish guy.

He convinces his brother to loan him two of his four children, for companionship. Wakdjunkaga is given specific instructions on the care and feeding of the children, which he ignores and, in his carelessness, kills them, bringing predictable wrath and a long chase—kill the Wabbit!—where Wakdjunkaga of course escapes. So much like a cartoon.

There are more stories of Wakdjunkaga foolishness. Where he is swimming for miles, looking for the shore but unable to see it as he only looks out into the ocean, when all he has to do is look the other way and he would see the shore. Where he is infuriated by a man on another shore who continues to wave at him. No matter the ignoring, reciprocating, commanding, challenging, the pointing man refuses to change his pose; Wakdjunkaga eventually figures out that the 'man' is a tree stump with a protruding branch.

It's of some reassurance to know that fart jokes go as far back as Trickster tales, as there is one where Wakdjunkaga has captured and is roasting some ducks, but leaves his anus to guard the ducks while he sleeps. Initially, his anus is able to ward off a marauding fox with farts, but the fox eventually overcomes the defense and eats the ducks. Wakdjunkaga punishes his own anus, resulting in burning it and somehow cooking and spreading about his own intestines, which he later eats before realizing what that delicious entrée is.

Wakdjunkaga has both shape-shifting and gender-bending powers. Despite his ability to wrap himself in his extraordinarily long penis, Wakdjunkaga can also take a female form and give birth when the story calls for it or the mood suits him. Radin explains:

> Trickster himself is, not infrequently, identified with specific animals, such as raven, coyote, hare, spider, but these animals are only secondarily to be equated with concrete animals. Basically he possesses no well-defined and fixed form..... He is primarily an inchoate being of undetermined proportions, a figure foreshadowing the shape of man. In this version he possesses intestines wrapped around his body, and an equally long penis, likewise wrapped around his body with his scrotum on top of it. Yet regarding his specific features we are, significantly enough, told nothing. [6]

In this final set of tales from the cycle, Wakdjunkaga teams up with fox, jaybird, and a hetcgeniga.[7] They find a place to live together but lack enough food to prepare for an anticipated difficult winter. Their scheme is for Wakdjunkaga to take on the form of a woman. He fashions a vulva from an elk's liver and breasts from elk kidneys. Through a parody on the Winnebago mating and courtship rituals— he observes some and blasphemes others—the attractive Wakdjunkaga marries the chief's son and bears him three sons. The purpose of all this is to obtain food, which Wakdjunkaga devours on a regular basis. We then take a tangential turn to a tale of the third son, who against normal Winnebago behavior, cries and cries until he is appeased first by a piece of a cloud, then by blue sky, and finally by green leaves and roasting ears of corn.[8] The very next day, however, Wakdjunkaga's disguise is exposed, and she skedaddles with her companions.

Trickster's Cherokee version signifies an African-Native American literary tradition and bestows supreme divinity upon Br'er

---

[6] Radin, *Trickster,* xxiii-xxiv.

[7] Unknown but thought to be a nit/head louse.

[8] Raven tales of the Northwest Indians echo their own versions of this story, but on a grander scale.

Rabbit, the folk character originating in West Africa as Anansi the Spider. This Trickster character, speaking to the oppressed status of the American slave, used his cunning towards survival, outwitting his oppressor, Br'er Fox.

## Èṣù-Elegba

The Yoruba have a vast and rich culture on the West African coast, in Benin, Ghana, Togo, Ivory Coast, and Nigeria. One of their core origin stories is that of Èṣù-Elegba, or Eshu. This Trickster demigod represents a spirit of playfulness, creativity, and potentiality that lives on today in both Africa and the Americas.

In a contest of the deities before God to see who was most supreme, Eshu outwitted his competitors, by making a sacrifice the day before the contest, and was thus instructed to distinguish himself by wearing a red parrot feather on his forehead, signifying that he was not to carry burdens. As reward for this cleverness, God bestowed on Eshu the personification of *àshe*.

This central ethos, àshe, is the Yoruba word for spiritual command. àshe, the power-to-make-things-happen, the human capacity for the divine, creativity. This force to make all things happen and to multiply is highly complex, with multiple and contradictory meanings. When possessed by the spirit of àshe, a person takes on the literal form of the mask they are wearing. The mask is the conduit and expression of a pretend reality, playful but with awesome power.

àshe is characterized by generosity, the highest form of Yoruba morality. We might also understand it as embodying play, playfulness expressing generosity of spirit. Play is a form of "be here now" and acceptance of the moment. àshe is also translated as "so be it" and "may it happen." Thus, the meaning of playfulness deepens to include appreciation of the moment and also an openness to potentiality.

Eshu is the "owner-of-the-power," a royal child, a prince, and a monarch. He is the embodiment of àshe, full of contradictions, a great god who represents many myths in one being. He is both a humble maker of sacrifices and a powerful god worthy of them. While he is supremely generous, he is also a great devourer. He is depicted sucking his thumb, smoking a pipe, and in other images of flagrant orality. In one tale, his mother offered him enormous quantities of fish. After eating them, he devoured his mother as well. Then in an act of generosity, he gave his mother back to the world, along with a spreading of his presence through yangi stones and shards. This is one example of Èṣù-Elegba's power to endlessly multiply his force. And if we see the Trickster as an adult who still plays like a child, then Eshu quintessentially represents this as the "...fusion of valences that are both childlike (insatiable eating) and mature (restitution of what is right to those who sacrifice)."[9]

Avatars of Eshu always have the protuberance from his head, but the feather is sometimes represented instead as a knife or even a phallus. Eshu is often painted in red and black, red being the color of àshe, black to trick those who do not look closely enough.

Èṣù-Elegba's purposes and behaviors are as changeable as the transient nature of play. His elusive and provocative nature was threatening to Westerners, who, when he emerged in early African-American slave culture, branded him as the devil. But he is honored even today in Africa, Brazil, Cuba, New York, Miami, and parts of the southern United States.

He is frequently misunderstood, dismissed as the fool or condemned as the devil, because the imperatives of domination require clear distinction between good and evil and resist empowering a character who is, first of all, at play and, furthermore, amoral. Though one eventually sees the highest Yoruba value, generosity, in Èṣù-Elegba, he comes to us with tricks, demands, and evasion.

---

[9] Robert Farris Thompson, *Flash of the Spirit: African & Afro-American Art & Philosophy* (New York: Vintage, 1983), 27.

Eshu is complex. As a child, he was known to tell tales and lie. So when he met up with a pair of glowing eyes emanating from the shell of a coconut, no one believed him. He was left alone in the woods to die beside the strange eyes. When his death and the still shining eyes were not respected or sacrificed to, disasters and death suddenly erupted throughout the world. Divination priests went to the site of the eyes and the boy's death, selected a special stone, and brought the spirit of Eshu back, to live within the stone. Thus was Eshu ultimately honored, and from Africa to Cuba to Brazil, Eshu's spirit is worshipped in the form of laterite cone altars.[10]

Eshu is a god of opportunity and referred to as the God of the Crossroads.[11] Reimagine the common legend where Robert Johnson meets the Devil at the Crossroads, writes a song by that name, and becomes the world's greatest blues singer and guitarist. While such a legend might satisfy Western hunger for exoticism, Robert Johnson's blues are more accurately appreciated as a blessing from Eshu than as a deal with the Devil.

To the Yoruba, attention is fixed upon whether this god has received the proper sacrifices. To Westerners, Eshu represents the potentiality (threat?) of a different social order. The Trickster is always the one who gives up power—the jester, the fool, or prankster who was "only kidding." In French fairy tales, at every opportunity to assume power, the heroic Trickster seeks more modest rewards like food or comfort.

Indeed, original and disruptive play, in contrast to our culture's mammoth obsession with contest, represents a noncompetitive opting out of the power game. The disparity is between the non-Western ideal where play disintegrates power, and Western folklore and literature where play surrenders to power's status quo.

Thus, the Puritan mindset could not accept a player, a prankster, the Trickster—names that strongly infer one who is not to be taken

---

[10] Thompson, *Flash of the Spirit*, 20-21.

[11] Hyde, *Trickster Makes This World*, 108.

seriously—as one of the most powerful (yet noncompetitive) forces in the universe. Except for God, that is precisely what Eshu represents. So we have a concept of play that reigns, a precedent for the Play Society, and a tradition of play, yet it is so foreign to our conditioned range of possibilities that even when we come in contact with this West African culture, we fail to recognize it.

European imperialism and slave trade wreaked havoc on African culture, and Western ways of war, government, technology, and economics covered the African landscape with their sheath. Yet powerful aspects of African spirituality, dance, music, art, sexuality, and humor survived conquest and made a historic transition to the West, becoming a major influence on popular culture. Such influence was particularly powerful in music and gave birth to some of the greatest rhythms and music of the world: in Cuba, the US, Brazil, and throughout the Western Hemisphere. The spirit of Eshu lives on in the soul of African-American culture. And this generous and powerful Trickster informs North and South American culture.

Besides Wakdjunkaga, what other indigenous Trickster tales met the New World arrival of Europeans and Africans?

## Raven

Raven tales are just one example of folklore that, through oral tradition and tribal migrations, imparts many different variations. The exaggerations and contradictions of folktales testify to playfulness and to earlier and older cultures that embrace the irrational and the coexistence of multiple versions . . . the ephemeral nature of folktales is itself a form of play.

Northwest Raven folklore comes from tribes that lived in what is now Oregon, Washington, and British Columbia, and extending to Siberia, Manitoba, and northern California. In fact, Raven shows up all over the world. Sometimes the Raven is the one who tricks, and sometimes Raven is the tricked fool. North American tribes also tell stories of Coyote, Blue Jay, Old Man, and Hare as Tricksters.

Raven has a voracious appetite and doles out rewards and punishments, but not with any system of morality to which our Western sensibilities are accustomed. In true Trickster fashion, the Raven can change appearance or gender, impregnate, take the form of a child, exert power, but also be harmed by the power of others.

A major Raven tale takes place long ago when the world was dark. There is an uncle/grandfather who is the keeper of the sun, moon, and stars. Raven gains entry into his lodge by becoming a speck of dirt; he impregnates the daughter when she drinks him in water, and then Raven is born as an incessantly crying infant. This is Raven's original trick.

The infant is appeased only with escalating treasures. First, he cries and is given the sack that holds the stars, which he releases through the lodge's smoke hole and into the skies. Then he uses the same routine to trick grandfather into giving him the sack with the moon, which he also releases and gives to the world. Grandfather sighs with regret but is all-loving of his grandchild. Raven baby resumes his insistent crying, this time more demanding and annoying than ever. Finally, and with great reluctance, grandfather appeases the crying baby with the sack that holds the sun. At this point, Raven shifts from infant back to his white Raven shape, takes the sun into his beak, and escapes through the smoke hole himself, releasing the sun into the world. And it is the smoke hole that turns the white Raven black. Grandfather and his family have been tricked!

This is the Tlingit tribe's version of The Theft of the Sun. There are many variations.

From all over the world come tales of a deluge that covers the earth, and tales of earth-divers who, through exhausting trips to the bottom of the sea, restore the land one dirt clod at a time. Raven is frequently one of these earth- divers. One version from the Haida tribe embodies the same kind of serendipity, plundering, and amoral free association found in the Winnebago tales. Yet in the end, it is Raven who rescues the earth and restores the land after the flood.

In another tale, Raven is the son of a chief, and he will not stop crying until his father's sister holds him. Thus situated, Raven puts everyone to sleep and then has sex with his aunt. And Raven's cousin has sex with Raven's mother. When the chief finds out, he exiles his wife and son Raven, sending them to live with the wife's brother.

In his new home, Raven is noisy, shits everywhere, and casts spells on his father and uncle, beaching them while they are in the form of whales. By wearing the skins of animals he has killed, Raven assumes their powers—not unlike the Yoruba and their masks—being able to swim like a duck or fly like a raven. He also seduces another aunt.

Raven is a frisky and insatiable Trickster who seems not to care about anything but his appetites, yet ultimately, he performs deeds that save the world.[12] In this same tale of seductions, it rains and rains and floods the earth, and it is Raven who flies to the sky and stops the flood by kicking the water.

Raven is frequently a great creator in native lore. In a Chukchi tale, Raven is credited with bringing water, rivers, the sea; fish, walrus, whale, and seal; bear, wolf, Red-Fox, and Arctic-Fox. Finally, he tires of giving out gifts, becomes invisible, and takes the form of thunder in order to create fright.

In one particularly Bugs Bunny-esque tale, Raven is with his friend Cakaku. They each pick up fish and boil the grease out of them. Raven is able to fill a small bladder, but Cakaku, who had also gone after whales, fills an entire house.

Raven has this dream and the next day tells Cakaku that he dreamed that they were about to be attacked. Raven assembles all the birds to form a defense, but it's a diversion, for when Cakaku goes to inspect the birds, Raven sneaks into Cakaku's house and starts drinking up all of his grease. Cakaku returns, catches Raven in the act, and throws him into a grease box. When he starts to tie him into the box, Raven

---

[12] Peter Goodchild, *Raven Tales: Traditional Stories of Native Peoples* (Chicago: Chicago Review Press, 1991), 32-33.

persuades him to use straw instead of strong rope. Raven uses the straw to drink up all the grease so that when Cakaku tosses the boxed Raven off a cliff and the box breaks up, he is able to easily escape and fly away.[13]

Raven tales often come with rich ambiguity. In the Tlingit tradition, both the grandfather from whom Raven steals light and Raven are Ravens. In other words, the light-stealer is the Trickster hero of the story, but his foil shares some of the same qualities . . . we could say that the grandfather is merely Raven-ish, but a deeper interpretation might be that the Raven activates a raven-like quality that is in all of us, just as everyone is considered to have some measure of àshe. Furthermore, there is the added ambiguity in the Tlingit tale that the raven-like grandfather wanted to give light to the world through a grandchild, yet when Raven came to fulfill that wish, grandfather became possessive of his light and had to be tricked into releasing it.

Author and folklorist Peter Goodchild[14] deems this part of the legend illogical, but maybe it isn't. It explains the principle that even when a wish is about to be fulfilled, we all tend to hold on to our old ways. We fear success when all we've known is struggle . . . what will we fight for when the struggle is over? This is a profound explanation of why the simple truths and playfulness of the Trickster/player are commonly rejected or dismissed. When the thing that we have been looking for all along is staring us right in the face, we resist it, or we fail to recognize it.

In eastern Siberia and North America, Raven, not Eagle, is the principal shamanic figure. But in Greek and European cultures, the Raven (or Crow) is deposed, punished, and relegated to the sidelines. This foreshadows the marginalized jester role Raven and other tricksters play in Western culture. In Norse mythology, we witness that passage.

---

[13] Goodchild, *Raven Tales*, 24.

[14] Goodchild, *Raven Tales*, 13-14.

## Loki

The Norse god Loki is a genuine Trickster, but his saga also introduces the more vengeful, less playful, and confined Trickster of Europe. His story illustrates the binding of the Trickster and the Western laziness and fear that make Trickster into the devil or the fool. And Raven moves from a central role to a subordinate one.

Chief god and all-father Odin is flanked by two ravens. Hugginn, representing thought, and Muninn, who is memory or mind. On a daily basis, Hugginn and Muninn reconnoiter the world and return, briefing Odin each evening. Raven retains a place of honor and respect but is stripped of his Trickster qualities. In Hugginn and Munnin we recognize Raven's divinity, but also a demotion from demigod to advisor.

In Greek mythology, Zeus, symbolized by the eagle, deposes his father, Cronos, the crow. The eagle represents the fighting side and social order established through conquest. The raven-crow suffers diminution but still pesters. Raven's role is mutating from the indigenous Trickster, culture hero, deity, and creator to the Christian era advisor, jester, and fool. Still divinely playful, but clearly down several rungs of status. Shape-shifter, gender-bender but one of the main gods, Loki is an apt figure to represent this change.

In many cultures, Trickster invents the fishhook or net early in the story cycles. Consistent with this, Loki designs a fishnet, which he then burns, but when he later angers the gods with mischief, they discover his fishnet design and use it to capture him. This is classic because of the common and cartoonish plot device wherein a Trickster is the architect of his own undoing.

Resentful of their exclusion from the gods' table, the Jötnar, giants who are rivals of the gods, seek vengeance. Loki is a god but also a Trickster and boundary crosser, and as thus he'd already mingled with the rival giants. He even fathers his children through a giantess.

In one of two tales, Loki sides with the giants and tricks the goddess Idunn, the keeper of the Golden Apples of Immortality, into being captured by them, apples and all. When Loki orchestrates this trick between the giants and the gods, the giants get a taste of immortality through the apples, while the eternals get a taste of time. This is why the gods appear old, as they lost their immortality for a time, until the Golden Apples were retrieved.

The gods were not amused. At the conclusion of this tale, Loki's punishment is prelude to the jester role when he is commanded, as penalty for stealing the apples, to compensate Skadi, the daughter of a giant whose death Loki had caused. He ties one end of a rope to a billy goat's beard and the other to his own private parts. He squeals in pain at this self- abuse, all for Skadi's amusement.[15]

The second story is of Baldr. He's the perfect god, a golden child, handsome and good, and associated with the sun. But after nightmares predict that some harm will come to him, his mother Frigg gets everyone in heaven and earth, including animals and fire and water, to swear not to harm Baldr. Her attempt to outsmart the prophecy through absolute control annoys Loki, who gender-shifts, and as a woman, interrogates Frigg. He finds out that she neglected to get the oath from mistletoe, it seeming so harmless, and so Loki tricks the blind god Hod into killing Baldr with a mistletoe dart. In this way, Loki the Trickster restores the inevitability of accident and accident's key role in rebirth.[16]

But the gods inflict a Promethean punishment upon Loki. He is bound beneath the earth and lashed with the guts of his own children. Acidic poison drips on him, and though his wife Sigyn is able to protect Loki with a dish, whenever she has to empty it, the poison drips onto him, and his writhing agony is what we know as earthquakes.

---

[15] Neil Gaiman, *Norse Mythology* (New York: W.W.Norton, 2017), 194-196.

[16] Hyde, *Trickster Makes This World*, 100-107.

Thus, two elements that are typically minor or even absent from Trickster tales, resentment and punishment, have now moved front and center. To what can we attribute this?

There are two eras of Norse mythology and two Loki's. The main source of pre-Christian Norse myths is the *Poetic Edda*. Though written down between the ninth and thirteenth centuries, they tell older, pre-Christian tales. *Prose Edda* was compiled and written by Snorri Sturluson in 1220, well into the Christian era, and influenced by Christian values. The Christian lens turns Snorri's Loki darker and more demonic than the Loki who inhabits the earlier poems. "When Snorri says that Loki is the 'father of lies,' an epithet that does not occur in the *Poetic Edda*, he doubtless knows that this is what Christians call Satan."[17]

So, through Sturluson, the Norse gods are reborn in a Christian frame and are no longer indigenously Scandinavian. The binding of Loki and other such Trickster tales like depriving Coyote of a ride on the Sun-lodge or not bringing the Taoist Monkey with you on your journey are examples of suppressing Trickster and inviting apocalypse when playfulness would have released the pressure and avoided, for example, earthquakes.[18]

Pre-Christian Norse mythology portrays Loki the Trickster as a necessary component of life, death, and rebirth. Revisionist Loki must become Satan once empire's and Christianity's need for control forces down such a playful and wily character. Indeed, in many tales, both Odin and Thor seem obsessed with devising punishments for Loki.[19] Christian text corresponds to Baldr's mother Frigg (like Mary), protecting Baldr, a Christ-like figure.

In contrast to Baldr, the slippery Loki appears as a bird, a flea, a woman, a mare, a fire. His shape-shifting causes us to wonder what

---

[17] Hyde, *Trickster Makes This World*, 100-107.

[18] Hyde, *Trickster Makes This World*, 172.

[19] Gaiman, *Norse Mythology*, .

his true self is. And he is thus demonized by those who are disturbed and intolerant of such ambiguity.

And he would seem to have the last word, being the bringer of Ragnarök, the apocalyptic battle that kills off the gods. There is a rebirth and a new reign of the six surviving young gods, including a resurrected Baldr. There is no getting around the emphatic portrayal of Loki as cunning villain, and only a more holistic embrace of the myth reveals the wisdom of chaos on the road to rebirth and human progress.

Hyde advises "There is no way to suppress change, the story says, not even in heaven; there is only a choice between a way of living that allows constant, if gradual, alterations and a way of living that combines great control and cataclysmic upheavals. Those who panic and bind the trickster choose the latter path. It would be better to learn to play with him, better especially to develop styles (cultural, spiritual, artistic) that allow some commerce with accident, and some acceptance of the changes contingency will always engender."[20]

Ultimately, this relates to the suppressive puritanism that has influenced US culture for so long and whose harness may finally be slipping. In tales of the Raven, of Eshu, of Loki, the Trickster in them is the boundary crosser between heaven and earth, between the gods and humans, and the one who tears enough at the fabric of the universe to reveal chance, chaos, play, and the uncertainty that brings opportunities to make a world that is more than what we ordinarily perceive. Societies intent on notions of absolute good and absolute evil, that bind the trickster, invite apocalypse. And how does that happen?

## Till Eulenspiegel

The spoils of war and conquest were too delicious, the sacrifices a Trickster god requires too steep. European warlords and monarchs confined the playful and imposed order and hierarchy. European culture

---

[20] Hyde, *Trickster Makes This World*, 107.

diverts the power of pranksterism, relegating the Trickster's power to mock what is "serious" and "adult" into conventional arts, entertainment, and buffoonery. This sidelining depletes and delays play's potential…to upset adult seriousness, to make a crack in the universe, to venture into the possibility of a more playful world. To inject play onto the stage where power struggles are fought, to direct play and pranks towards creating that opening—*disruptive play*—engenders great and necessary risks. So Europe instead chose the path of outsized control and inevitable cataclysm.

Till Eulenspiegel is the hugely popular European Trickster character who stars in a story cycle of ninety-five episodes.[21] He originated in Germany and Austria but is also popular in Denmark, Belgium, The Netherlands, Bohemia, Poland, and Italy, and there are three museums dedicated to him in Germany. True to Trickster ways, he is rumored to have actually lived, in the fourteenth century, but it's only a rumor, and we do not know who or what lies in the grave that bears his name in Mölln, Schleswig-Holstein, Germany.[22]

There are many versions of his tales, numerous books, Richard Strauss's famous tone poem, operas, and, later, movies and TV shows, almost all of European origin. He has within him genuine Trickster traits. He has a big appetite and will make mischief in the interest of getting a good meal. He deliberately misunderstands any communication by taking instructions literally. When, in one of his many jobs—this one with a beermaker—he is told to boil some hops, a dog by the same name suffers a horrible death. When he is hired by a priest to work half-time, he does half of every chore he was assigned. He leaves an enormous shit on the floor of a bathhouse named "House of Cleaning." And this is one of his other most notable traits, the use of excrement as a comedic tool, fart jokes and poop jokes, often

---

[21] N, *A Pleasant Vintage of Till Eulenspiegel*, trans. Paul Oppenheimer (Middletown, CT: Wesleyan University Press, 1972).

[22] There are even tales of a second grave.

including the tricking of someone into eating it. Such scatology proliferates throughout the Till Eulenspiegel tales.[23]

But unlike Raven, Wakdjunkaga, or Eshu, who could be considered either premoral or beyond morality, Till Eulenspiegel is deeply mired in European morality. He was traumatized as a child when he fell off a bridge into the mud and the townspeople laughed at him… and he is thus motivated by revenge, to create misfortune for others and escape it himself. But he is not evil and uses his prankster talents with moral intention: to expose greed, hypocrisy, and other failings of religion, craftsmen, and nobility. He is also a rebel champion against the Spanish who killed his father, and thus a participant in conflict.

But he is generally a champion of play. He avoids work and offers critiques of people who work too hard or are too serious. And like other Tricksters he has a great appetite (for food, not sex) and plays tricks for the thrill of it. In one movie version, Jester Till retains this Trickster mode of getting things done via tricks, but he is motivated by clichéd hero quests to save a town, get the girl.[24] He does have the totem/sidekick of the owl, with whom he is traditionally associated.

In other words, he is defined and confined by European Catholic (he lived before the Reformation) sensibilities of morality and lacks the moral mystique and divinity of the non-Western Trickster. Whether they are bad guys, hypocrites, or just plain mean, there is a persistent, moral avenger undertone to the Till Eulenspiegel tales. "They got what they deserved" . . . the non-Western Tricksters provide no such anchor, no such rationality, no such reassuring morality.

## French Fairy Tales

People in power have depended upon this defanging of the Trickster for centuries. In the realm of seventeenth century fairy tales, particularly those from France, the heroes are sly pranksters, but given

---

[23] N, *A Pleasant Vintage of Till Eulenspiegel*, 24.

[24] Getting the girl is an artifact of contemporary filmmaking. In the original tales, Till Eulenspiegel's life is devoid of love and sex.

the opportunity to overwhelm their villains, they consistently stop short of total victory. Robert Darnton's study of fairy tales shows that when they overcame their opponents and were granted *whatever wish they wanted* . . .

> Wishing usually takes the form of food in peasant tales . . . their wishes usually remained fixed on common objects in the everyday world. One hero gets "a cow and some chickens"; another, an armoire full of linens. A third settles for light work, regular meals, and a pipe full of tobacco . . . the tales remain rooted in the real world. . . . The clever weakling makes a fool of the strong oppressor by raising a chorus of laughter at his expense . . . but laughter . . . has limits. Once it subsides, the tables turn back again . . . the old order regains its hold on the revelers. Tricksterism is a kind of holding pattern. . . . Ultimately then, Tricksterism expressed an orientation to the world rather than a latent strain of radicalism. It provided a way of coping with a harsh society instead of a formula for overthrowing it.[25]

Thus, the mischievous, playful instinct was intimidated, and peasant fairy tale heroes would simply seek as their reward a good meal or, at most, the temporary humiliation of the ruling class, not a reordering of power and class structures. Let's take one more example of perhaps the quintessential premodern Western Trickster.

## King Lear's Fool

We most often read that Shakespeare's *King Lear* is the story of a king's descent into madness. Though portrayed as an almost sympathetic character, the more we learn about Lear's past, the more we realize what a malicious tyrant he was. The play is as much about the madness of power as the madness of Lear, and Shakespeare's lesson echoes that of Frigg and Baldr, that those who lust for power, control, and domination—Lear, his daughters, their spouses and suitors,

---

[25] Robert Darnton, *The Great Cat Massacre and Other Episodes in French Cultural History* (New York: Vintage, 1985), 33, 34, 59.

enemies and allies—invite catastrophe and conflict. Thus, blinded by their greed, it takes Fool, the King's court jester, to expose the folly.

Lear enters as a king we know nothing about except that he is retiring and turning over his kingdom to his three daughters. He offers the largest share to the daughter who demonstrates the greatest love for him, unknowingly inviting the lies of his two eldest, Goneril and Regan. The youngest daughter, Cordelia, speaks a blunt truth, telling her father that to profess love so blatantly in order to increase her inheritance is distasteful and she will not stoop to that. Lear is offended and enraged, and Cordelia is banished. Lear's most loyal aide, Kent, is also banished for protesting this unfair punishment. While one of Cordelia's suitors from France loses interest in her, now that she is stripped bare of her dowry, the king of France is enamored by her integrity and marries her.

The love and devotion competition thus collapsed, Lear saves for himself a retinue and tells Goneril and Regan that he'll live out his days visiting them in their respective castles. But both daughters have tasted their inherited wealth and power and immediately begin to scheme against him.

As the plot thickens with forgeries, lies, and betrayals, the Fool increasingly mocks Lear and amplifies his misery. The Trickster Fool refuses to take seriously the power Lear personifies.

There is intrigue and betrayal within the competing kingdoms of Lear, Goneril, and Regan, and they all eventually fight to destroy each other. No alliance is honored, and infidelity, political scheming, gouging of eyes, suicide, and poisonings, as well as good old-fashioned stabbings, ensue. It all goes to hell in grand fashion.

When Lear finally admits that he needs help, his pride prevents him from apologizing to Cordelia and gaining her support.

This pride is pathetic. Lear feels that he cannot function as a full human being without his power. He has no humility and thus never was a full human being. The feeling of fullness that came with power was an illusion. But there is an ultimate compassion in Shakespeare such that, if we see him as the Fool's foil, Lear mirrors in his flaws the deficits that would be filled by a human with the virtue of Trickster traits. In this light, he is a sympathetic character.

This is Shakespeare's deliberate indictment against the folly of making power paramount. Shakespeare is quite clearly stating that this is not the way to behave. Amassing power will only corrupt and cause upheaval, misery, and killing.

In contrast, the Fool matches the elusiveness of power with a dance of his own. By definition and decree, he has no power, and thus he can see the madness for what it is. The Fool is of no determinate age, though clearly, he will not grow up. Is he altogether human, or is he a Trickster? The Fool accepts Lear's sublimity and uniqueness in a way that the other characters in the play cannot. The Fool is understood only by the audience. Even though he may represent Lear's inner voice, Lear refuses to understand him. The Fool makes Lear's madness worse, drives him crazy. And he dances on the play's mushrooming graves, using his power of prophecy to make a social critique (of priests, brewers, nobles, squires, usurers, tailors, bawds, and whores).

But wait, there's more. Shakespeare delightfully endows this uncanniest of characters with the power of time travel. In his final lines, The Fool invokes Merlin: "The prophecy Merlin shall make, for I live before his time."[26] Fool is suggesting his transience in time (*Lear* takes place in the eighth century BC, and Merlin would have lived at least thirteen centuries later).

After making this prophecy, the Fool mysteriously vanishes from the play, challenging the audience to reflect on the meaning of this strangest of characters. The Fool becomes an absence still provocative to the audience, not to the king. Though trapped in Lear's endgame, the Fool is also free of time and presumably drifts out of the play and into another era.[27]

---

[26] William Shakespeare, *King Lear*, ed. Russell Fraser (New York: Signet Classic, 1987), 2.3.95

[27] Harold Bloom, *Shakespeare: The Invention of the Human* (New York: Riverhead, 1998), 494-499.

Lear's Fool is the truth-teller, gaining the privilege of speaking truth to power in exchange for having none. This is the Western order of things.

And this being a story of the West, the Fool is not as formed as a Trickster character and plays within a confined role and circumstances. As we learn of his origins and surface acceptance of abuse at the hands of nobility, we see a character resentful and driven by revenge, gaining it by tormenting and mocking Lear. Not a deity.

The Trickster is powerful, the Fool is not. Yet there is prescience in this play. *King Lear* was *The Godfather* of its time, the story that exposes the folly of power through a narrative of it slipping away. Akira Kurosawa's film adaptation *Ran* takes a few liberties and substitutes sons for daughters, but the core message and the critical role for the Fool endure. Shakespeare's enduring political wisdom is that power is a fool's game, and it takes a Fool to reveal this. It is through the depth of *Lear's* characters and their rampant, almost comic, villainy, that Shakespeare offers a narrow but transcendent lifeline to the possibility of a world based less on power but more on complex and joyful humanity.

In his comic retelling of the story, American author Christopher Moore discovers that divine potentiality of the Fool: "The fool's number is zero, but that's because he represents the infinite possibility of all things. He may become anything. See, he carries all of his possessions in a bundle on his back. He is ready for anything, to go anywhere, to become whatever he needs to be. Don't count out the fool . . . simply because his number is zero."[28]

Thus, King Lear's Fool is a transitional character to a future that yet lies ahead, bound by Western fear of Trickster power to be a fool and a jester, but given enough depth and prescience to hint at liberation and the transcendence of power.

So let's time travel, too, and see how a more fully formed Trickster character, through the supposed harmlessness of animated fiction, has been roaming among us for the past eighty years.

---

[28] Christopher Moore, *Fool* (New York: Harper, 2009), 138.

## Bugs Bunny

There is a Zulu tale where Trickster is a weasel who manages to move in with a leopard mother and her cubs, whom he successfully plots to eat. Knowing he will be discovered, he creates multiple tunnels for his escape. When the leopard mother pursues him, thinking that there is only one tunnel and she will overtake and kill him, he doubles back, sets spears at the entrances and exits, and kills the leopard mother as well.

In Native American tales, Coyote traps his pursuer in a tunnel by setting fires at both ends, catching and cooking his adversary at the same time.[29]

Does this sound familiar? Most of these indigenous tales are short enough that they could be retold in the five- to eight-minute time span that classic cartoons run. It is more than coincidence that children's cartoons, especially those from the golden age of American animation (1930s to early 1970s), tell similar Trickster tales and typically run for about seven minutes. And the hare is one of the common forms of Trickster in Native American and African folklore.

Enter Bugs Bunny. Trickster Bugs lives in a warm and comfortable underground home, but he is also a wanderer, and his stock in trade trick is the tunnel, which makes, blocks, and blows up opportunities and pranks. Bugs' persona expands into our culture through satire and mimicry, especially with the kindred Groucho Marx, whose lines ("Of course you realize, this means war!") and props (carrot = cigar), stooped pacing, and eyebrow-raising Bugs regularly appropriates.

The ten most frequently portrayed characters in film—Santa Claus, the Devil, the Grim Reaper, Jesus Christ, God, Adolf Hitler, Abraham Lincoln, Sherlock Holmes, Count Dracula, and Bugs Bunny—include only one cartoon character. A gang of artists, writers, and directors created Bugs, who quickly rose from guest role to star and became Warner Brothers' corporate symbol. One of his developers was animator Ben "Bugs" Hardaway, and notes referring to Bugs's Bunny

---

[29] Hyde, *Trickster Makes This World*, 48.

eventually morphed into the name that stuck. Bugs Bunny debuted in 1938 and 1939, with the first definitive version being the 1940 Academy Award-nominated *A Wild Hare.*

While he was initially characterized with a hayseed country boy persona and accent, Bugs soon adopted a Brooklyn/Bronx accent and more urbane perspective. I should like to suggest, first, that Bugs Bunny is the leading American manifestation of the Trickster archetype, and secondly, that he emerged as such unconsciously through the creative efforts of this gaggle of artists.[30]

One of his very first appearances, in *Elmer's Candid Camera* (1940), features the country version of Bugs and is reminiscent of Native American and African tales. He behaves amorally, in one scene, attacking and pranking Elmer, putting him in mortal danger; in the next, feigning compassion and rescuing Elmer from drowning; and then finally, throwing him back in the lake once he has made sure that Elmer is okay. The only consistency is that Bugs is always pulling our leg, never serious. His response to his own endangerment is to fake suffering and pleading. We like him for his redeeming virtue of refusing to take anything seriously.

Including his gender or gender role. In 1940's *A Hare's Tale*, Bugs kisses Elmer. On the lips. Twice. And once on the nose. Bugs, like most Tricksters, wanders alone, but he's a sexy wanderer where the sex is tricky too. Cross-dressing is as common as wolf-whistling in Bugs Bunny cartoons.

---

[30] "Bugs was not the creation of any one man but rather represented the creative talents of perhaps five or six directors and many cartoon writers. In those days, the stories were often the work of a group who suggested various gags, bounced them around, and finalized them in a joint story conference." Some of the twentieth century's greatest talents shot Bugs, like a cannonball, into the heart of the American psyche: directors Tex Avery, Chuck Jones, Fritz Freleng, Robert McKimson, and Bob Clampett; voice actor Mel Blanc; and composer and conductor Carl Stalling. [Ipfs.io. (2018). *Bugs Bunny.* [online] Available at: https://ipfs.io/ipfs/QmXoypizjW3WknFiJnKLwHCnL72vedxjQkDDP1mXWo6uco/wiki/Bugs_Bunny.html [Chase Craig recollections of "Michael Maltese," Chase Craig Collection, CSUN, Accessed 2 May 2018]. And by the same token, and as future chapters will show, Alfred Jarry's *Ubu Roi* or Andy Kaufman's *Tony Clifton* characters were unconscious renderings of the Trickster.

Elmer's facile morality binds him, while Bugs is liberated by his lack of one. The nonsensical plot wanderings are characteristic of Bugs cartoons and Trickster story cycles.

Grown adults create these cartoons, grown adults very much in touch with their own childlike capacity for play. Bugs, the consummate modern Trickster, plays in the larger field of Play as well, with nonsense and silliness that connects to all children. In 1944's *The Old Grey Hare*, the creative team is well into their stride, and in Trickster fashion, Elmer time-travels to 2000, where he and Bugs play out their routine in their creaky twilight years. "Eh, what's up, prune-face?" hails old Bugs, who is suffering from lumbago. In a tour de force of phony sentimentality, Bugs fakes a mortal wound when shot by Elmer's Buck Rogers Lightning-Quick Rabbit-Killer. He whips out a scrapbook he'd apparently been keeping, and we time-travel once again to their first chase as infants. After reenacting the "What's up, doc? I'm looking for a little baby bunny. What's he look like, doc? He looks . . . just like you!" routine, the chase ensues, but is suddenly halted. Baby Bugs says, "Uh-oh, time for little babies to have afternoon nap." The two curl up together and nap. "Okay, nap over," declares Bugs, and the chase resumes.

Sure, it's a typical smart-aleck gag, but it also means these grownups are remembering their own infancies. Sweet and childlike and broadly playful.

The Trickster is thoroughly profiled by Lewis Hyde in *Trickster Makes This World*,[31] but I should like to make connections beyond and apart from mythology, to where players/Tricksters shine the light on political and cultural potential. And I offer Bugs as a grounding mechanism. Think Trickster, think Bugs. But also let Bugs open our minds to greater playfields. This begins by returning to our definitions of original, cultural, and disruptive play, the play of animals (Tricksters are usually animals) and of infant and toddler humans, and

---

[31] Hyde, *Trickster Makes This World*.

our main query of how, in the real world, an adult who has retained the ability to be playful fares in the worlds of politics and culture. In short, Tricksters and players who inhabit the even larger world of play.

We've come some ways from Jack and the Beanstalk (*Petit Jean*), Loki, Lear, and Till Eulenspiegel. In the twentieth century, Trickster makes his jailbreak, led by dada, continued by the hippies, and found today with tricksters like the Yes Men and as yet to be discovered figures. As a transcendent influence, power required that play's early showing in Western history be humbly framed as nonthreatening mischief and humor. But I would suggest that our historical arc bends towards a meeting of the Trickster orientation to the world with what would be considered a radical vision of a Play Society.

So with Bugs taking his seat in the peanut gallery of our minds, we turn to a modern, true-life tale of two young men with intellectual disabilities, not necessarily Tricksters but most definitely adults vibrantly in touch with play.

# TWO

# Arturo and Remus, Players among Us

> May your heart always be joyful,
> And may your song always be sung.
> May you stay forever young.
>
> Bob Dylan[1]

THE TRICKSTER embodies many attributes of play. And *disruptive play* draws heavily on the Trickster archetype to shape its political and cultural role and unlock potential. But play itself is larger still. We've explored definitions of play and connected the dots to the Trickster archetype. The following story further answers the second part of our question: "What happens when adults are able to conserve the ability to play that they naturally experienced as an infant or child?" We follow the adventures of Arturo and Remus, two young men with developmental disabilities. In my own experiences as a special educator, I often found that such individuals—whom we stereotype in even the most charitable of perspectives as being "less than"—retained the capacity for play and playfulness.[2] Measurable intelligence is an extremely unreliable correlate to a person's

---

[1] Bob Dylan, "Forever Young," *Planet Waves*, Asylum Records, 1974, vinyl recording.

[2] Joseph Chilton Pearce, *Magical Child* (New York: Plume, 1977), 131, 144.

ability to help society advance and grow. I came to value highly the contribution people with intellectual disabilities make to the public commons and offer the following true story[3] to illustrate this point and broaden our appetite for what we might discover and experience in a more playful society.

Arturo was bound for glory. Everything about him—his expansive gestures, his full range of emotions, and the way he grabbed on to life—said the same thing: I am a glorious person, a special human being. Revel in me, and give to me fully when you are with me. I will laugh with you, be angry or hurt, I will cry, I will cry out, I will tease, deceive, I will be your best friend. I am Arturo Montealegré.

Arturo's family dressed him in polyester hand-me-downs, and he had a habit of cinching his belt too tight. His clothes could never impress, so his brazen style made his glory more naked. There were no pretensions, no pandering to fashion. He had no need to depend on social support or the crass development of image. Arturo was an original. His pride was personal, and if he owed any points of reference, they would be to his family.

It was 1987. His family had been in the United States only a few years. Arturo's father was a truck driver who had left Nicaragua for the US and eventually brought the rest of his family—parents, nephews, nieces, siblings, and children—to live with him. They all found some work and jumbled their lives together in San Francisco's Outer Mission District. Their house was just a little bit mad. Arturo had an uncle who lived with them, and he would pace the house, mumbling, smoking, pointing, nodding, smiling. This was all a little hard on Arturo's brother and sister, who were both attending the public high schools and trying their best to fit in and be cool. The father, also Arturo, was out of town a lot, delivering goods with his truck. The family had managed to somehow spread the word that

---

[3] Names have been changed.

they would pick up newspapers for recycling on the same day the trash was collected, and on early mornings, I would see them in their beat-up, oversized mid-1960s Pontiac, filling the back seat with everybody's old papers. The Montealegrés were now, and perhaps had always been, individualists in the mold of the mythic individualist American. Clearly, Arturo saw the world on his own terms as well.

I worked as a job coach for a program whose mission was, through the school district and the state rehabilitation system, to serve young people with disabilities who were within a couple of years of high school graduation. I would help find jobs for these young folks and then go out on the job with them, providing whatever assistance was necessary to enable them to learn the job and eventually maintain it with minimal or no assistance from me . . . supported employment. And Arturo was one such individual I had the honor of serving.

Remus, about nineteen or twenty, was another young man in the program. He came from a large Filipino family and spoke with a clipped singsong accent. He had some intellectual disability and a persistently sunny outlook. To me, he was a wise man who put the rational, serious, and stifling matrix our culture imposes on daily life in its proper perspective.

Remus was hired by a Jack in The Box fast-food restaurant on Market Street. He showed up for work with his friendly, abundant spirit and moderate intellectual limitations. He learned all his job duties pretty quickly, but his approach to one of them taxed my ability to teach. He was to wash the windows with a glass cleaner and polish the rails with a special polish. These things he could do, and he was supplied with cleaner, polish, and paper towels to do them; but he would not continue to use a towel once it was even slightly soiled. Remus could go through five rolls of paper towels in as many minutes. I would show him how to use the towels, how to fold them back and reuse them until they were saturated, and then move on to fresh ones. He nodded and smiled. "Okay, okay," he would say, with his clipped accent and singsong voice . . . and then use them properly whenever I was within eyesight of him. But whenever I left the worksite to check in on others I was supporting, he would return to his wanton squandering of this valued resource; his satisfaction surpassed only by the glee of watching me steam and rage when I returned to the scene, him resplendent in mounds of used paper towels, utterly without guile and thoroughly amused.

I had a sense of being the indulged child, being Remus's student, when I would persist in my hopeless commitment to training him to hold down a job and share in the daily grind with the rest of us. It wasn't a matter of him preferring a disability check, being lazy, or fooling the system. The economics of gainful employment and self-support were beyond his understanding. What he did understand better than most were the joys of greeting the day and taking a breath of fresh air. He reveled in the sparkle of the world and the lovingness he reflexively shared with everyone he met. Clearly, it was more fun to unroll endless paper towels and watch Mr. Siegel sputter and fume than it was to obediently learn his job duties.

Remus died of leukemia less than a year later, and I wouldn't change a moment of our relationship or think that my gift of job training was any more valuable than the gift of play he shared with me. Without romanticizing the challenges of living with a disability, people like Remus keep our minds and hearts open to the insights provided by an atypical existence.

It was while working as a job coach in this program that I met Arturo, who was also to become my client. And these young men came into my life because my job sanctioned me to serve people with intellectual disabilities. But to remember them thusly is as unfair as calling anyone else "normal." For Remus and Arturo, the stigma and narrowness that come with descriptors like retarded or emotionally disturbed does not do them justice. Remus should instead be remembered as a man at play in the world, an angel sent to remind us to take ourselves more lightly. And Arturo . . . Arturo was a man on a train bound for glory.

Arturo was referred to the supported employment program by his two teachers. Clearly, they knew Arturo better than I, and their greater experience with him showed. For instance, they could usually understand what he was saying, whereas I could not. His speaking style was one of rapid-fire retorts of English phrases, one to five words, perhaps in the vocabulary of a second- or third-grader, but peppered with Spanish, and using too few words spoken too fast. His teachers always got it the first time. I required a few repetitions each time he spoke. Arturo would invent his own words too; it would take time to get used to his speech.

But speech was just one aspect. Arturo had an assortment of idiosyncrasies, all adding up to a princely and cogent style. There was a lot to know about this man, and I could read this partly from the practical hints and conventional wisdom the teachers shared with me:

"Arturo is very proud, but don't let him push you around. Make sure you don't let Arturo get carried away in public; he'll talk to anyone. He's smart, but he won't let you know what he does or doesn't understand; he'll act like he understands even when he doesn't."

But more revealing and portentous were the knowing smiles and winks the two teachers exchanged with each other as they coached me through my experiences with this amazing man. Once, I reported back to them how he would involve himself in the conversations of anyone he met on the streets, gesticulating, exclaiming, picking up on the tones and affect of the conversation even though he didn't understand the content.

"Yes, we know," the teachers would say (wink, wink, nod, nod), "You do have to keep an eye on him."

Like any self-respecting Horatio Alger, Arturo took on the work world with gusto. He was on the ground floor, but ready to work his way up, and reach for the top. At the McDonald's down by the Civic

Center, also on Market Street, his main task was clearing the customers' trays off the tables, but he also swept and mopped the linoleum floor. He had to learn the routines, such as where to find the mop and when to use it, how to restock the napkins, where to dump the trash bags, and so forth.

The job was not without its subtleties. Arturo had to be able to tell the difference between half-eaten food legitimately cast off and meals temporarily left by a customer who went to get more ketchup or go to the restroom. Before he mastered this, it wasn't safe to leave your table during Arturo's shift until you were through. Truth be told, Arturo saw nothing wrong with helping himself to unattended food. He was instructed that eating off the customers' trays was clearly against the rules. And when he protested against wasting these remnants of real food, well, his argument was not completely without merit. So Arturo had one of his first encounters with the realities of the work world. This up-and-comer thought he knew a better way, but he had to at least make a showing of following the rules and quietly go along with them. He suffered our foolishness gladly, but it was not easy for him. Why couldn't we recognize his ambition and set him loose?

The McDonald's personnel and I did know the rules, and how to communicate them. Arturo clearly thought us inane, but he tolerated our attempts at assertion, gently patting us on the shoulder with a condescending "Okay, boss," to reassure us that he now understood the task or the rule and to let us believe we were in charge. We were then dismissed; he would no longer be needing us. Of course, if we insisted on hanging around, he was happy to indulge us. With an eager-to-please smile, Arturo would continue with his work, but you could almost see the wheels turning in his head as he quietly formulated his next career move.

For Arturo was never satisfied with his accomplishments, and though he mastered all of his job duties within a few weeks, including window washing, refilling the condiments, and running the trash compactor, destiny compelled him with the urge to be more.

For example, he was willing to add security guard duties to his job description, and at no extra cost. This McDonald's restaurant was in one of the seedier blocks of the downtown area, and we had our share of street types coming in and occasionally hassling the female cashiers, or not having the money, or panhandling right there in the dining room. Arturo was quick to rescue any distressed employee who might be trying to settle a dispute, and unwanteds who were eventually ejected had to suffer the further humiliation of having Arturo shake his upraised fist at them as they left, shouting obscenities and threats no one could quite understand. But the effect was tremendous and the emotion unmistakable: they were no longer welcome at the McDonald's protected by Señor Montealegré.

I was consistently on the job with Arturo in those first several weeks. I really wanted to help engineer his success, and the manager, Letty, seemed to appreciate my presence in her store. In fact, once Arturo was approaching mastery of his tasks, and the regular employees found ways to work with him, my role changed. Letty would use me as a sounding board for all of her managerial problems, and I got a closer glimpse of the mostly Filipino youth who ran this McDonald's. I made some new friends and occasionally went bowling with the group after hours. Working here was a little like getting adopted by a family, and I was feeling pretty good about Arturo being a part of this social group, and having a good time myself.

But I had other young clients around the city, and other job placements to monitor. Since I was so comfortable at this McDonald's, and the location was central, I started making occasional calls from Letty's phone[4] to keep tabs on my fast-food fiefdom, my mail messengers and clerks, gardeners, cooks, and cashiers who were graduat-

---

[4] No cell phones around, this is the 1980s.

ing from San Francisco's special education high school classes. My job was to add to the already incredible diversity of this town by helping Arturo and his age-mates carve a niche in it. An incidental benefit to me was observing close-up the business of managing stores, hotels, and restaurants in an urban community.

One day I arrived at the work site and was met by one of the cashiers. "There's been a problem with Arturo," she informed me, "You'd better go talk to Letty." I experienced a sinking, *omigod, what's he done now?* feeling, a feeling that was becoming an occupational hazard.

My man, it seems, had shown some real initiative. Letty told me that she had noticed that the large pad on which she made her weekly orders of buns, beef, fries, and other supplies was missing. After a thorough search, it was discovered that Arturo had fashioned an office for himself in a corner of the storeroom. He had also absconded with an unused telephone, pencils, and a hat and set up shop on an empty cardboard crate. He was discovered there, barking orders over the disconnected phone, scribbling angry strokes on the page, and just generally rehearsing for his chance to run the whole show. The man was clearly on the fast track.

"Well, Letty, looks like Arturo wants your job," I said through a broad smile. "He's ordering buns and burgers, just like he's seen you do."

"No, I don't think so, Shep. He thinks he's you. He sees you coming in here all the time, using my phone."

Well, this mystery was never quite resolved, and Arturo got a dose of Letty's anger, which he understood and forgave, but the incident did put to rest doubts anyone might have had about Arturo's star quality. We also tend to assume that satire is a deliberate act, but it ain't necessarily so.

---

Part of my job was to train Arturo to ride the bus home independently. We had to walk a block from Market Street to Mission. From there, we had to take a number 14 bus and transfer a mile or so later to a 26, which took Arturo to within a block of his house.

The 26 was generally filled with other high school students by the time we got on. Arturo might see someone he knew, and occasionally, his brother would be coming home from school on the same bus. It was a safe and friendly, if rowdy, ride to Arturo's neighborhood.

The Mission 14 was another story. From where we had to pick it up, in the midafternoon, it attracted all sorts: office workers, students, bohemians, and shoppers to be sure, but a dose of bums, winos, addicts, and unpredictable street people as well. I had been assured that Arturo's teachers and family had let him out in the community on his own often and he had used the buses before. This was not supposed to be a difficult assignment.

One afternoon was particularly warm; the Civic Center area was particularly congested; I was particularly tired. I just wanted to get Arturo home, get work over with, and get home myself. We got off work at about five o'clock; it was crowded in the streets and on the buses. I got on the 14 with Arturo. I was in the early stages of gradually "fading out" my presence and leaving Arturo to travel to and from work without me. Eventually, I would board well after him, letting him choose the correct bus. Towards the end of the travel training, I would follow the bus in my car to make sure that he got off at the right stop. But in this phase, we buddied up like a couple of working stiffs on our way home together, having put in another tough day at the office.

City dwellers who use buses generally agree that the seats in the back of the bus are the most dangerous places to sit, and they get taken last. And even though San Francisco is a reasonably safe city, many would rather stand than sit in the back. Since I had begun the very initial stages of fading, I let him board the bus ahead of me, and of course he marched straight to the long row across the very back of the bus, in his mind a choice and comfortable place from which he could hold court. His mood was jolly as ever. I was borderline morose, I wanted to get home, and I was too tired to care where I sat. We took two of three open seats.

At the very next corner, a small crowd boarded. One of the new passengers was a black man, homeless or at least down on his luck, about thirty. You could tell that he had at one time been quite handsome, but he was pretty well into what either heroin or too much cheap wine could do to you. I noticed him, and I couldn't escape having that clichéd reaction: this guy had talent and intelligence, and they got wasted, in both senses of the word. He sat next to me, so there I was, with him on my right and Arturo on my left.

No, he didn't smell or anything, though he wasn't clean and his clothes were worn. My act was something in between tolerant and unnoticing. I didn't have to try too hard to adopt the urban stance, look bored and look away. It's not like his condition was uncommon. We never became friends, but let's call him Joe.

"Hey, man, you got a cigarette?" he drawled at me. Imagine a voice sleepy and aggressive at the same time.

"No," I barely said.

"Hey, man," a little louder, a little annoyed, "give me a cigarette."

"I don't smoke."

I stopped looking straight ahead and gave him a little eye contact. Some would say that was my fatal error. Even a glance will provoke someone who's looking to be provoked. Arturo had been quiet throughout but now started hitting my arm with the back of his hand, maximizing my discomfort, egging me on to do God knows what. His gestures were visible enough, unfortunately, for our interloper to see that we were together.

"How about your friend? Hey, man, *you* got a cigarette?"

Arturo showed about as much restraint as he was going to; he didn't respond beyond a facial snarl and a squinting of the eyes, no speech, somehow realizing that ignoring Joe might be the best course of action.

"No, he hasn't got any cigarettes either." I lost a little of the flatness in my voice, showing just enough irritation to escalate the situation. That wasn't my intention, just a lapse, another minute error, large enough to do damage.

"Hey, motherfucker, I was talking to your friend. Why don't you let him speak for himself. Mind your own fucking business." And then continuing to address Arturo, "Hey, man, give me a cigarette!"

We now had the attention of the back third, perhaps even half the bus. Only a few heads turned, but the reduced noise level indicated that several passengers were now bystanders observing whatever the hell was going to happen next. Among them was a man, also black, in the aisle seat to my right, about three rows in front of us. He was built like a halfback or a body builder, he wore wire-rimmed glasses, and he carried books. A student, an athlete, mid to late twenties.

"What's the matter, can't you talk? Gimme a cigarette." Joe was feeling powerful and arrogant, on some kind of mission, having some kind of mean fun. He was after Arturo.

"He doesn't talk, alright, just leave him alone." I tried to simplify and close off the event. Arturo had other plans. My credibility lasted less than a second.

"No, man, no!" Arturo refused. Arturo barked. Arturo bristled. I don't know whether he even knew what the guy wanted. But Arturo made it clear that a citizen's indignation and a giant's wrath had been aroused. One "no" from Arturo said a mouthful. His no said: No, I have no cigarettes, I have no affection, no obligation, no respect, and no patience for you.

"You faggot, where are you faggots getting off the bus?" Joe said. "I'm gonna get off and beat the fuck out of you. Let's go, I'm gonna fuck with you. Gimme a fuckin' cigarette, you faggots."

Arturo sprang into action. He jumped to his feet and came across me to Joe, digging in in the aisle just two feet from him, so that when he gave him a double dose, flipping him the bird with both hands thrust out, the middle fingers were not six inches from Joe's face.

"Fuck you, fuck you!" Arturo was shouting. All of a sudden, he's got perfect diction. "Come on, I fight you, man. Come on, fuck, man, fuck, come on!" He made fists, then resumed flipping him off. I'm struggling to get Arturo back to his seat, scolding, trying to put our team together, protect my man. I'm hapless, hopeless, but I'm part of the cyclone raging in this spot. Joe's getting to his feet, and then he sits back down, content to shout threats at us "faggots," letting us know what he's going to do to us when we get off the bus.

"Hey, you want a cigarette?" The athlete-student had just turned and spoken, clearly, with anger, but more with an authority that paralyzed the action. By now we had a pretty good audience.

Joe was taken aback. "Huh?" was all he could manage.

"Go ahead, ask me for a cigarette."

Still caught off balance, Joe played along. "Alright, you got a cigarette?" He was tentative. I guess he thought maybe he was going to get one.

"Yeah, I've got a cigarette." Pause. "And I'm not giving it to you. You want to get off the bus and fuck with me? Cause I'm not giving you one of my cigarettes. You wanna call me a faggot?"

The energy in the bus was completely transformed. It was out of a comic book. I had not expected to encounter and witness Black Panther in action when we boarded. The Marvel hero had been out of print for over ten years and wasn't due to be back for another thirty.

"Come on, why don't you call me a faggot?"

"Hey, man, I was just asking him for a cigarette."

"God, I can't believe that you're a brother. Are you a total idiot? How can you call yourself a black man? You've got no pride. You're nothing. Can't you understand a man with the world going against him? Can't you even see the guy's got a handicap?"

Our rescuer stood up. He was awesome. He was in control, a god. He had nothing more to say. His physicalness, his anger, his presence completely overwhelmed Joe into defeat. It was over.

"Handicapped? I didn't know your friend was handicapped. Why didn't you tell me he was handicapped?" Joe whined. All of a sudden, he's my friend, and I've let him down. Yeah, the last incident was over, but now this asshole is on to the next one, and every time he says the word "handicapped," it's really loud and emphasized; it stings like acid, and the fool has found exit in his shamelessness . . . and an amazing ability to miss the point.

"Hey, man, if you'd've told me he was handicapped, I wouldn't've said anything. Shit, man, why didn't you tell me he was handicapped? I couldn't tell he was handicapped."

Arturo grumbled; his lips had spittle on them, and he was ready to take the man on again. I was in awe of Arturo's pride, and I remembered the way his family treated him. He was special because he was their eldest son and the protector of the family during his father's frequent absences. Unbeknownst to Joe, Arturo was still a threat to him. The divine interceding had neutralized the chances for violence. But Joe continued to whine, Arturo continued to snarl, and I coached Arturo to just stay in his seat.

Joe, of course, had nothing to apologize for. It was my fault for not balancing the bigotries. If we follow Joe's logic, it was my civic duty to clarify the situation in the beginning before it got out hand. When first approached for a cigarette, I guess I was expected to say, "No, sir, I have no cigarettes, and neither does my friend. Although you are addicted, impoverished, arrogant, and perfectly entitled to harass people of average intelligence, please leave my handicapped friend alone. But you may continue to threaten me. In fact, if you believe it will truly challenge my self-esteem, you may proceed at this point to call me a faggot."

And we witnessed the battle between the sensibilities of the great avenger and the insane nonsense of Joe. Our rescuer was not a god, though; he was a man behaving as a true hero and acting when he must, but rewarded only with sorrow. In the aftermath of the clash, he sat in his seat, contained but perspiring, fuming, feeling rage and disappointment.

Arturo was redeemed. The protector of his family had lived to work, and survive, the rat race another day. He was not just a legitimate member of society but a proud one, and he was prepared to continue his challenge to the mainstream and forge his own ascent of the career ladder. He would fight his way to the top and fight for his place in the world, which was no longer on the bottom but securely above Joe, Joe whose handicap reduced him to making pathetic threats, running from his own despair.

---

We will be spending time with playful trickster characters as we explore *disruptive play*. But not all playfulness indicates trickster. And while *original play* is an encounter with the chaotic, not all chaos is playful. People like Remus and Arturo, who can find and enjoy playfulness on a regular basis and for good long moments, can be shaken from that tendency and enter a chaotic fray that is anything but playful, is its opposite, fighting. Thus, this story provides a caveat to the coming narrative.

And it's the fact of Arturo and the truths of this story that hint at the profound lessons people with intellectual differences have to teach us: how rationalism goes awry, how limited our knowledge of and exposure to the variability of the human condition is, and what we miss when we ignore or stifle the child's play sustained by such individuals. When their antics inadvertently satirize the so-called sanity of our workplace and we neglect to give pause and reflect, when their anguish signals that play has ceased, they show us ways in which our society must yet heal and grow. When they offer to shepherd us through the gates of the Play Society . . . well, there "comes a time, when the blind man takes your hand, says don't you see?"[5]

---

[5] Jerry Garcia and Robert Hunter, "Comes A Time," *Reflections*, Round Records, 1976, vinyl recording.

# The Sin of Sins

# THREE

# It's Ubique!

*The 19ᵗʰ century seems to leave little room for play. Tendencies running directly counter to all that we mean by play have become increasingly dominant. Even in the 18ᵗʰ century utilitarianism, prosaic effi-ciency and the bourgeois ideal of social welfare— all fatal to the Baroque—had bitten deep into society. These tendencies were exacerbated by the Industrial Revolution and its conquests in the field of technology. Work and production became the ideal, and then the idol, of the age. All Europe donned the boiler-suit. Henceforth the dominants of civilization were to be social consciousness, edu-cational aspirations, and scientific judgment.*

*Johan Huizinga[1]*

HE COMPLETED his best work by the age of twenty-five and wrote what is arguably his masterpiece at the age of fifteen, a tale of his incompetent physics teacher told through marionettes. He was under five feet tall, lived on a half-floor and developed a deep affec-

---

[1] Johan Huizinga, *Homo Ludens: A Study of the Play Element in Culture* (Boston: Beacon, 1955), 191-192.

tion for alcohol, in particular absinthe. He died at thirty-four but is credited with inventing modern art before the twentieth century had even dawned. His life could be summarized as potently playful, an unshackling of the trickster spirit, smuggling in the files, escape plans and explosives that would make Trickster's jailbreak via dada possible.

His name was Alfred Jarry.

Jarry (1873-1907), playwright and cultural revolutionary, successfully distilled and lived in the world of play. His art is indistinguishable from his life, and he fashioned make-believe from everything he touched. If protest is energy projected against the dominant culture, then Alfred Jarry's life proves that to be playful in a society that is not . . . is protest that can reach the level of violence.

Like Monk or Mozart, Hendrix or Picasso, Henri Rousseau or Erik Satie, Jarry seemed to spring forth fully formed. Like play, his creations—The Ubu Cycle, poems, essays *(How to Construct a Time Machine; The New Rifle; Virgin and Manneken-Pis)*, and fiction, especially *Exploits and Opinions of Doctor Faustroll, 'Pataphysician*—come to us fully formed and confound efforts at a developmental theory. His style can be described as scenic, where everything is happening at once, and dialogue emerges from the scenery, starts to make sense, but then dissolves back into hallucination. The perturbing question of *Ubu Roi*—the fictional King of Poland emerging from the caricature of physics teacher Hébert—is answered at the end of his career with the dream vision of 'Pataphysics, his nonsense science of imaginary solutions to the world beyond metaphysics. Evidence of that science of exceptions is present in his early works. He made art of intensity and violence and fully fused it into his being.

A life so rebellious could not be sustained; he had to die young. Jarry's artistic vision was so advanced that some view dada and Surrealism as mere postscripts, adding not much more. He lived completely in the realm of play. He became his key fiction, *Père Ubu*, who in turn was a parody of the rational world.

In Jarry, we have proof of the connection between play and the dream world, and we are confronted with the uncomfortable fact that disruptive play, in our culture, sets loose a monster, yet in monstrosity, we can find inexhaustible beauty.[2] And therein lies the challenge.

The painter Gauguin, a friend of Jarry's, commented that Père Ubu was "the man who has a human body and the soul of wood louse."[3] Whether coincidence or Jungian synchronicity, the louse is also a character in one of the Winnebago Trickster tales. And Ubu springs from Jarry's imagination as a fully formed Trickster archetype, in all his glory and inscrutable mess.

A scene from his play *Ubu Enchaîné* concerns a "disobedience drill" of soldiers in an anarchist army, where every order must be disobeyed, thus putting freedom first. Père Ubu rebels by actually following orders, declaring himself a slave. A revolt ensues where the free men fight for the right to be like Ubu, enslaved and following orders.

One short work alone, *Ubu Cocu* (Ubu Cuckolded), overflows with dream imagery. Ubu and his family, through aggressive language, move into Achras's (a keeper of polyhedra) home uninvited then later impale him on a stake without killing him.

PA UBU, *then later, his* CONSCIENCE.

PA UBU: Have we any right to behave like this? Hornstrumpot, by our green candle, let us consult our Conscience. There he is, in this suitcase, all covered with cobwebs. As you can see, we don't overwork him. *(He opens the suitcase. His Conscience emerges, in the guise of a tall, thin fellow in a shirt.)*

CONSCIENCE: Sir, and so on and so forth, be so good as to take a few notes.

PA UBU: Excuse me, Sir, we are not very partial to writing, though we have no doubt that anything you say would be

---

[2] Taken from an Alfred Jarry quote: "I call monster every original inexhaustible beauty." Alfred Jarry Quotes. BrainyQuote.com, Xplore Inc, 2018. https://www.brainyquote.com/quotes/alfred_jarry_157114, accessed May 2, 2018.

[3] Roger Shattuck, *The Banquet Years* (New York: Vintage 1968), 245.

most interesting. And while we're on the subject, we should like to know how you have the insolence to appear before us in your shirt tails?

CONSCIENCE: Sir, and so on and so forth, Conscience, like Truth, usually goes without a shirt. If I put one on, it is as a mark of respect to the distinguished audience.

PA UBU: As for that, Mister or Mrs. Conscience, you're making a fuss about nothing. Answer this question instead: would it be a good thing to kill Mister Achras who has had the audacity to come and insult me in my own house?

CONSCIENCE: Sir, and so on and so forth, to return good with evil is unworthy of a civilized man. Mister Achras has lodged you; Mister Achras has received you with open arms and made you free of his collection of polyhedra; Mister Achras, and so forth, is a very fine fellow and perfectly harmless; it would be a most cowardly act, and so forth, to kill a poor old man who is incapable of defending himself.

PA UBU: Hornstrumpot! Mister Conscience, are you so sure that he can't defend himself?

CONSCIENCE. Absolutely, Sir, so it would be a coward's trick to do away with him.

PA UBU: Thank you, Sir, we shan't require you further. Since there's no risk attached, we shall assassinate Mister Achras, and we shall also make a point of consulting you more frequently for you know how to give us better advice than we had anticipated. Now, into the suitcase with you! *(He closes it again.)*

CONSCIENCE: In which case, Sir, I think we shall have to leave it at that, and so on and so forth, for today.[4]

Ubu has lit a green candle that emits a perpetual single note as from a flute. The Conscience and Achras conspire unsuccessfully to

---

[4]  Roger Shattuck and Simon Watson Taylor, eds., *Selected Works of Alfred Jarry* (New York: Grove Press, Inc., 1965), 28-29.

do away with Ubu by dropping him through a trap door. Rebontier and Achras recite different soliloquies simultaneously. Ubu and his Conscience argue over whether a crocodile is a whale or a snake.

This brand of disruptive play was not confined to Jarry's writing but leapt into his real-life exploits as well. Jarry built a shack elevated by four supports, which he called a medieval dungeon and dubbed "the Tripod." Jarry and his pals would dress up and impersonate monks; they would stage mock attacks of people in the marketplace with sabers.[5] They performed strange chemical experiments. And they were jocks, enthusiasts of the latest sporting trends (bicycles), canoeing, boxing, and fencing. When the French army sought to equip its troops with a new rifle, Jarry published an objection that the repeating mechanism on the current rifle jammed and made it useless. Therefore, it should be retained so that in defeat the conquering army would be unable to use the weapons.

Such sarcasm and acrobatic logic were not departures for Jarry but typical of his writing, his worldview, and his behaviors. He was simultaneously hilarious and dead serious. He never laughed. He wrote that laughter was born out of the discovery of the contradictory. Such discovery was a given for Jarry, inborn or at least so well trained that it was with deadpan delivery and no further explanation that he enlightened others by adopting a contrarian view. Even his speech patterns reflected it. He never favored one syllable over another, and seventy-five years before computerized voice programs, Jarry deliberately affected a clipped mechanical tone that he became known for, freeing language from the prejudice of accent and inflection, projecting it into a sphere of greater ambiguity.

Who was this exceptional genius who fully embodied the essence of the avant-garde, whose life and art were indistinguishable, who confounded rationality at every turn? He never abandoned the basic insight and rebellion that came when the adult world was first coerced

---

[5] The first flash mob?

upon him as an adolescent schoolboy. Faced with a so-called rational world he could not accept, he held steadfast to the precepts and joys of childhood play and chose to live in the inevitable train wreck.

To take the perspective of the child at play is in this case likened to dreaming while awake. What distinguishes Jarry from a child, then, or from a person with a developmental disability, was his genius intellect that could grasp culture, transform the child/adolescent perspective into guerrilla art, and confront rationality head on. In Jarry's case, this meant to challenge the truth of every statement and expose absurdity . . . that everything considered rational is simply a single perspective selected from many. He lived by the principle that no state of being excludes its opposite; everything is not only possible but also real. In his words, "God is the tangential point between zero and infinity."[6]

The absurd explains the real. There is always another perspective. When a black man ran out of a bar without paying for his drinks, Jarry explained that he was most likely an explorer from Africa investigating European civilizations, and he was embarrassed by his lack of native currency.

One night, Jarry and a friend arrived at a light opera with a note from the composer entitling them to complimentary seats in the orchestra. Jarry had on a white canvas suit with a paper shirt onto which he had painted a tie. Embarrassed, the house manager seated them in the balcony instead. Jarry took his revenge by commenting loudly as the curtain was going up and the musicians were finding their seats: "I don't see why they allow the audience in the first three rows to come in carrying musical instruments."[7]

We are not immune to his perspectives. Jarry's deep satiric bent is alive and well in contemporary pop culture. Monty Python is his beloved

[6] Jarry, Alfred, *Exploits and Opinions of Doctor Faustroll, Pataphysician,* in Roger Shattuck and Simon Watson Taylor, eds., *Selected Works of Alfred Jarry* (New York: Grove Press, Inc., 1965), 256.

[7] Shattuck, *The Banquet Years,* 211-212.

grandson. Jarry was in the room when DC Comics took his contrarian absurdism mainstream with Bizarro world, populated by inversions of Superman, Lois Lane, Jimmy Olson, etc. The internet is littered with absurdity as well.

## Dark Dreaming While Awake

One of the qualities of play is that all things are valued, or none is valued more than another. So, as in a dream, the most trivial image receives as much intention and attention as the most colossal, a paper clip is as significant as a world war.

When a schoolboy, his teachers at the Lycée were his prime targets, and among them was a physics professor Hébert, a boob who the students ridiculed mercilessly. He was to become Jarry's foil and most essential character, Ubu Roi. Hébert metamorphosed from incompetent physics professor to marionette, (as Héb and Hébe), and ultimately to the vanquished King of Poland, Père Ubu. Père Ubu is pure id. Jarry needed a character whose every utterance, whose total behavior, exposed the absurd.

Physics is the most precise and rational tool of the Western mind, describing the world as we believe it to be. But play is spiritual physics animated, an alternate vision. Play challenges time, sequence, and rationality. Thus, it is precisely fitting that Héb would be attempting to teach physics, this bastion of rationality—and be so bad at it that its absurdity became an irresistible target for Jarry to pick and reshape for us as the science of 'Pataphysics.

The catastrophic implosion of Western rationality, World War I, was still almost twenty years away. Yet Jarry was prophetic in forging his alternative universe—to many he seemed crazed, yet he was the sane one in the asylum, comprehending the insanity of the hellbent system.

Jarry's key character, Père Ubu, embodies play, but he is like the Looney Tune tasmanian devil Taz, play's dark side, the archetype for Andy Kaufman's Tony Clifton character, and Jarry's ultimate weapon.

Because in order to build a society that supports the multiple realities of play, a society of conscious life illuminated by dreams, existing society must be vanquished:

> Jarry molested and destroyed, for in the end he knew that his function would be constructive. It is the meaning of the inscription that prefaces Ubu Enchaîné:

> Père Ubu: *Hornsboodle, we should never have knocked everything down if we hadn't meant to destroy the ruins too. But the only way we see of doing that is to put up some handsome buildings.*

> Only new construction can ultimately destroy the old. Beyond Jarry's nihilism there is a positive side to his work. Creating in Ubu a one-man demolition squad twenty years before Dada, he incorporated this figure into works that go on to broach transcendental values.[8]

So the introduction of disruptive play demands a massive rejection of the not-play or cultural play contest that dominates society. The inevitable conflict is toxic to cultural play (see Chapter 10, *Abbie Hoffman, Lone Warrior of Play* and Chapter 11, *Andy Kaufman, Holy Fool*) and confrontational. All this is embodied in Père Ubu.

Père Ubu's most distinctive features were his immense belly and his three teeth, one each of stone, wood, and iron. He was a glutton incapable of even picking himself up off of the ground. His behavior was consistently reprehensible, his assassination of Achras typical.

*Ubu Roi* debuted on December 11, 1896. The first word of the play, *merdre*, "shit," caused fifteen minutes of pandemonium in the theater before the performance could proceed. The story itself, told with much scatology, parodies Macbeth, as Père Ubu murders his way to the throne of Poland, pillages the country, and is then vanquished and forced to flee to France, from whence he threatens more havoc.

---

[8] Shattuck, *The Banquet Years*, 226-227.

Ubu is an obscene sinner, but in truth not a sinner because he never acknowledged or knew any difference between right or wrong. He is more accurately described as pure id or a trickster and is thus completely free and completely selfish. Jarry needed to unleash this monster upon us to cleanse the world of an order and sense of morality that was constraining the human spirit and obstructing our true propensity towards play. Centuries repressed, it is naïve to believe that disruptive play could be released gracefully. Shattuck comments:

> Baudelaire had a theory of the comic which took as its premise that an angel tripping over its wings would not be funny in the manner of a man slipping on a banana peel.

> ... Human laughter is intimately linked to the circumstance of our ancient fall, or our physical and moral degradation. . . .

> Let us try, since the comic is an element of damnation and of diabolic origin, to consider an absolutely primitive soul, one which so to speak has escaped nature's hands. *(De l'essence du rire.)*

> Baudelaire takes as his example Virginie from Bernardin de Saint Pierre's romantic novel *Paul et Virginie.* Yet the innocence of Virginie's virtue is as nothing beside the innocence of Ubu's evil. Both are oblivious of human values. Ubu has only his appetites, which he displays like virtues. When we try to injure him with our laughter ("satanic" laughter, Baudelaire would call it), we discover that his behavior is so abject that we cannot reach him. He does not have traits of either a great hero or a great villain; he never deliberates. Can we really laugh at Ubu, at his character? It is doubtful, for he lacks the necessary vulnerability, the vestiges of original sin. Not without dread, we mock, rather, his childish innocence and primitive soul and cannot harm him. He remains a threat because he can destroy at will, and the political horrors of the twentieth century make the lesson disturbingly real.[9]

---

[9] Shattuck, *The Banquet Years,* 234-235.

Thus we confront the scary power of play's dark side. This is why the practitioners of deep play and original play sometimes balk at the thought of disruptive play, though the three need to be connected. Without the spiritual grounding of deep and original play, disruptive play becomes contaminated by the power game it could otherwise transcend. Play is not a moral affair, yet the undoing of power games must be complete before play can be released beneficially, thus there is a moral (and mortal) battle before us. Père Ubu is a nightmare, but he is completely free, and in an uncontaminated world, that freedom is precisely the evolutionary goal of human society. Thus he, and Jarry who became him, are critical martyrs. Ubu has deliberately infected himself with society's illnesses. Absurd?

Jarry was popular among the literati of Paris, to the point where the term *ubique*, inspired by his Ubu plays, entered the vernacular. But such notoriety is not sustenance. To fully inhabit play in a world inimical to it—even in *la belle époque* Paris (1871-1914)—requires a special combination of ego strength and vulnerability that can be deadly. For Jarry it was; he died at the age of thirty-four. Aspects of a stable and socially acceptable personality had to be sacrificed in order to expose and bring play out into the open. Jarry made that sacrifice, and most likely made a conscious decision during his adolescence to forsake some of the tradeoffs that a socially acceptable adulthood required. Like the Trickster, he had few sexual or romantic relationships; and he lived in constant poverty, regarded by many as a freak.

Though the cause of death was tuberculosis, the condition was exacerbated by poverty and alcohol. The cheapest alcohol and even ether were his tools for sustaining the hallucinatory state. There were no workshops available on how to play and survive as an adult. As a true forerunner, he put a strain on his existence, which Shattuck describes as such: "The conscious and the unconscious fuse into a continuum which coincides with the fusion of thought and action, art and life, childhood and maturity."[10]

---

[10] Shattuck, *The Banquet Years*, 201.

His reward was to live a life that strived for the limits of absolute freedom. Jarry made high art of adolescence. And adolescence is a time when play is not completely forgotten and adulthood eyed with great suspicion. What Jarry established as a juvenile perspective at the turn of the century came to dominate humor a hundred years later. Be it *Saturday Night Live*; Amy Schumer; *Monty Python's Flying Circus*; Stephen Colbert; Zach Galifianakis; *National Lampoon*; *MAD* magazine; Martin Short; *In Living Color*; Sarah Silverman; *South Park*; the movies of Terry Gilliam; the antics of Andy Kaufman, Gilda Radner, Jonathan Winters, Lily Tomlin, Bill Murray, Chevy Chase, Jim Carrey, Adam Sandler, John Belushi, Chris Farley, Chris Rock, or Robin Williams; comedy at the millennium routinely exploits the absurd and goes for the juvenile jugular.

His price was self-sacrifice in the interest of teaching us that reality is in fact subjective, that the stuff of dreams can be lived. Fortunately, he lived in a time and place that amplified these possibilities. Though Parisian tolerance ultimately killed dada with kindness, Paris gave Jarry enough room to play, and without the splendid fertility and open spirit of *la belle époque* Paris, we might never have known him.

## Jarry's Enormous Influence

The aspect of disruptive play most difficult to convey is the element that requires destruction, for this is what most scares people. Like the anarchists prominent in his time, Jarry called for a full destruction of the ranking and institutionalization of art and the society that spawned it. Most react to the call for destruction before they hear that it is made in the interest of discovering a new and higher order. Sometimes the decks must be cleared, and I will attempt to answer this difficult question of disruptive play in a later chapter, but it is made conspicuous by Jarry's life.

There are virtually no standards by which to judge the role Jarry created and the decor with which he surrounded himself in order to sustain it. He discarded every standard, ethic, maxim, golden rule, and secret of success. In the end, his role implies new, almost non-human standards, evidenced by the completeness of his transformation. Everything in his universe had to yield to his power to change it. Nothing escaped, neither the conventions of eating, which he destroyed by the simple expedience of devouring meals backward from pastry to peasant soup, nor common sense itself, which he stalked with the brilliant antireason of 'pataphysics.[11]

As radical as Jarry was, some mainstream trends supported and made sense of the absurdities he acted out. And the key word here is **act**. In previous centuries, station preempted self. You didn't have to wonder about who you were because your birth determined it. As democracies took hold between the seventeenth and nineteenth centuries, the idea that one was born into a malleable citizenship, that one could make an identity, gained currency.[12] At the same time, the status and recognition of the actor rose, and people began to connect what the actor does on stage with what people do in life. Shattuck quotes lines from Sartre, who describes a café waiter carefully playing the role of a café waiter—in his rapid and precise movements, his inflexible stiffness, the acrobatic juggling of dishes and balancing of trays . . .

> . . . All his behavior seems to us a *game*. . . . He is playing, he is amusing himself. But what is he playing? It doesn't take long to see: he is playing at being a café waiter. . . . The child plays with his body in order to explore it and take inventory of it. The waiter plays with his condition in order to attain it.

> . . . [But] this waiter in the café cannot immediately be a café waiter in the sense that this inkwell *is* an inkwell. . . . He knows his condition means getting up at five o'clock, the right to tips, etc. . . . But all that is a matter of abstract possibilities, of rights and duties conferred on a "person possessing rights."

---

[11] Shattuck, *The Banquet Years*, 211.

[12] As influenced by the Romantic movement and the philosophy of Jean-Jacques Rousseau.

... It is a "performance" for others and for myself, which means that I can be he only in performance, by impersonation. But if I impersonate him I am not he; I am separated from him as object from subject. . . . I cannot be he, I can only play at being he, that is, imagine to myself that I am he . . . yet there is no doubt that I *am* in a sense a café waiter.[13]

Jarry realized this to the point that he walked the line of sanity, and in public, he became his primal character Ubu Roi. To help us imagine Jarry, we have the modern example of Andy Kaufman, whose friends testify that towards the end of his career he lost track of his "real" personality and affected his many characters. There are lessons in this. We live in an insane asylum, but within a consensus on what roles each of us play. So-called crazies like Jarry, Duchamp, Kaufman, Vaché, Cassady, and Cravat are elevating the game and pointing to the genesis of the Play Society, where roles are more flexible. "If everybody lives roughly the same lies about the same things, there is no one to call them liars: they jointly establish their own sanity and call themselves normal."[14]

Every day we read about another billionaire or maverick politician who garnered great success by "breaking all the rules" and just "following their bliss," playing. Such individuals perform interesting refinements of "the rules." which attract dollars or votes, but they are fakes. True rule-breakers are extremely rare and tend to be those who challenge a ranked and unplayful system. Play is the revolutionary force that breaks the rules and allows the occasional glimpse into a world beyond the rational, the dream world of transitory rules. Jarry was just such a character, and the difficulty of being Alfred Jarry testifies to the awesome power and daunting challenge that play presents in Western society.

---

[13] Jean-Paul Sartre, *Essays in Existentialism* (New York: Citadel, 1993), 167-169.

[14] Ernest Becker, *The Birth and Death of Meaning* (New York: The Free Press, 1973), 221.

# FOUR

# Trickster Meets the Twentieth Century

> As everyone knows, the Impressionists were preoc-
> cupied with light; they sought to seize its fluid play
> at single points in space and time. To achieve that,
> they had to abandon all preconceived notions of
> color, to abjure dark pigments and adopt bright
> ones, to ignore local tones in order to capture
> general Impressions, to blur the outlines of objects
> by applying paint in perceptible strokes. All this
> was necessary in order to capture the scintillating
> quality of the play of light itself.
>
> Sir Peter Hall[1]

ORIGINAL PLAY is the play of very young children and other life forms, a spiritual activity that connects humans, with each other and across species, and with an essential life force. Deep play is a blissful state that adults find while engaged in artistic and adventurous pursuits, but most often solitary and apart from social reality.

In Alfred Jarry, we encountered an artist who immersed himself in a third form, disruptive play, play in the midst of a society inhospitable to it. He embraced, clung to, and embodied a number of trickster characteristics and lived a rigorously playful persona inseparable

---

[1] Sir Peter Hall, *Cities in Civilization* (New York: Pantheon, 1998), 202.

from his art. He exposed the terror and horror of rationalism. The antagonism he provoked was lethal. And so he bore the intense punishment of not going along with the program, of his loyalty to the absurd. His sacrifice made the world safe(r) for the players to come.

Jarry played around ahead of the times and in a solitary performance. It would take a somewhat less notorious and more accessible group of artists to create a bigger bandwagon for play in culture. Playful, rebellious, antitraditional, and anticommercial, Impressionist art lit up modernity's dawn. Impressionism brought unprecedented success to poor, starving bohemian outsiders, artists who also opened the door for play to animate Western politics and culture.

We perceive the Trickster archetype as durable yet elusive. And while Trickster is revered, respected, and sacrificed to in non-Western cultures, Westernism represses and casts out play and the Trickster, Jarry being no exception. Playful adults, artists, the poor, people with disabilities, and deviators are all sent to the margins. From the seventeenth century development of military tactics and the industrial revolution of the eighteenth century came a more prescriptive sense of the normal and the suppression of carnival celebrations and urges . . . thus the binding of the Trickster spirit.[2] The concentration of power, by its very nature, requires divesting this spirit, treating the Trickster as the Fool or court jester. But eventually the Fool makes fools of those who would constrain, punish, and repress Trickster spirit.

In *Trickster Makes This World*,[3] Lewis Hyde delves deeply into the mythology around the trickster god Loki. Much is devoted to Loki's binding. While the elaborate tale of how Loki is bound is what draws attention, it was his boundary-crossing tricksterism that brought

---

[2] Barbara Ehrenreich, *Dancing in the Streets: A History of Collective Joy* (New York: Metropolitan, 2006), 122-127.

[3] Lewis Hyde, *Trickster Makes This World* (New York: Farrar, Straus and Giroux, 1998), 100-107.

on this controlling and Christian punishment: stealing the Golden Apples of Immortality and the killing of Baldr. In the scriptures of Norse mythology, the transition of the Trickster from respected god to punished outcast can be seen in the Loki of the *Poetic Edda*, based on pagan folklore, and that of the *Prose Edda*, which seeks to put Norse mythology into a Christian context. It is not just the punishment but the deed of playfulness and the punishment it provokes that shed light on the symbolic design of the Christian Era.[4]

For example, when nineteenth century anthropologists encountered the collective joy and playfulness of ecstatic dance, trance, and other rituals of nonwestern cultures, they described them as grotesque, savage, disgusting, and hideous. The prevailing theory was that such rituals were evidence of the inferiority of these non-Western races. By the 1930s, these beliefs of a less evolved human were discarded by the academics, but the rituals and drives toward a playful *communitas* still stirred the entrenched fears of the repressed Westerner, fears that persisted deep into the twentieth century and continue to poison our collective psyche.[5] The demonizing of Èṣù-Elegba by a slave-owning society bent on punishment is another tragic example.

But Trickster cannot be indefinitely confined, and in the volatile and sweeping changes in Europe and the US that announced the twentieth century, tricksterism and play made their jailbreak, bursting the bonds of the dominant order and setting the stage for a world liberated from war and hierarchy. And this tale is not one of mythological gods but of a historical phase presaged by Jarry that challenges and taunts seriousness and the foundations of power itself.

In the twenty-first century, it is self-evident that the arts are where rebel spirit, social critique, levity, playful gibing, and radical proposi-

---

[4] Christianity came to Scandinavia after 1000 AD; the Loki myth as told before and after differs accordingly.

[5] Ehrenreich, *Dancing in the Streets*, 1-16.

tions find platform and refuge. They provide a reasonably safe place for the trickster spirit to play. But this was not always the case.

## Four Things You Find In A Golden Age

The institutionalization of art in France dates to the establishment of the Academy of Painting and Sculpture[6] in 1648. The government did not control art through censorship but through rigid rules that defined aesthetic quality—there was a stranglehold on what paintings and sculptures reached the public. Acceptance of this system was indisputable. It was official, and it was popular. By the nineteenth century, biannual Salons—the government's exhibitions of approved art—could attract close to a million people over the course of its fifty-five days of show.

Two hundred years later, Europe saw a concentration of wealth amongst a new bourgeois class that would build railroads, internationalize trade, accelerate investing, and, for the first time, create a significant and broader market for paintings. Art was commodified, and the governmental grip loosened. Soon thereafter came new concepts in painting, and artists who adopted an anticommerce view. Being outside the government system that supported a more staid style, they created their own bohemian subculture. They met in cafés and formed alternative schools and studios, which would come to characterize the impending golden age.

In *Cities in Civilization*,[7] Sir Peter Hall identifies four characteristics consistently found in a cultural, urban golden age. Firstly, a culture, "a long accumulation of psychological and social traits, a kind of cultural reproduction over generations, among a people living together in a country or a region or a city, that makes them especially amenable to art or to thought."[8] Secondly, the chaos of cre-

---

[6] The Académie Royale de Peinture et de Sculpture, which was absorbed by the Académie de Beaux-Arts in 1816.

[7] Hall, *Cities in Civilization*, 15-20.

[8] Hall, *Cities in Civilization*, 20-21.

ativity, borne of an instability. After a defined path and means of passing knowledge on from generation to generation has developed, the knowledge and competence synergize and give birth to creative energy.[9] Eras of creativity are preceded by an apparent stagnation that is actually more of a gestational moment of styles and talents accumulating before the new age is born. Thirdly, outsiders. The interest generated by the culture and nascent creativity attracts people from other countries and cities, from other cultures, and from other walks of life: examples include the talents attracted to Athens through its mercantile empire (500-400 BC), the critical influence of Jews in Vienna (1780-1910), and the first tech boom of the San Francisco Bay Area and Silicon Valley (1950-1990).[10] And fourthly, economic factors, though not necessarily wealth. A golden age can also be a transformation from a traditional aristocratic order to a new system based on merit and enterprise.[11]

Impressionism in Paris met all four criteria. The culture of painting was a national treasure. Paris entered that phase of seeming stagnation, pregnant with possibility, in the second half of the nineteenth century. Competence in painting was widespread, and there was an incredible archive in the Louvre. The players themselves were outsiders from Spain (Canals), Holland (van Gogh), the Danish West Indies (Pissaro), and the provinces of France (Monet, Bazille and Cézanne). Manet, Degas, Sisley, and Renoir were Parisians, but from troubled family circumstances that made them outsiders in some sense, all benefitting from emergent individualism.

Hall's fourth requirement, economic transition, was met by capitalism's expansion into a market economy—industrialization, economies of scale, and sustained demand. In the case of art in France, it

[9] Hall, *Cities in Civilization*, 18-19.

[10] And a meshing of outside talent with that of "Exemplary Creators", i.e., Howard Gardner, *Creating Minds: An Anatomy of Creativity Seen through the Lives of Freud, Einstein, Picasso, Stravinsky, Eliot, Graham, and Gandhi* (New York: Basic, 1993), 40-41.

[11] Hall, *Cities in Civilization*, 22.

was a matter of critics functioning as publicists, ideologues, and theorists, educating a public as to why this new art was good. The dealers kept their fingers on the pulse of this bohemian culture, purchasing and reselling the latest undiscovered genius's *oeuvre*. And voilà, you had a movement known as Impressionism. In economic terms, it was the birth of the modern art industry.

Huizinga makes a similar observation of the transition from an agonistic to a decadent phase that arises when there are fewer common enemies to surmount. Whereas aristocratic leaders establish new orders through military victories and conquests, the peaceful eras that follow typically advance commerce and democratization. Paris from 1871 until World War I, enjoyed one of these peaceful and golden ages, *la belle époque.*

But in these transitions from one system of commerce to another or from one social order to another, there is a hiccup in the historical cycle. Play as a revolutionary vision has a moment, shows its potential, and the Trickster spirit breaks free and takes the opportunity to "oil the joints" and influence the new, emerging orders.[12] The overwhelming power of the repressed Western psyche and the tempting rewards of a capitalist system that would rather dub a new avant-garde than effect authentic social change stifle this impulse as quickly as it appears, but the imp shows its Trickster self nonetheless, each time with greater presence and recognition. Before a modern market economy took over (fraught with the elements of contest), the game was exposed just long enough for playful artists to name it and propose an alternate vision. This began with the Impressionists, peaked with dada, and withdrew into Surrealism.

## Four Artists, Four Traits of Play

The seeds of modern art were as old as Voltaire in the eighteenth century, and Delacroix, Miller, and Courbet, who in the mid-nineteenth century turned to common walks of life and international

---

[12] Hyde, *Trickster Makes This World.*

influences for material instead of utilizing the aesthetically correct and ancient domestic myths—angels, gods, and aristocracies. Creative artists seized upon the technological innovations of photography and portable paint to make it possible for these influences to be brought together in a coherent and less inhibited revolutionary art movement, Impressionism, after which fine art would never again resemble itself.

Impressionism's crashing of the gates—formally prescribed aesthetics, government patronage—was largely unintentional; the Impressionists' commitment to play enlivened their daily lives, but they pursued commercial success: for their paintings and for their careers. Had the judges running the government Salons decided to like the Impressionists' paintings, the (mostly) starving artists would have gladly accepted the offer, and eventually benefitted from the new commercial system.

Roger Shattuck identified four artists—a playwright, a critic/poet, a composer, and a painter—who stood outside the Impressionist stream, yet characterized *la belle époque* and set the stage for dada.[13] Three of them—impresario and poet Guillaume Apollinaire, composer Erik Satie and writer Alfred Jarry—are dadas, but all four expressed a supreme innocence of play in their creations and tilled fertile ground for the play-element to thrive in art. As far as leading the modern art movements, the four's iconoclastic contributions did not represent a specific stylistic direction. Rather they gave permission for artists to strike out in whatever direction they pleased.

Shattuck describes four traits that Apollinaire, Jarry, Satie, and painter Henri Rousseau share. All are characteristics of play as well.

The first emerges from *the cult of childhood* established by the Romantics.[14] It is the idea of the "child-man," where a grownup has refrained

---

[13] Roger Shattuck, *The Banquet Years* (New York: Vintage, 1968). Also, *dada* will not be capitalized here. Lowercasing the first d in dada was a style adopted by many Dadaists (née dadas, by which I shall call them). They were playing with us and with convention.

[14] The Romantic movement, for example, was heavily influenced by the philosophy of Jean-Jacques Rousseau.

from putting off childish things. Thus, the Romantics revise the idea of maturity and question the stifling of childhood by education and society. Such reconsideration opens the door to adult play. To some extent, all four artists explore themes of childhood. The refreshing innocence and vulnerability of Henri Rousseau's paintings—*The Sleeping Gypsy, The Dream, Boy on the Rocks*—are realized through the eyes of a child.

The second is *humor and absurdity*. Humor, laughter, and play are inextricably tied together. Humor emerged in *la belle époque* as a method and a style. Satie composed funny music even though music most challenges the conveyance of humor. Satie music is like playful wisecracks artfully scrawled on the walls of "classical" music. Like graffiti artists who have to run away as soon as they've painted, Satie pieces alight with unexpected melodies and chords, and then, like a sprite, they are gone.

His music and his scored musical directions ("With profound respect," "Take off your glasses") were sincere quips that entertained and suggested music's potential to bring a laugh. Listening to his music is, in fact, often a comedic experience. Humor invites an exploration of the absurd, clearly revealed in Jarry's *Ubu* character or Satie's antics.

The third characteristic results from a further extrapolation of absurdity, and that is *exploration of the dream state*. Play is make-believe, a bridge between waking consciousness and dreams. Jarry in particular considered the dream as merely another way to illuminate the world, a reality as valid as the wakeful one. He took on the lives of his fictional characters—he would actually go out in public as one of his characters and stay in character as easily as one puts on a pair of pants.[15]

And the culminating synergy of these three traits gives rise to the fourth, *ambiguity*, the expression of two or more meanings in a single

---

[15] Foreshadowing an eerie connection to Andy Kaufman, which will be explored in a later chapter.

symbol or sound. The contrast between play and a life rationally lived creates the basis for satire. Imagine a clown performing in the somber arena of a courtroom à la Monty Python. *Dr. Strangelove* is satire on the deadly rationality of nuclear brinksmanship run amok. Ambiguity as perspective, as philosophy, as reality. Ambiguity affords equal weight to multiple meanings of a song, poem, play, or painting (or life).

This is a central quality of play, that of extending belongingness and creating an open space where there is no one right answer, no exclusive claims of membership or of correctness. The idea of deliberate ambiguity is conspicuously absent or at least esoteric in Western art and thought prior to this era. Thus, Shattuck's four progenitors and their creations, which greatly influenced all modern art, embody play's child-likeness, humor, dream state, and ambiguity. Their work was prelude to a full expression of original play socially engaged, or disruptive play.

The Impressionists revealed just enough of the absurdity of Paris society and Western life in general to set the stage for dada, which would lay bare the even greater absurdities of rationalism and hierarchy that were holding the human spirit hostage. The more criticism and bad press Impressionism received—though there were always some favorable reviews—the more people came out to view these controversial works. Being excluded from the state-endorsed Salon competitions added notoriety and made an Impressionist artist more interesting to the public. As the popularity of these renegades grew, more people saw the obsolescence of the old order, and conditions ripened for artistic revolution and play.

Impressionists rebelled against the traditional, academic art of the period, with its emphasis on romantic or allegorical subjects and its worship of craftsmanship and polish. Instead, they responded to the world through their senses: Berthe Morisot's *A Summer's Day*, Degas's *After the Bath, Woman Drying Herself*, Picasso's *The Dream*, Renoir's *The Garden in the rue Cortot, Montmartre*.[16]

---

[16] Robin Updike, "Lasting Impressions," *The Seattle Times, Impressions* June 6, 1999, 2.

Impressionists painters, somewhat innocent in their pursuit of an aesthetic vision, were following a muse as seemingly innocuous as light. But the idea of breaking away from the state-supported Salon was radical, the fine arts equivalent to Luther's rebellion against the Catholic Church. The Impressionists' independent show of 1874, even though it was a commercial failure, provoked denunciation by the right wing as an attack on the government.

Before their commercial success, Impressionists[17] adopted an anti-commerce view that bonded them. To provoke government-regulated taste made their camaraderie even tighter. Their styles were sometimes indistinguishable from each other, not from lack of originality, but because of close relationships and a collective spirit. The artistic product was secondary to the life of the community that created it.

The French government lent vigorous support to the arts, which could be viewed as progressive. But the independent Impressionist shows challenged that establishment, politically and aesthetically. In other words, the government-sponsored Salons and the Académie des Beaux-Arts were anathema to play. But if art at its essence is play, the Impressionist movement instigated sensual art as playful revolution, and the great uprising of disruptive play known as dada.

## Not That Revolution, This Revolution

Hall compares Impressionism, the art revolution of *fin de siècle* France, to industrial revolutions such as the rise of the cotton industry in Manchester (1760-1830) and shipbuilding in Glasgow (1770-1890). But while all these revolutions changed relationships between people, common folk played a passive role in these transitions to a more advanced form of capitalism. Modern art in Europe probed on the level of ideas, not goods. It raised questions about the social order and thus the agency of the citizen. Even if it was just a hiccup. Even

---

[17] Most notably Monet, Pisarro, and Cézanne.

if those questions were quelled by the new economic order of the art dealer/critic/collector symbiosis. Even if, like the Impressionists, political revolt was not the intention of the artists.

The rebellion began as a style. Impressionists affected bohemian dress and unkempt hair. They dispensed with the *de rigueur* umbrellas, gloves, and shirt collars. They discovered that radicalism could bring notoriety. But they came undone. While the cabarets were the birthplace and weaning ground of a new social vision, they were also the showrooms where dealers would bring new artists and their work together with potential customers. Capital investment quarantined social statement, a contradiction that artists have been struggling with ever since.

There had been independent dealers in Paris dating back to the 1830s, but they posed no serious challenge to the state system. In the 1860s, the Salon was still the only way to get known and have a career. But by the 1900s, the Salon had become a ridiculed sham; now you needed a critic, a publicist, and a dealer on your side. The paintings were fetching high prices. Social statement would only screw up the new system, which was now in place; dealers had neutralized the politics of Impressionism.

To understand how Impressionists vacated their budding social commitment and dada embraced it is to understand the difference between emerging commercialism and true anticommerce. Was anticommercialism simply an attitude for artists to adopt and make their art more chic, or was it a deeply held conviction that meant producing art that confounded the marketplace, that intentionally had no commercial potential? All forms of modern art growing out of the Impressionist movement capitulated to the rules of the new marketplace system; art became an industry and a product.

Except for dada.

Cubism, the first major new movement to emerge from Impressionism, provides the best example. Few dispute that Picasso's *Les*

*Demoiselles d'Avignon* (1907) and Duchamp's *Nu descendant un escalier, n°2 (Nude Descending a Staircase, No. 2, 1912)* are among the first great cubist paintings, yet Duchamp left this school to pursue ready-mades in 1913, a more random, playful, and challenging art form. Picasso, on the other hand, was eager and ready to run with the form and begin building his career. Picasso, for all the wonder and genius of his contribution, defined himself within the role of artist and would be the most successful exponent of the dealer/critic/publicist system. As we shall see, other artists had their minds on a bigger game: dada, the antiwar, anti-celebrity (anti-)art[18] movement inspired by Alfred Jarry and prolonged by Marcel Duchamp.

---

[18] Hans Richter, *dada: art and anti-art* (London: Thames and Hudson, 1997), 9: "Dada invited, or rather defied, the world to misunderstand it, and fostered every kind of confusion. This was done from caprice and from a principle of contradiction."

# FIVE

# Who Is to Blame for dada?

*What dada proposed was not the end of art as such but a radically new conception of creative activity, a fresh equation between the variables: art-self-reality. It was here that dada's originality lay...dada, like Surrealism after it, envisaged the artist as a spiritual adventurer for whom productivity was of secondary importance.*

*Robert Short*[1]

*Cubism was a school of painting, futurism a political movement: DADA is a state of mind. To oppose one to the other reveals ignorance or bad faith.*

*Free-thinking in religion has no resemblance to a church. Dada is artistic free-thinking.*

*André Breton*[2]

*Dada was child's play, literally and figuratively...*

*Roger Shattuck*[3]

---

[1] Robert Short, *Dada and Surrealism* (Secaucus, NJ: Chartwell Books, 1980), 20.

[2] Short, *Dada and Surrealism*, 18. Short is quoting from *Geography Dada*.

[3] Roger Shattuck, "The D-S Expedition," in *The Innocent Eye: On Modern Literature and the Arts* (New York: Farrar, Straus and Giroux, 1984), 41.

NEATLY TUCKED between Cubism and Surrealism, one is tempted, perhaps even encouraged, to digest dada as merely one of many art movement isms from before World War II—Postimpressionism, Cubism, Social Realism, Futurism, Expressionism, Fauvism, Constructivism. But even a cursory examination of dada reveals it to be as much a political as an art movement. Dig a little deeper, and you find that it superseded other politically minded art movements like Futurism, Social Realism and Expressionism by holding that most fragile quality, a sense of humor, and by going beyond the presentation of painting, literature, and poetry into activist public theater and performance art. dada represents the Trickster's jailbreak from Western rationality and Puritan binding. Peel away the onion layers surrounding dada, and at its core lives the miracle of play, fantastically animated in a social context.

The emergence of Impressionism (and all the liberties it implied) and the stark contrast between the ensuing bohemianism and the agony and absurdity of World War I collided to forge dada. Through a remarkable serendipity and the logical thrust of the art movements and historical events that immediately preceded it, dada dissembled logic and presented play as society's only viable future. dada delivered its timeless message and made a hasty exit. When the dust settled, we were left with questions of dada's impact. Where did the scent of disruptive play left by dada's energy lead in the years that followed? Was dada a futile gesture, a joke, or a heartfelt effort to point the way to the next phase of human progress?

## Vive le France! Vive le Paris! Vive dada!

The social potential of art has always carried the greatest intrigue in France, particularly in Paris society. From 1885 onward, Paris was the leading edge—the avant-garde—in politics, fashion, architecture, lifestyle and the arts, and particularly theater. After Hausmann's completion of its urban renewal that brought broadened boulevards, Theatre Francais, the new Opera House, and city hall, Paris "...had become a stage, a vast theater for herself and all the world. For thirty years the frock coats and monocles, the toppers and bowlers . . . seemed to be designed to fit this vast stage-set, along with the ladies' long dresses and corsets and eclipsing hats. Street cleaners in blue denim, gendarmes in trim capes, butchers in leather aprons, coachmen in black cutaways, the army's crack *chasseurs* in plumes, gold-braid, and polished boots—everyone wore a costume and displayed himself to best advantage."[4]

Most importantly, there was a civic self-consciousness to this role-playing, which translated into a theater consciousness. "The theater reigned supreme. Yet it was all a show within a show. The frenzy on hundreds of stages all over Paris reflected the gala life around them. At the Opera . . . the performance never stopped the fashionable goings-on in the boxes. The city beheld itself endlessly and was never bored or distracted."[5] Thus at the heart of Western art comes a significant and indisputable blurring of the separation between play confined to the stage or the canvas and the daily lives of the audience. There was a mass quest to discover the self.

One indication of this spiritual and artistic birth was a proliferation of adulterous affairs and liberated sexuality. Sarah Bernhardt was the reigning artist and sexually liberated pop figure; in this case, play is sex play. As the prototype for the Hollywood star, Bernhardt created the mold Madonna, Christina Aguilera, and Lady Gaga were to exploit many decades later. She brought talent, irreverence, and play to her personal, professional, and public life. In the United States, celebrities with the luxury and wealth that allow them a more playful life continue to infuriate the Puritan core of the American

---

[4] Roger Shattuck, *The Banquet Years* (New York: Vintage, 1968), 5-6.

[5] Shattuck, *The Banquet Years*, 9.

psyche and breed scandal. American permissiveness always bears the stigma of licentiousness—in France, no such taboos existed, and play was given freer reign.

And the Parisians could not ignore the disconcerting anarchist movement that romped onto this stage; they were sympathetic to its ultrademocratic theories and the bravura of its leaders. The challenge of the anarchists—question all assumptions—was taken earnestly, which meant that the emerging movements in the arts could no longer rely upon any formulated aesthetic. Thus, the sense and rationality of the previous century was shattered, and a window opened. "Anarchism itself can be seen as a form of political primitivism trying to return to an earlier stage of social evolution. What one can overlook most easily in all this demonstration is its stubborn purpose to change the aspect of both life and art. There was a connection . . . between the irrepressible frivolity of the upper classes and the resolute gaiety of young artists."[6]

The hard lesson for Parisians was that the energy of play has implications far beyond the "frivolity of the upper classes." Disruptive play challenges the political systems that protect and sustain those classes. The upper classes and the bohemian artists are thus locked in a paradoxical embrace: disruptive play (anarchism or dada) will expose the contest-play that, through capitalist exploitation, creates a false play-space for the elite . . . a false or decadent play-space because it is achieved through economic exploitation. Bohemians and elite feed off each other at the same time that they seek each other's exploitation or overthrow.

The outrageous prank was to become the hallmark of dada. As disruptive play, it illuminated class tension. Around the turn of the century, a group of young artists of the Lapin Agile Cabaret, just gaining in notoriety and earning an income but by no means wealthy, filled a canvas with paint applied by the swishing tail of a donkey. It was submitted to the *Salon des Indépendants* as "And the Sun Went Down

---

[6] Shattuck, *The Banquet Years*, 24.

over the Adriatic" and was praised by a number of reputable critics. The "What Is Art?" question thus made its rude entrance.

And for a while, play begat greater play. As early as *fin de siècle* France, the avant-garde ran the dual risks of either getting too far ahead or else becoming too commonplace for the mainstream. Thus, to preserve the potency of their statement and sustain momentum, artists would quite deliberately manufacture scandal and invent lies that would continue to shock and attract sensation. Performance artists continue this battle today, to "venture far into the realm of pure buffoonery without abandoning their loyalty to artistic creation."[7] These Trickster artists crossed boundaries—of the stage and the conventional performer-audience relationship—inciting social transformation. None of these pioneers is pure, and many "went astray and lost touch with human values. But their vices lie so close to their virtues that they cannot be separated without careful scrutiny. . . ."[8]

But we are not seeking out heroes, we seek the elements of social transformation—the possibilities of the Play Society—that dadas like Arp, Duchamp, Ball, Richter, Breton, Huelsenbeck, Cravan, Vaché, Ernst and Tzara energized.

So Paris, a beacon of liberalism and free thought, inspired the world and opened up possibilities for artists and revolutionaries alike—in art, music, poetry, literature, philosophy, and political action.

Then upon this vibrant and playful cultural gestalt came a war of unprecedented scale.

## Draft Dodging in Zurich: dada's Greatest Hits

While some dismiss art and artists as peripheral to politics and economics,[9] dada's roots indicate the contrary. They were intentionally antiwar and confrontational of the war machine. World War I was

---

[7] Shattuck, *The Banquet Years*, 26.

[8] Shattuck, *The Banquet Years*, 28.

[9] i.e., An early modern sign of this was the failure and ineffectiveness of the First International Congress of Writers for the Defense of Culture in 1935. Shattuck, "Having Congress," in *The Innocent Eye*, 3-31.

quite possibly the most powerful impetus for dada to elevate and transform the ways in which we perceive, experience, and digest creativity. The artists' sensibilities are not extraneous to the purposes of government. In Hugo Ball's unpublished novel of 1919, *Kritik der deutschen Intelligenz* (Critique of the German Intelligentsia), he foresees the horrors of Hitlerism. Hans Arp, a leading dada, predicted Stalinism and more as early as 1915:

> Revolted by the butchery of the 1914 World War, we
> in Zurich devoted ourselves to the arts. While the guns
> rumbled in the distance, we sang, painted, made collages
> and wrote poems with all our might. We were seeking an
> art based on fundamentals, to cure the madness of the age,
> and a new order of things that would restore the balance
> between heaven and hell. We had a dim premonition that
> power-mad gangsters would one day use art itself as a way
> of deadening men's minds.[10]

dada's lack of easy definition was more than a deliberate ploy. It was also the chaos of the circumstances—an absurd war—that brought German, American, French, Austrian, Romanian, Ukrainian, Alsatian and Swiss artists to Switzerland (Zurich), a country with no significant artistic traditions of its own. It was its political status as a neutral haven for pacifists that drew this eclectic group there. Switzerland's political displacement, coupled with its lack of a fertile artistic culture meant that dada was uniquely free to birth itself unbound by cultural tradition (notably not meeting Hall's conditions for a golden age), and to make direct contact with sources beyond culture—like play.

In February of 1916, Hans Arp's friend and fellow idealist Hugo Ball opened the Cabaret Voltaire in Zurich. And with great glee and playfulness, they deconstructed art there nightly. It was, in Ball's mind, a cleansing process to precede the real task of rehabilitating art as a meaningful instrument of life.

---

[10] Hans Richter, *dada; art and anti-art* (London: Thames and Hudson, 1997), 25. Richter is quoting from *Dadaland* by Hans Arp.

The complex story of dada, which spanned the geography of Western civilization—from its origins in Zurich, to its heyday in New York and Berlin, its branches in Lausanne, Barcelona, Hanover and Cologne, and its colorful demise in Paris—is well-recounted by the likes of Robert Short,[11] Hans Richter,[12] Robert Motherwell,[13] and other art historians. Our concern here is to identify the energy, this thing, this disruptive play element—collectively realized and expressed—which fully informed dada.

First and foremost, consider dada anti-art as the residue of an activist life. dada was an attitude that left pieces of art in its wake, most of them destroyed and dissolved. The soul reveals its true qualities through action, making static art secondary. dada put its best work into "one shot" periodicals printed on cheap paper or on wall posters or stickers to make the statement: this is not art, this is a creative visual act.

This compelled spectators to rethink their position not merely by the novel force of the image or sound presented to them but by deliberately changing the context. In other words, dada, using art as its power tool, let play out of the box. You do not see a public poster or sticker in the same way you view art in a museum. Thus, there is the opportunity for the image to stimulate a novel response—come to this cabaret, join this demonstration, insult your government, quit your job, stop making sense.

dada challenged the whole dominance of technique as a measure of an artist's worth. While postimpressionism was a detour into technique for its own sake, dada went punk, rejecting technique and democratizing creativity; everyone was capable of the same creative freedom as the artist. André Breton, who would further define dada when founding Surrealism, declared all human acts art and all humans artists. This reduction of competence to a transient aspect of art—emphasizing

---

[11] Short, *Dada and Surrealism*.

[12] Richter, *dada: art and anti-art*.

[13] R.B. Motherwell, *The Dada Painters and Poets* (New York: Wittenborn, 1951).

play over art—upset the apple cart of the new market system that was promoting new schools of modern art, and it certainly risked the credibility of dada as an art movement.

Which is precisely what the dadas wanted, for by eliminating culti-vated competence (another of Hall's golden age characteristics) from the prerequisites of art and artists, they brought dada into the realm of play, making clear their intentions to create an inclusive reality and not exclusive showpieces. They mocked style and substance, thus cre-ating a stylistic tour de force and possibly making the most import-ant political statement in modern history.

A chronicle of dada events and pranks that were being pulled throughout Europe at the time depicts this play (non)sensibility. Also, we should observe the wide range of people who participated in the movement and successfully responded to rational society through play. There was not a dada "type" but rather a broad spectrum of personalities who were able to perceive the world and come to the same realizations, bringing their own unique contribution into play.

And it all starts with the original six of the Cabaret Voltaire in Zurich. There was Hugo Ball, the serious and spiritual idealist and talented painter, and Emmy Hemmings, the sole female, the outra-geous and shrill singer of cutting-edge brothel poetry and folk songs.

Tristan Tzara, Ball's opposite, was a Romanian poet whose acid wit and necessary nihilism he directed to the heart of the political machine: "Art falls asleep . . . "ART"—a parrot word—replaced by Dada . . . Art needs an operation. Art is a pretension, warmed by the diffidence of the urinary tract, hysteria born in a studio."[14]

Hans Arp was a talented Alsatian-born painter who experimented with new formats in wood carvings and torn-and-pasted-paper con-structions (all temporary, mostly disappeared). Richard Huelsenbeck was in love with African rhythms and would lead great drum ensem-

---

[14] Tristan Tzara, "Dada Manifesto of 1918," in *dada; art and anti-art*, by Hans Richter (London: Thames and Hudson, 1997), 35.

bles. The pugnacious poet would swish a riding crop in the air as he recited absurd verse peppered with nonsense syllables.

And, amongst many others, there was the quiet Marcel Janco, who produced thoroughly modern masks that nonetheless carried the suprahuman characters and emotions of the Japanese and Ancient Greek mask heritage. The larger-than-life masks—with bright greens, reds, and blues; large open mouths; twisted noses; gaily arched eyes—demanded full costumes and improvised dances, which the Zurich dadas provided along with great and constant laughter. Hans Arp gives a description of the chaos of playfulness Cabaret Voltaire ignited:

> Total pandemonium. The people around us are shouting, laughing and gesticulating. Our replies are sighs of love, volleys of hiccups, poems, moos, and miaowing of medieval Bruitists. Tzara is wriggling his behind like the belly of an oriental dancer, Janco is playing an invisible violin and bowing and scraping. Madame Hennings, with a Madonna face, is doing the splits. Huelsenbeck is banging away non-stop on the great drum, with Ball accompanying them on the piano, pale as a chalky ghost.[15]

The Cabaret would nightly stage performance art, for example the poème simultané, a contrapuntal recitation of three poems by three poets all at once. They would speak, sing, whistle, etc. to create a total cacophonous effect and an organic work of art that was open to the effects of chance.

The Cabaret also hosted African nights that featured Janco's masks and the novel introduction of African rhythms into Zurich night-life. This represents a significant first effort to link the aspirations of utopian Western artists to the democratization of art found in African culture. That is, though there are class differences in African culture, the role of the artist is distributed throughout the tribe and universally shared, precisely what the dadas were seeking. African culture has had

---

[15] Short, *Dada and Surrealism*, 32. Richter is quoting from *Dadaland* by Hans Arp.

immense effect on American blues, jazz, and, later on, rock and roll. The dadas also picked up on its power:

> Huelsenbeck was obsessed with Negro rhythms, with which he and Ball had already experimented in Berlin. His preference was for the big tomtom, which he used to accompany his defiantly tarred-and-feathered "Prayers." Hugo Ball writes: "He wanted the rhythm [Negro rhythm] reinforced: he would have liked to drum literature into the ground." Imagine the combination of Ball's piano improvisations, Emmy Hennings' thin, unrefined, youthful voice (which was heard alternately in folk-songs and brothel songs) and the abstract Negro masks of Janco, which carried the audience from the primeval language of the new poems into the primeval forests of the artistic imagination—and you will have some idea of the vitality and enthusiasm by which the group is inspired.[16]

In the Cabaret, bells, drums, cowbells, and the like were spread about, and the previously passive audience encouraged to join in.

Hugo Ball performed the first "abstract poems." Marcel Janco and Ball designed a costume: a tight-fitting, cylindrical pillar of shiny blue cardboard that reached to the hips, then a huge coat collar, fastened at the neck so that Ball could flap it like wings by moving his elbows. It was topped off with a blue and white striped cylindrical hat. Since Ball could not move in this dress, he was carried onto the stage in a blackout. When the lights came up, he recited the first of three poems:

> gadji beri bimba glandridi laula lonni cadori
> gadjama gramma berida bimbala glandri galassassa laulitalomini
> gadji beri bin blassa glassala laula lonni cadorsu sassala bim
> Gadjama tuffm I zimzalla binban gligia wowolimai bin beri ban
> o katalominial rhinocerossola hopsamen laulitalomini hoooo
> gadjama

---

[16] Richter, *dada: art and anti-art*, 20.

rhinocerossola hopsamen
bluku terullala blaulala looooo . . . [17]

More than merely shocking the audience, Ball reports actually entering a state where more influences entered the performance, and by the third poem, his majestic recitation had taken on a liturgical style. While in some venues he would certainly have been booed, Ball was applauded and lauded by supporters who had come to expect the unexpected.

Not that dadas were afraid of taking their outrageousness to the broader public commons. One night, a troupe of them made the rounds of the Zurich restaurants with the older and respectable-looking Augusto Giacometti (uncle of the sculptor Alberto). They would open the door, Augusto would enter and shout "Viva dada!" They would proceed to the next. Hans Arp described how "the diners nearly choked on their sausages."

The media and the idea of fake news were not safe from dada either. dada did it first! A duel between Hans Arp and Tristan Tzara was fabricated, and the story planted in the Swiss newspapers placed the sentimental poet J.C. Heer at the scene as one of Tzara's seconds. Heer, not a dada, sent a furious disclaimer to the newspaper. Yet another story later that day was published, acknowledging that it would have been embarrassing for Heer to have been there, but respect for the truth compelled them to say that he had . . . all a hoax to infuriate and deflate the importance of such events reported as news.

Tristan Tzara discovered that the warring nations were eager to wage propaganda wars in Switzerland, so he was able to obtain art works from Italy, Germany, and France free of charge and upon request; instead of displaying them in the manner requested by the hosting nation, he used them for dada propaganda himself.

---

[17] This poem was inserted into a song by the art rock group Talking Heads. "I Zimbra" by Hugo Ball, David Byrne, and Brian Eno on Talking Heads, *Fear of Music*, Sire Records, 1979, vinyl recording. And this style of antiperformance would be echoed by trickster Andy Kaufman almost sixty years later.

Johannes Baader claimed to be "Super-dada" and founded "Christ & Co. Ltd." At one point, he invaded the Weimar Diet and hurled down armfuls of leaflets, declaring himself "President of the Globe."[18]

And sometimes the public responded. At the final soirée of Zurich dada in April of 1919, the elegant but scandalous Walter Serner sat astride a chair in the middle of the stage with his back to the audience. During the ensuing recitation of his manifesto, *Final Dissolution*, a group of young men from the gallery tore apart the theater's balustrade, chasing Serner off the stage and into the street, smashing his props. Twenty minutes later, the mob's rage subsided, and the performance resumed.

## dada, International Man of Mystery

Arthur Cravan was the prototype for the beat/hippie Neal Cassady, claiming to have burgled a Swiss jeweler's shop and traveled on forged passports across Europe and North America. He described himself as a confidence man, sailor, muleteer, orange picker, snake charmer, hotel thief, nephew of Oscar Wilde, lumberjack, ex-boxing champion of France, grandson of the English queen's chancellor, Berlin chauffeur, etc. . . . clearly a man willing to play diverse roles in the world, and perhaps tell a tale or two. He let off random pistol shots at a lecture in Paris in the 1910s. During a lecture he was delivering to an invited audience of society ladies, he got most of his clothes off before the police took him away.

Cravan was a dada first, and then an amateur and not very good boxer. He had the audacity to challenge the great Jack Johnson to a fight. This they did on April 23, 1916, and Cravan was knocked out in the first round. Was he pulling our leg, indulging his own fantasy, or creating new realms of disruptive play? Cravan disappeared after setting sail from Mexico with the intent to cross the Caribbean. Like

---

[18] Short, *Dada and Surrealism*, 38. Fifty years later, Yippies would shower the New York Stock Exchange with dollar bills in a similar comic feat.

Cassady, Andy Kaufman, and the soul of all dadas, Cravan believed that personal action must supersede art. Thus, his *ouevre* is evident in his résumé more than in any preserved pieces of art, though he was a writer.

The medium of the magazine was cheap, disposable, and fast, and thus served the dada movement well. Corporate capitalism understood this and appropriated the medium, converting it into a vehicle for consumer advertising. But in the early twentieth century, the magazine was a flexible medium, amenable to the transitory lightning-flash, anti-art politics of dadas. The 'zine sustained the medium's rebel potential in the plethora of alternative rags that flourished in the 1960s '70s, decreased by the 1980s, but proliferated again in the last turn of the century. 'Zine energy has since migrated to the internet, a super-sized morass. But thank you, dada.

Preceded by the publication *Cabaret Voltaire*, *dada Journal* was edited by Tzara, but Janco, Arp, Ball, Huelsenbeck and Richter, along with others on the scene, all contributed. In protest of the new order of valuing, selling, collecting, and preserving art, the magazine was a vehicle for dadas who were more concerned with eliciting reaction and creating action; poetry, art, manifestos, and music were incidental. Stylistically, dada and dada events—creative use of typography and stock images, alternating sounds with words in poems—owed a debt to futurism. But unlike futurism, dada had no articulated program; it was, like play and the trickster, anticonceptual. It proceeded on the faith principle that there is an attainable human state that is revealed when people are provoked but not contested.

dada had no program, was against all programs . . . and it was just this that gave the movement its explosive power to unfold in all directions, free of aesthetic or social constraints. This absolute freedom from preconceptions was new to Western art. The fragility of play in a not-playful world meant that such a paradise could not last. But there was a brief moment of absolute freedom.[19] The commitment to NOT having a program, to the view that all human creation was raised to the level of art, all people to the level of artists, naturally led to the use of chance to create art. As chance democratizes circumstance—chance also unshackles play. Ball's idea was to create "... a fusion, not merely of all art, but of all regenerative ideas. The background of colours, words and sounds must be brought out from the subconscious and given life, so that it engulfs everyday life and all its misery."[20]

As the editor of the journal, the great networker, the believer in the worldwide transformative power of dada, Tristan Tzara would also establish relations with poets, writers, and artists in other countries, bringing dada international status.

## dada and Surrealism Fight, Play Loses

dada's assault on rationality was carried out through premeditated acts that induce spontaneous play. So a dada might plan to fire off a gun in a theater or disrobe during a lecture, but without being quite sure what will happen or what a dada would do next. The point is to release play and let spontaneity take over . . . in a social context. dada provocation is in your face and compels a total and immediate change of behavior. dada is the foremost example of tricksterism and disruptive play.

Under Tzara's leadership, dada crystallized and narrowed, losing some support of visual artists, becoming more literary. Tzara's initial partners, Arp and Ball, carried a spiritual vision that brought heart into such antics, through their painting and their cabaret shows, that veered away from nihilism. For them, the dada assault was indeed a clearing of the decks in search of a higher spiritual order that was

---

[19] Short, *Dada and Surrealism*, 34.

[20] Hugo Ball in Hans Richter, *dada; art and anti-art* (London: Thames and Hudson, 1965), p. 35.

accessible to all. But by the time dada reached Paris, two key changes had occurred.

One, World War I had ended, and so Paris dada was postwar dada. The Parisians had not fled the war, they had fought, and Paris was delighted and tickled to receive the dada that arrived from Zurich. But it was a victory celebration and a joyous foray into silliness without a foil. This firmly established dada as an important art movement, but kindness was killing it. Paris refused to produce any decent villains worth mocking.

The second change was that Ball had left the movement for a more pastoral existence. Tzara's influence overshadowed Arp and others, and thus the more literary, nihilistic side of dada is what met Breton and the Parisians. On the surface and at first, the emigrating Zurich dadas were joining Breton and the Surrealist movement, and the Surrealists shared dada's utopian hopes, but there were key differences.

For dadas, the unconscious was a place you visited on your way to making your anti-art. It was a component of the play element stripped bare—the raw material of the unconscious, enhanced by the employ of chance and thrust into a social context.

For the Surrealists, the unconscious was a frontier that needed illustration. Rather than attack rationality like the dadas (external, social, political), the Surrealists sought to fire the pistol off in the theater of the mind, to evoke "convulsive beauty" through painting and automatic writing (internal, personal, spiritual). Rather than fight social reality, the Surrealists evaporated all social reference through automatism. The idea of automatic writing, for example, was to make a direct connection from the unconscious to the paper, like the free association Freud was using. To bypass culture rather than attack it. dadas like Arp had experimented with but not embraced automatism as Breton, Comte de Lautréamont, and Max Ernst did. Short and Shattuck both agree that it was automatism that initially separated the dadas from the Surrealists.

In the search for the imagic analogue to automatic writing, Surrealist artists set about to illustrate the dream world, to paint as if in a dream, to unify the dream with waking consciousness. Such art was their pistol shot. Notable Surrealist images include Max Ernst; Yves Tanguy's and Salvador Dali's otherworldly landscapes; Dorothea Tanning's realistic images of vulnerable and somber pubescent girls; Joan Miró's happy and random colors and shapes, suspended in liberated space; Jindrich Styrsky's distortion of the Statue of Liberty; Man Ray's stark and stunning photography; Rene Magritte's apple-face, feet-shoes, or transposition of genitals to make a face; André Breton and Tristan Tzara's intellectual and nihilist screeds; the poetry of Robert Desnos; and Paul Éluard's unreal scenes of intense emotion, like a wild elephant crashing through a "civilized' tavern". All Surrealist art has been hugely influential throughout modern times, in advertising, aesthetics, perspectives.

The Surrealists were highly ambitious and intent on changing the world; they believed that they could through the psychic triggers of their art. Art to astonish. The provocation of Surrealist art is intended to reach the unconscious mind and ultimately have an impact on behavior and society. As Breton defined it, Surrealism was "psychic automatism in its pure state by which one proposes to express . . . the actual functioning of thought."[21] To the extent that this is fun, it is play, but more like deep play than disruptive play. Despite noble and conscious social goals and its other revolutionary qualities, and perhaps without intending to, Surrealism retreated into the conventional and ordinary art experience. They willingly put play back into the box—a new and irrevocably changed box—but a box nonetheless. Rather than sustaining any performances on the stage of society, they accepted their new role as artists, convinced that they could still effect social change by raising consciousness. As Roger Shattuck put

---

[21] André Breton, *Surrealism and Painting*, trans. Simon Watson Taylor (London: Macdonald and Co., 1972), 70.

it, "the cultural police have now herded those rowdy crowds back onto the sidewalk of literature and art."[22]

While retaining some wit and humor, Surrealists got very serious, stopped playing, and refused to misbehave.

This contrast is similar to the fracturing of the sixties movement into special interest groups. All had their merit; in narrowing their program, advocates enhanced the likelihood of political victories but lost sight of the larger vision. The first casualty in such regrouping is play. The sense of humor, the ability to not take either "side" of an issue or its protagonists too seriously, evaporates. In the 1910s, Tzara's faction is likened to the Leninists of the sixties who worked on specific single issues and evolved into the autocrats of political correctness. The Surrealists correspond to the more spiritual side of the sixties counterculture, best represented by the human potential movement, where play, instead of being confined to the canvas, found itself in the compartmentalized retreats and workshops characteristic of that movement.

It seems that for play to flourish in a social context, the movement that supports it must have elements of the artistic/spiritual and the political. This is for lack of better terms, and the point is that the movement really has to be a full-blown social revolution that is broad enough to include a true range of participants—this is the recipe that releases play. The isolation and danger of players like Jarry or Oscar Wilde are testimony to the even greater fragility of an individual player exploring frontiers without cultural support.

It is fairly easy to understand the elusiveness of disruptive play and what would seem to be its intrinsically short lifespan. To build a challenge to that dictum, and thus the aftermath of any sustained movement of disruptive play requires analysis.

To have pursued substance would have meant for art and political action to merge. dada's progeny, the Fluxus movement of the sixties,

---

22 Shattuck, "The D-S Expedition," in *The Innocent Eye*, 40.

sought the elimination of all boundaries between art and life. Political action doesn't necessarily mean waging an insurrection, but it does mean to live a life where what was art becomes functional and universal behavior. If to be an artist means to bring beauty, or at least authentic expression, into this world, isn't that a viable goal for all humans? But that would mean giving up all the money to be made from the new art movements and all the decadent fun and special status attached to artist chic. More simply put, the end of World War I brought a return to normality. And since artists do have to eat, economics compelled them to find a way to make a buck off of the new movements.

There was a painful split between dada's nihilistic destroyers and the idealistic dreamers. Both wanted to do away with the established order, but only the idealists ventured into imagining what might grow from that. Generally speaking, the painters tended to be more idealistic and the writers more nihilistic. Living through World War I could make a cynic of anyone, but art, and dada in particular, had become transnational and had successfully built bridges between Germany and other cultures—Switzerland, France, United States, Spain—birthing a globalist optimism. World War II is testimony enough to the fact that those bridges and the artist dream for world peace did not prevail. Robert Short observes:

> Realism, said the Dadas, required that men acknowledge the persistent fact of their own violence, that they accept the complex nature of the psyche and the world rather than seek to impose a simple order upon reality. The mastering of man's fear of his own irrational powers, the conquest of psychic freedom and personal autonomy, Dada insisted, was a prerequisite of any social revolution.[23]

It was just this sort of personal commitment and dada influence that drove André Breton and his colleagues to found Surrealism. Artwise, Hans Arp had introduced elements of chance into his collages,

---

[23] Short, *Dada and Surrealism*, 40.

and this would influence Surrealism's exaltation of the unconscious, ultimately through automatism, to wit: *The Hyperbole of the Crocodile's Hairdresser and the Walking-Stick,* by Tzara, Serner, and Arp; *Lessons in Automatic Writing,* by Max Ernst; and *Self-Portrait: Automatic Writing,* by André Breton. While a critical and meaningful innovation, it is equally important to note automatism as a turning away from social context—the activism and disruption that defined dada.

As critical as dada is to the progress of humanity, it was easily dismissed and sidelined by the more serious Surrealism, by seriousness itself—like anything else that embraces the silly. The demise of dada can clearly be traced to the play element taking flight. Tristan Tzara's leadership—lasting from Ball's departure in 1917 to dada's vague demise somewhere in the mid-1920s—sustained the movement, but the serious nihilist argument and the dominance of the literary faction over the artists took all the fun out of it. The play element is like light dancing on the water, and until we can solve the seeming contradiction of establishing the irrationality of play, its appearances were destined to be short-lived. The split within dada sends Tristan Tzara into a more absolute, play-less nihilism and to Surrealism. The element of play has taken flight.

# SIX

# Eros, That's Life

*The Dadaists despised what is commonly regarded as art, but put the whole universe on the lofty throne of art. We declared that everything that comes into being or is made by man is art." The original dadas . . . were united in their belief that life was what mattered, not art. The great masterpieces in the museums were tainted, along with the books and the noble ideas of a murderous society that was tearing itself to pieces on the Western front.[1]*

*Hans Arp*

NOTHING IS QUITE so serious, yet quite so absurd, as war. Its horrors and contradictions urge creative souls to inspired opposition. And World War I provided ample quantities of blood and stupidity, the pitiable foil for a heroic and sustained provocation. dada dramatically injected play into daily life as the antidote for a civilization possessed by war's curse.

As the ecstatic and chaotic birth of the absurd in art, dada held the aggressive bias that art is made in service to creating peace in the world.

---

[1] Quoted in *Duchamp, A Biography* by Calvin Tomkins (New York: Owl, 1997), 191.

That art does not glorify power, it challenges it. A wild and unstoppable gush of ideas, dada burst out with simultaneously joyful and liberated art among a crowd of artists scattered throughout Europe and the US. It could never be embodied by one person; its transformative program defied description and containment. Yet in Marcel Duchamp (1887-1968)—painter, prankster, sculptor, chess master, cross-dresser, inventor, trickster—we find an individual who sustained a dada identity beyond dada's death and created seminal examples of disruptive play. He jolted the world with playfulness—urination was involved—in the midst of a somnambulant and serious art market.

World War I shut down the burgeoning modern art movement in Europe, particularly Paris. Energetic artists opposing the war took refuge in Zurich, birthing baby dada with the debut of the Cabaret Voltaire and challenging the seriousness that traps men into making war. Europe's politicians ignored them, opting for the idiotic stridency and deadly violence of World War I.

Duchamp refused conflict and championed the essential magic of play, humor, laughter, and even dared his dada colleagues to look at their own tactics: "They were . . . fighting the public. And when you're fighting you rarely manage to laugh at the same time."[2]

Many forms of competition and ranking are at their core absurd. Sports, beauty contests, stock markets, top ten lists, elections, corporations, and wars all have their legitimate detractors. There is fun and excitement and sometimes improved services and products that come of competition. But competition runs rampant, it's out of proportion. At its worst, it breeds political games that collapse into war. Duchamp the pacifist chose to attack competition within the art world, part of the same malady; and this arena allowed his brilliant wit its full range.[3]

---

[2] Marcel Duchamp, quoted in *Duchamp, A Biography* by Calvin Tomkins (New York: Owl, 1996), 193.

[3] Dan Franck, Bohemian Paris: Picasso, Modigliani, Matisse, and the Birth of Modern Art (New York: Grove, 2007).

## The J.L. Mott Iron Works

The entry and rejection of Duchamp's ready-made, *Fountain*, would be a declaration of play, in art and in life. His humble porcelain piece would sow a vision of a world where war was not possible. Elegant and notorious, Duchamp confronted the art world's establishment, creating street theater that is a handbook on how art liberated leads to a playful life.

The Impressionists had crashed the gates of the government-controlled art industry in France by mounting their own exhibitions apart from the Salons. Beginning in 1874, the *Société Anonyme des Artistes Peintres, Sculpteurs et Graveurs* presented the works of Monet, Pissarro, Renoir, and Morisot, and the *Société des Artistes Indépendants* did the same, beginning in 1886. The public considered where an artist showed to be more important than the painting's actual style. So anything not in the official Salon was by default Impressionist.

Cubism had managed to distinguish itself and had been the rage. Picasso delivered the first stunner with *Les Demoiselles d'Avignon* in 1907. By 1912, Duchamp matched him with *Nu descendant un escalier, n°2 (Nude Descending a Staircase, No. 2)*, arguably the more essential Cubist example. But Duchamp was already bored. "Cubism is a dead end!" he declared. Impressionism and Cubism, were radical, but not liberating. Duchamp went after bigger game in a bigger city. In the middle of June 1915, he arrived in New York. In that freer, more permissive air, he would resonate, match, and reverberate dada's public noise across the Atlantic.

Duchamp was part of the Society of Independent Artists, a small group that formed in 1916 with the intention of mounting annual exhibitions for underexposed artists in a noncompetitive show. They would feature two works by any artist who could muster the five-dollar annual dues and a one-dollar initiation fee. "No jury, no prizes" (no competing) was its policy.

How far could this breakaway from convention go? No competition meant that the artist was freed to explore more novel ideas.

Duchamp set out to take ART to the level where it would mix freely with modern LIFE. *What choice connects them?* he mused. *I will present the Independents with everyday objects raised to the dignity of a work of art by the artist's act of choice. And I choose…the urinal.* He titled it *Fountain* and signed it with the name "R. Mutt," taken from J. L. Mott Iron Works where it was purchased.

The dealers whined. *No, no, no, we can't display a urinal as a piece of art. We're building a new commercial enterprise here. We can't sell that. We can't approve that.*

The collectors complained. The critics protested. *We reject you. Bring us art. You've gone too far, Marcel. Can't you be more like that Picasso guy?*

But there was no stopping him. In a public airing out of the controversy, the editors of the magazine *The Blind Man* (most likely Duchamp, Henri-Pierre Roché, and Beatrice Wood) declared:

> Whether Mr. Mutt with his own hands made the foun-
> tain or not has no importance. He CHOSE it. He took an
> ordinary article of life, placed it so that its usual significance
> disappeared under the new title and point of view—created
> a new thought for that object.[4]

While not a classic trickster poop or fart joke, the scatology associated with *Fountain* comes close enough.

This was Duchamp; this was dada. Its insubordinate ethos challenged the sense and seriousness of art, and of existence, and exploded the art world with the playfulness of the child, positing café society as a social model. *La belle époque* opened a window on the play opportunity, and the dadas jumped eagerly through it.

Regardless of dada's intention to NOT be art, Duchamp was too popular, too important to be ignored. The critics had to make a show of understanding this, somehow squeeze this three-dimensional urinal—this piece of life—into the two-dimensional stock responses

---

[4] Tomkins, *Duchamp, A Biography*, 185.

of art criticism. *It's really beautiful, this is not just any urinal; it shows classic lines even as it thrusts us into the twentieth century. . . . You know, there's a sublime suggestion of sex here. . . . After all, the urinal is, well, you know. . . . Note the female passivity in the receptacle of the phallic and how Duchamp has carefully laid the piece on its side.*

No. No. And no. *Fountain,* the urinal experience, is not about observing the quality of the lines, any deep symbolism, the porcelain, or the inscription, though how sex meets modern technology is Duchamp's defining theme. Today, the shock value is past tense, but the intention is clear. To submit a common urinal as art was to playfully disrupt the transition from the old patronage system to the new marketplace of dealers, critics, and publicists. Duchamp dared them to try and market such an outrageous piece of "art." He sharply reminded these brash entrepreneurs that the revolution in art was not made to line their pockets; he did not create in order to sell but to introduce play into life and all that that suggests. Fifty years before Andy Warhol would beatify the Campbell soup can, Duchamp encouraged us to make ordinary life beautiful with the same tools of perception we use to make beautiful art.[5]

The story of Marcel Duchamp's *Fountain* provides a powerful example of dada as anti-art, of how the most mundane objects could become art by virtue of the artist saying so and altering the context through which we perceive that object. Or is he having a laugh at our expense? Ridiculing artists or elevating artisans? A rather playful attitude in the face of what was again becoming a serious subject, now that art was officially modern.

Considered the greatest artist of the twentieth century, Picasso produced paintings and sculptures that frequently embodied playfulness . . . but he put art first, play second. Duchamp and dada lived

---

[5] And in the 1960s, the original urinal having been lost or destroyed, Duchamp commissioned seventeen replicas.

the reverse ethos that put the release of play into daily life first, with works of art the mere residue.

What fun Duchamp is having, what masterful play. What nerve Duchamp had in submitting a common urinal as a piece of art! Or painting a moustache on the Mona Lisa! What adjustments the strait-laced observer must make to avoid being drawn into the play of it. How am I to react to this? Am I being mocked? No, I am in on the joke; it's all those other snobs who have become rigid in their concepts of art and beauty. The genius is that the contestmongers were desperate to have him join their game, but he was always several steps ahead. And so, in an artistic manipulation of chance and rude brandish of dada aesthetic, Duchamp the trickster discovered and brought the ready-made into the world. In his own words:

> As early as 1913 I had the happy idea to fasten a bicycle wheel to a kitchen stool and watch it turn.

> A few months later I bought a cheap reproduction of a winter evening landscape, which I called *Pharmacy* after adding two small dots, one red and one yellow, in the horizon.

> In New York in 1915 I bought at a hardware store a snow shovel on which I wrote *in advance of the broken arm.*

> It was around that time that the word "ready-made" came to my mind to designate this form of manifestation.

> A point that I want very much to establish is that the choice of these "ready-mades" was never dictated by aesthetic delectation.

> The choice was based on a reaction of *visual indifference* with a total absence of good or bad taste . . . in fact a complete anaesthesia.

> One important characteristic was the short sentence which I occasionally inscribed on the "ready-made."

That sentence, instead of describing the object like a title, was meant to carry the mind of the spectator towards other regions, more verbal.[6]

Can people be shaken from their rigidity on a mass scale? Can such provocative "art" alter the course of human affairs? The realm in which dada attempts to stimulate this change is the realm of play, and no one was able to play—or to provoke resistance to play—better than Duchamp. He was fully detached from the idea that there is any purpose to life that would make it necessary for him to believe in something. Thus, as a very pure nihilist, he holds a most objective mirror up to us. Because he presents no agenda or program, our reactions to Duchamp's creations are very much our own, and thus, he goads us to take responsibility for our own beliefs and actions.

And, like the Trickster, like Bugs Bunny, Duchamp bent his gender, springing a cross-dressing second identity on the world as Rose (and later Rrose) Sélavy in 1920. This alter ego would sign some of Duchamp's pieces, flirt with folks of all sexes, and stimulate various capers and frolics. She disappeared just as suddenly in 1941. Rose is an anagram for eros, and Sélavy a phonetic for c'est la vie . . . Eros, that's Life.

His *The Bride Stripped Bare by Her Bachelors, Even* (most often called *The Large Glass)* confounds the viewer: is it the twentieth century's most profound statement on the relationship of men to women and humans to machines, or is it, as Short comments, "An immensely elaborate joke, a game which throws doubt on the seriousness of all human endeavor."[7] Duchamp abhorred the notion that his creations would be put back into any box, analyzed and compared, and considered art with a capital "A." His courage and his genius were to lay traps in his art that would snare such classifiers. Because he would

---

[6] Marcel Duchamp, quoted in dada: *art and anti-art* by Hans Richter (London: Thames and Hudson, 1997), 89.

[7] Robert Short, *Dada and Surrealism* (Secaucus, NJ: Chartwell Books, 1980), 27.

rather play. Duchamp lived in a world of playfulness and, from that ether, grasped the central theme of the twentieth century, reconciling the contradictions and confluences of sex and technology.

## The Price The Trickster Pays

dada, like play, is irrational *and* meaningful. Thus, dada was the end of the line for art as we knew it; for if art was on the threshold of transforming society into some merged version of art and life . . . it didn't. We have instead an altered status quo, mainly an art *industry* that persists. In such a case, all that is left to the artist is nihilism, the denial of meaning (the depression of a failed effort) or style, the illusion of meaning (making money from a failed effort).

And nihilism and empty style have been the persistent threads of modern art since World War I, since Surrealism. In *The Painted Word*, Tom Wolfe humorously describes modern art's detours and retreats from its activist origins.[8] When the dada challenge—for disruptive play to alter our very definition of *what is art*, to dare ask *what is the matrix that confines our daily life?*—went unmet, art veered into two cul-de-sacs. One was social realism, a more harmless form that commented on political struggle rather than engaged in it, i.e., propaganda. The other was art for art's sake, and the silly debates and theories of what can and can't happen in painting and sculpture. Overlooked or dismissed is the great dada alliance between writers and artists and the revolutionary potential of disruptive play. The next dynamic association was two generations away, between writers, poets, and musicians.

Impressionism reinterpreted light, leading to artists' reinterpreting reality, leading to dada and artists questioning reality, which then divided itself over nihilism and style, leaving social engagement behind. Thus defanged, modern art proceeded upon a course of breaking reality down into more and more abstract forms. Its experts

---

[8]   Tom Wolfe, *The Painted Word* (New York: Farrar, Straus and Giroux, 1975).

follow a theoretical strand whose only relation to people is to illustrate existential isolation.

A good example of this cul-de-sac, this endgame, is the explosions of chance in the yellows and blacks, the vibrant reds and blues and grays, the fantastic drip art work of Jackson Pollock, beauty in the abstract. For this discussion, it is evidence of the fully emasculated artist. The revolution that never occurred in society is fought out on the canvas. It's even possible that Pollock's pained life and premature death was borne of the frustrating chasm that had opened up between art and the impact it could possibly have upon life. As an artist fully connected to the lineage that emerged from France at the turn of the century, Pollock bore this weight.

The price the trickster pays: when the divinity of play is rejected, it hurts. Society exiles trickster-types to a lonely place and busies itself with so-called serious matters.

Wolfe may see disruptive play as unimportant and, as a social conservative, seek the purely sensual pleasure of viewing a painting that is pretty. But the social conditions and creative explosion of *fin de siècle* France challenged us to change our ways, to discard war and the love of power, to allow our lives to become works of art. Let art perform its ultimate function, which is to spiritualize daily life. Dispense with beauty as a relative term. To call something beautiful is to imply other things must be ugly. This was unacceptable to the dadas.

But what happened was that the marketplace took over, and artists awarded themselves the consolation prize of a new special status: theory, nihilism, and style hopelessly yoked to the ultimate commodity, fashion.

So play goes into hiding, takes refuge in philosophy, while political movements grow more serious and art more detached. The muse took flight, and it was not until the 1950s that it emerged again to spark a complex and international social movement in the sixties. In this case, the art of the times—rock and roll—was again socially engaged, and the politics of the time—hippies, Yippies, European revolutionaries—were playful enough to incorporate beauty into their social vision. With the Beats playing the prelude analogous to the Impressionists and early moderns, the game got bigger, the stakes higher, and the vision of a society that plays made one more step towards something more than a momentary realization.

Our previous chapter recounted the death dance as dada left the political stage and entered the dream world of Surrealism. It's worth noting that Jarry, who died seven years before dada's birth, and Duchamp, who endured and thrived beyond its death, reveal play's resilience. In their playfulness, they floated above the political scuffles that killed dada, killed play. Such escapes keep the play spirit alive and available for future generations to reinvent.

dada effectively dismantled art by challenging the foundations of its economic and social hierarchical structure, the dealer system that itself was less than forty years old. But ultimately it failed to achieve its vision because capitalist systems, like water, will simply seek other avenues when one is blocked, when the artist does not cooperate. So the system that perpetuated art as compartmentalized commodity ultimately ignored or absorbed dada, but the intentions of its creators cannot be forgotten, its reverberations on history and the unfulfilled vision of a playful life indistinguishable from artistic creation lies before us still.

# History Doesn't Repeat Itself, but It Does Rhyme

# SEVEN

# Hearts' Beat

*When the mode of the music changes,*
*the walls of the city shake.*

*Attributed to Plato and*
*to Allen Ginsberg*

*They celebrated the jagged moment of experience,*
*which is intuitive rather than rational;*
*it moves on as soon as reason catches up.*

*John Leland[1]*

CASSADY OPENED the throttle wide. In a green Cadillac going 110 miles an hour across the Nebraska plains, Jack Kerouac, Neal Cassady and the rest of the Beat Generation were about to write the next chapter in the fitful but sweet history of play as a way of life. As mid-century approached, these Buddhist bebop bohemians put art, life, and America together and came up with the inevitable: Play is the thing.

They eschewed the straitlaced life that a prosperous postwar America laid out for the many—tract homes, GI Bill college educations, in-home television entertainment, mass consumption, enlist-

---

[1] J. Leland, *Hip: the history* (New York: Harper Perennial, 2005), 140.

ment in the Cold War—and instead chose life on the road, with its earthy passions and cosmic awareness. As the masses retreated into mediated pleasures, the Beats became the torchbearers of disruptive play, and they played well with each other—speeding down America's highways on buses and in fast cars, exploring the possibilities of sex and relationships, wandering the darkness of the soul through drugs and the denizens of the underworld, and dropping off a major literary movement along the way. Reaching beyond the faltering of two world wars and an economic depression, the twentieth century finally announced that it was about speed and possibilities undreamed. In the shadow of the atomic bomb, it was, categorically, time to play.

The Impressionists bled colors into each other's styles. They laid the template for a Western life lived artistically. dadas jumped on this notion, brashly challenging the form and function of all art, summoning all daily life to the level of art, and making their lives their masterpieces. The Beat Generation revived this life-as-art idea. Their poems and novels were the harmonic overtones, the tracings and the residue of their living. From that intensity came throbbing vibrations that shake the world still.

And what better, freer, more fun and fantastic stage to play on than the heart of American romance and adventure, the Wild West? The scout elected to guide Beat culture into this cosmic frontier was Neal Cassady.

Reduce play to a chemical reaction. Purple and green molecules gleeful and purposeless as they giggle and bobble off of each other in excited and playful chaos. Personified as Neal Cassady—Dean Moriarty in *On the Road*, Cody Pomeray in other Kerouac novels. He could be across the room but be right at your side, bouncing off the walls literally, figuratively, poetically. Capital *P* Presence. Later on, when he joined Kesey and the Merry Pranksters, he was known to juggle a hammer while driving a bus filled with tripped-out proto-hippies and the Grateful Dead. Um, driving a bus REALLY FAST.

Cassady was a trim, blue-eyed boy with an Oklahoma accent and sideburns. He had what he called his "crooked Grecian curve," a broken nose he got in an accident when he asked a friend to steer the car he was driving while he kissed one of his girlfriends. On his first visit to New York, he worked parking cars and wore oily coveralls. Or a sleeveless white T-shirt.

He had Hollywood good looks that attracted women from afar and the rock and roll swagger that brought them near. He was Burt Lancaster untamed by Hollywood and Elvis stripped bare of his more manufactured music. But nothing describes him, nothing demonstrates his play, more than his rap.[2]

With him, arms moving constantly, talking unceasingly, sometimes making sense, word sounds, word rhythms, more like the Beating wings of a griffin than the Italian style of gesticulation. He was the Beat Generation's con man, Lenny Bruce doing Howard Cosell with Tourette's syndrome, a mobile Delphic Oracle. Ferlinghetti said Neal Cassady's voice was "like a speeded up Paul Newman from *The Hustler.*"[3] The semi-smirking bursts of brilliance and nonsense spit out constantly from the whirring consciousness that was Cowboy Neal, the high-voltage generator taking in the vibes of a new culture in its birth throes and spurting them back out at a yet higher energy level. The fountainhead. Not poetry he wrote, just the way he was. Like this:

> I said I'm just about America deMarco Greg
> At the uh last year you know
> We arrived just in time
> Double parkin' Winnemucca speeder endurance
> Six days it was finally she grabbed the of course the Vicks
> VapoRub
> Instead of the Vaseline
> That was what ended it
> My first child forty-two then, Charlie Valencia
> On Temple where we had Nasser Dezz

---

[2] The way he talked, not unlike but not rap music.

[3] Lawrence Ferlinghetti, editor's note to *The First Third*, by Neal Cassady (San Francisco: City Lights, 1971).

For thirteen fifties father half Mexican half Irish like
Anthony Quinn
So he loved her you know, there was a triumph of us
The only three-way I ever had Kerouac's not queer
But my present wife the fourth and he
It was just a New Year's Eve sort of a,
Well he was always looking for a colored girl, Cara Lastee
Finally found her Bedford-Stuyvesant and
That was the last time I committed suicide I knew
Toward the Ford sign across the Hudson
Get across this long Missouri
That preacher said Van held her I didn't see it
Move on
Hah hah!
Menopausal
Don't ask me how
Twenty years I held ten on the railroad and ten more for
And I'll be dead a thousand years you see, so if I don't do
right now
. . . right in it . .
You can work yourself into anything, how can you get out
of it?[4]

In Kerouac's dreams of the West, riding through his novel as Sal Paradise in Greyhound buses to Denver with Dean Moriarty, or speeding across America in one of the more than five hundred cars Cassady would steal, they staked out a new playground. No coincidence those fast cars; for in postwar America, the car was the symbol and the vehicle for fun, speed, freedom, and play. And no coincidence that Cassady, play incarnate, was the least prolific of the Beat writers.

The primary literary producers all had their playmates and mentors, more involved in their play than their artistic output. Allen Ginsberg (1926-1997) met Carl Solomon (1928-1993) in the loony bin. William Burroughs (1914-1997) sought out Herbert Huncke (1915-1996) on the streets of New York to learn about the underworld and

---

[4] Transcribed from a tape of Neal Cassady at an Acid Test, circa 1966, in *The Dead Book: A Social History of the Grateful Dead*, by Hank Harrison (New York: Links Books, 1973).

drugs. These men made a solemn pact and devotional commitment to a freed life.

All Beats played, and whatever freedoms America could offer, Beats gobbled up and turned into fuel for their joyride. We might see these lives as reckless and undisciplined. Burroughs was seriously dedicated to exploring drug addiction firsthand, trying out marijuana, morphine, heroin, Dilaudid, amphetamines, basically anything he could get his hands on or grow in his Texas opium fields. He later shot his wife in a William Tell re-creation that didn't go quite right. Or did it? We'll never know.

Kerouac, inspired by a forty-page, single-spaced, unpunctuated letter from Cassady, typed *On the Road* over the course of a three-week coffee binge on a homemade scroll made of twenty-foot strips of teletype paper taped together.

Ginsberg, completely untamed. At a public reading of *Howl*, when an irritated professor asked him what he meant by "nakedness," he undressed. He invented the necessary American art of coming out of the closet and did so in a style that has never been matched—through his multiple lovers and his poetry depicting his multiple lovers and Kerouac's prose detailing his multiple lovers.

But if a person's every behavior, every thought, swears a passionate devotion to exploring the outer reaches of the mind, of America, writing directly from the soul without editing, and sharing fear and love no matter the consequences, then life locks and loads as a vigorous discipline. Life becomes your art, and art relies upon play. There's nothing reckless or weak about it. Steadfast repudiation of the resurgent puritanism of the Fifties. Bop Buddhism.

## The Years Between

The conditions between the two world wars (1918-1939) were right for novelty, but not for activism. The energy of the avant-garde that had been amassing for over twenty years unloaded itself in a great outpouring of modern art, but it was borne of a political tension that had already passed.

The writers, who were more cynical and nihilistic than the painters, got disgusted with Americans' stunted awareness and left the US altogether. They joined the antagonized bustle of activist artists, Communists, and pacifists of 1930s Europe, simultaneously trying to convince themselves that the Soviet Union had not sold out democracy on the left and that Hitler was not the totalitarian of the right that in their hearts they knew him to be.

In the last half of June 1935, the First International Congress of Writers for the Defense of Culture convened in a sweltering Paris summer heat. Surrealists, anti-Fascists, Communists, authors, poets, and pacifists all came together to avow that the artist would be taken seriously by the political powers of the time.[5] The Congress was reported as a great success; some consensus was reached. But to what end?

Artists and writers were well aware of the great advances they had made in the new century. Art had been liberated to mingle with all aspects of life, and these writers, of all categories—Aragon, Breton, Pasternak, Gide, Éluard, Malraux, Tzara, Forster, Huxley, Brecht, Feuchtwanger—were eager to cohere their diverse yet generally progressive perspectives into a social vision.

But as momentous as dada and Surrealism had been and were throughout Europe and the US, they were not mass cultural movements. Thus, artists had to deal with the painful possibility that they didn't actually matter to the actions of armies and governments. Success as an artist does not automatically translate into a popular movement of any influence. Who really cared what they thought, felt, saw? Before the assembled artists and their passionate speeches was the widening chasm between the hope they had placed in the 1917 Great October Socialist Revolution and the reality of Stalin's iron fist.

---

[5]  Roger Shattuck, *The Innocent Eye: On Modern Literature and the Arts* (New York: Farrar, Straus and Giroux, 1984), 3-31.

Politicians tried to turn the tables on the artists and dictate their agenda through them. They put forth socialist realism which "... requires of the artist that he provide an image that conforms to truth, a concrete historic image of reality in its revolutionary development. This truth and this precision in representing reality must ally themselves with the problem of the ideological reshaping and the education of workers in the spirit of socialism."[6]

Breton and the Surrealists were smart enough not to fall for this nonsense. Their explorations of the unconscious revealed a greater and less absolute world that the artist could not truncate to please a politburo. And the play spirit of dada is glaringly absent from socialist realism, for the political program of play is, as far as we understand it, no program at all.

On the other hand, the writers were overwhelmed by Hitler's skill and prodigious capacity to build a mass movement. So the Congress was reported a success for the insights and positions it aired, but it must be measured by how ineffectual it was in stopping Hitler's rise in Germany and by its endorsement of Soviet communism just as Stalin was showing his totalitarian colors.

As the world struggled with economic depression, the US invented new forms of democracy, giving the government permission to embark upon major works that would create jobs and sustain citizens as the economy regained footing. Dams, roads, public forests, and public arts sprang up under the Works Progress Administration (WPA), while Woody Guthrie gave voice and song to a populist spirit that connected America's struggles to a global workers' consciousness. James Agee and Walker Evans further documented the depth of American poverty.[7] The Roosevelt administration recognized it.[8] But

---

[6] Quote by Fedor Panferov, from "Having Congress," in *The Innocent Eye: On Modern Literature and the Arts*, by Roger Shattuck (New York: Farrar, Straus and Giroux, 1984), 20.

[7] Agee, James, Walker Evans, and Blake Morrison. *Let Us Now Praise Famous Men*. London: Penguin, 2006.

[8] H.R. Rep. (1937). Farm tenancy. Message from the President of the United States transmitting the report of the Special committee on farm tenancy.

Hollywood offered popular denial through Busby Berkeley musicals, screwball comedies, and sentimental, idealistic dramas. Playful denial, not play as social statement. Art had long since left the realm of play and was taking itself oh so seriously.

Nowhere in this landscape was play the thing. The Motion Picture Production Code, for example, forbade a couple to be in bed together unless one foot was on the floor. Sexual relations outside of marriage were to be presented in a way that would not arouse passion or make them seem permissible. All criminal action had to be punished. Neither the crime nor the criminal could elicit sympathy from the audience. Authority figures had to be treated with respect.

America's persistent puritanism proved too inhospitable for its writers, and the political excitement of Europe—crystallized in the Spanish Civil War—too attractive. Hemingway, Stein, and Fitzgerald, if they could not find room to play, could at least find hope for it in Europe's instability and frank consideration of socialist utopian visions. They were, as Stein announced and Hemingway echoed, a Lost Generation.

Then World War II, in its appalling seriousness, bound the Fifties. After the military powers had exhausted the world, cultural constraints became balder, conditions for play even worse, a sign of strain not strength.

The tales of the repressed Fifties have become familiar litanies. But we would do well to remember that the era cast more than just a mood, affected more than the harmless *Leave It to Beaver and Father Knows Best* families that we joke about today.

People were jailed for their beliefs. People were put to death. Hedda Hopper suggested that those suspected of disloyalty be kept in concentration camps. Accusers like Senator Joseph McCarthy and the House Un-American Activities Committee assumed that all American dissidents were under Soviet control. A Harvard scholar committed suicide under the pressure of investigation, and sixty professors at University of California–Berkeley were dismissed for refusing to sign a loyalty oath. Hollywood writers like Dalton Trumbo, Frances Chaney and Ring Lardner Jr. suffered blacklisting, as did Lillian Hellman, Paul Robeson, and Richard Wright.

The FBI conducted clandestine surveillance and prepared a list of millions of citizens who would be detained should there be a national emergency. Henry Kissinger and Ronald Reagan were amongst their informants. J. Edgar Hoover violated a great American principle—*writ of habeas corpus*—when he insisted on shielding informants' identities.

World War II had animated and inflated the cultural need for an enemy. The postwar economy fed on military contracts and weaponry to fight the new communist rivals. Nuclear bombs and people stupid enough to consider dropping them, including President Eisenhower, were a daily concern stoking mass anxiety. Sputnik, the Soviet Union's preemptive foray into space, further fanned the flames of the hysteria. This raging anticommunism and Cold War competition unleashed an angry and joyless behemoth of fear. Playfulness would be regarded with the utmost suspicion.

But when a society works itself into a lather of repression, competition, and hatred, it inevitably animates its opposite—noncompetitive, liberating play. Tricksters eventually break free of their bonds. And play, in its refusal to fight, is the response that truly threatens power.

## Beat is Play

This next rebellion would be homegrown. The folk and blues musicians left for New York, Memphis, Nashville, Los Angeles, and Chicago— not Europe—and this time, the writers stayed too.

The Beats would unlock the key to growing a nondoctrinaire mass cultural movement that was intuitively anti-Fascist, antibureaucratic, nonconformist, cool, and antitotalitarian.

Beat has lost none of its vitality over the years. The Beat Generation played insistently in a culture that could not accommodate their

vision then, and is only now catching up. Fifties America had done
the courtesy of not collapsing into a fascist state. Freedoms survived,
if barely. Artists grasped at the edges of a lost society and looked to
madmen and criminals for sanity and ethics. Beat.

The repressed, straitlaced anger holding down an underclass, binding
the Trickster, gave way to play and a new literary voice. A critical art-
plus-life-equals-play equation reborn; play wriggling free from society's hateful grip and teaching it how to dance again. But the wriggling,
at first, hurts. Beat.

Beat as in the beat of Max Roach's bebop drums. Beat as in beat-
itude—jazz, sex, meditation, or writing to the point where the self is
obliterated. Beat as in forged by the smith's pounding of hot metal. Beat
as in beat down by the authorities who censor and withhold release
of *Howl*,[9] *Naked Lunch*,[10] and *On the Road*.[11]

> Beat shoes that flap . . . old bums and beat cowboys.. . . .
> my eyes are closing, they're redhot, sore, tired, beat . . . like
> the man with the dungeon stone and the gloom, rising
> from the underground, the sordid hipsters of America, a
> new beat generation that I was slowly joining . . . I was
> so lonely, so sad, so tired, so quivering, so broken, so beat,
> that I got up my courage . . . I lost faith in him that year.
> I stayed in San Francisco a week and had the beatest time
> of my life. . . . Then he got his suitcase, the beatest suitcase
> in the USA. . . . as though tremendous revelations were
> pouring into him all the time now, and I am convinced
> they were, and the others suspected as much and they were
> frightened. He was BEAT—the root, the soul of Beatific. . .
> dealing with the pit and prunejuice of poor beat life itself in
> the god-awful streets of man . . . Beat Negroes who'd come
> up from Alabama to work in car factories on a rumor. . . .
> If you sifted all Detroit in a wire basket. the beater solid
> core of dregs couldn't be better gathered. . . . Houses by the
> side of the road were different, gas stations beater, fewer

---

[9] Confiscated by San Francisco customs police on grounds of obscenity.

[10] Right to publish established only after lengthy court tests of freedom of expression.

[11] Publication was delayed six years, partly due to publisher apprehension.

lamps. . . . . Real beat huts, man, the kind you only find in
Death Valley and much worse. . . . The mambo beat is the
conga beat from Congo, the river of Africa and the world;
it's really the world beat . . . In downtown Mexico City
thousands of hipsters in floppy straw hats and long-lapeled
jackets over bare chests padded along the main drag, some
of them selling crucifixes and weed in the alleys, some of
them kneeling in beat chapels next to Mexican burlesque
shows in sheds.[12]

So out of this foundry, liberated by having nothing left to lose, the
Beats rediscovered play . . . and set about disrupting.

As the catalyst for Kerouac's writing, Neal Cassady was play incarnate, a new and improved American brand where drugs, sex, and cars
energized a vision, a retort to the frenzy of modern advertising and
consumption, taking play to a new and unnatural level.

Carl Solomon, who could have coined the term "lunatic saint" to
describe himself, was a fringe character who traveled by sea to Europe,
soaking up Surrealist and dada influences. Upon his return, he declared
himself insane and was shocked up and locked down. When they
met in the Columbia Psychiatric Institute, he inspired Allen Ginsberg to play to the maximum, and it is to him that *Howl* is dedicated.
Ginsberg had just enough fame to insulate him from the authorities
and to direct his crazy play onto the critical social contexts and losing
contests of the time and beyond—conformity, Vietnam, the environment, gay culture.

*Howl* and William S. Burroughs's *Naked Lunch* exemplify a Beat
advancement over dada consciousness. The Beats shared the dadas'
disgust with a death-insistent establishment, but they saw that the
nightmare could not be rejected through the simplicity of the child
alone, it had to be experienced.[13] Thus the Beats narrate encounters

---

[12] Jack Kerouac, *On the Road* (New York: Penguin, 1957), 9, 37, 50, 54, 81, 171, 195, 199, 243, 244, 271, 277. 287, 301.

[13] For better or worse, some of the Beats had the benefit of knowing about or undergoing psy-choanalysis.

with the dark side of our souls . . . to exorcise, to fully embrace our humanness without any personal shame and without the need to project that shame externally through war, violence, or repression.

The Beats weren't writers, painters, and musicians who liked to play so much as they were dharma bums, children of the underworld—"players" who happened to write, paint, and make music. Their play was not taken as the innocence of a child but as assault. Beat collided, then leapt. Beat disrupted an unforgiving and square mainstream.

They were wild metaphor and brown dirt, black asphalt and untamed verse, neon glare and headlight vision. The Beats had the wide-open spaces of the West, true cowboys roaming the New Frontier of modern America. Like the ruling industrialists, the pioneers of a few generations before, and the colonists before them, Beats staked their claims in twentieth-century America and took their place alongside other icons like Henry Ford, Davy Crockett, or Benjamin Franklin.

Free-standing styles in dress, sexuality, music, and mores bespoke opposition to the mainstream establishment, but one could also taste a new perspective that did not as desperately need opposition in order to thrive.

Initially, Beats couldn't pin fears of nuclear war on any particular villain. In his poem "Bomb," Gregory Corso tried to nail the demon down:

> *Budger of history Brake of time You Bomb*
> *Toy of universe Grandest of all snatched-sky I cannot hate you*
> *Do I hate the mischievous thunderbolt the jawbone of an ass . . .*
> *Bomb you are as cruel as man makes you and you're no crueller than cancer*
> *All man hates you they'd rather die by car-crash lightning drowning*
> *Falling off a roof electric-chair heart-attack old age old age O Bomb*
> *They'd rather die by anything but you Death's finger is free-lance*[14]

---

[14] Excerpted from "Bomb" by Gregory Corso, in *The Portable Beat Reader*, ed. Ann Charters (New York: Penguin Books, 1992), 174.

Fear of nuclear war was abstract and indefinite, a more elusive opponent than the specific and finite World War I. Ultimately, this became a strength. dada wilted without the foil of a world war. But the Beats, and the rock and roll counterculture to follow, mirrored abstract nuclear anxiety with an even more elastic national imagination and rebellious youth movement that grew in the face of war but did not require it. "The Establishment" was a less definite and more fertile target that increased the popularity of the Beat revolution.

Like the dadas, but in greater numbers, Beat cultivated an attitude. Beat antics did not have the deliberate, showcasing, performance art qualities of dada.[15] The US was not engaged in a major war, yet. And because the Beats were mainly writers and the dadas were mainly painters—the muses and the characteristic personalities are drawn in different directions.

Like the Impressionists, the Beats sought acceptance and were rejected. But while the Impressionists eventually prevailed within the mainstream art establishment, Beats grafted their lives onto America's netherworld—hobos, addicts, queers, prostitutes, poets, and deviants—a subculture apart from the intelligentsia and so gained a less self-conscious play ethic that could romp in the subcultural catacombs of marginalized America.

The Beats cloaked the play element in cool, but they nonetheless advanced play through their eventual popularity. They made art that could merge with the organic networks of culture and also conquer the style machine of American advertising and hype that accelerates and/or co-opts cultural change. "I see a vision of a great rucksack revolution . . ."[16] Thus spake Kerouac.

The Beats stumbled into a crack in the universe where they were able to stay true to the ethos of their art—live now, write now—and where they had the opportunity to be popular and build a mass

---

[15] Up until the 2010s, Americans tended not to make the connections between daily life and politics that the Europeans do. Americans lean more into style than class struggle substance.

[16] Jack Kerouac, *The Dharma Bums* (New York: Viking Penguin, 1958), 97.

movement. They succeeded where their forebears of the thirties had failed, they found a sweet convergence of youth culture, music, romance, sex, literature, and playfulness that revolutionized American culture and politics. Unlike Hitler's Germany or the Cold War, which were built upon ultimate contest, the Beat's America summoned a mass cultural opposition to contest—play.

## Cool

In John Tytell's *Paradise Outlaws: Remembering the Beats*, he describes William S. Burroughs as a "sorcerer of fiction." Norman Mailer calls him "the only writer of our time to have been possessed by genius."[17] Burroughs was willing, eager, and dedicated to throwing his soul and creations open to the mad colors of chance. The routines of *Naked Lunch* are reputed to have been published in a random order—deadlines prevented any review. In collaboration with the painter Brion Gysin, Burroughs explored the cut-up, a means of writing analogous to the modern painting of Jackson Pollock and others, where the materials, be they paint or words, are freed to express a life of their own. In the cut-up, Burroughs would arbitrarily splice passages from Arthur Rimbaud, Joseph Conrad, and T.S. Eliot into his narrative. This was a fitting sequel to the automatism of Duchamp and dadas like Arp, Huelsenbeck, Janco, Tzara and Ball, who would compose poems with nonsense syllables or by tossing pieces of paper to the floor, each with a word on them.

If Duchamp could make a urinal into a piece of art by declaring it so as the artist's choice, then the next stage was to free and surrender choice itself to the universe and let random force compose. Burroughs thus created with chaos and chance painting. He would set a can of paint in front of a canvas or plywood panel. Then, with a

---

[17] John Tytell, *Paradise Outlaws: Remembering the Beats* (New York: William Morrow, 1999), 118.

double-barreled Rossi shotgun, explode the can and voilà, ART! . . .
I mean, PLAY.

Kerouac took a different approach and attempted to connect with
the play element the way jazz musicians, in particular saxophonists like
Lester Young and Charlie Parker, connect with music in the moment.
He spent many smoky evenings at Minton's Playhouse in Harlem,
listening to beboppers, observing how their improvised solos would
vary, yet be based on a lexicon of riffs, motifs, themes, hooks, melodic
morsels, chord substitutions, and basic schemes.

Kerouac's idea was to take the same approach to writing. But in
writing, this was heresy; it went against the rewrite, one of writing's
sacred cows.

To so combine writing and play creates a conundrum. You cannot
edit play. But to refuse to edit your writing and then still expect the
world and the marketplace to pay for it, to read it, to enjoy it as art . . .
is that asking too much?

It's not. Kerouac heroically aspired to live life as art. He wanted to
connect his writing process and the reader to the ferment of ideas and
images that populate the subconscious in the same spontaneous, raw,
and honest way the jazz improviser does. That we hear his ideas, his
stream of consciousness, that we get a close-up of his idiosyncratic
access to the play element.

If we understand the synonymy between creativity and play, not
just the physical play of wrasslin' but the less physical play of the
mind as well, then Kerouac's craft emerges as a successful attempt
to bring play and art closer together. By not editing, he brought the
play of his Beat life to the page unfiltered.

We speak of Huncke, Solomon, and Cassady as the pure players
and the inspirations for Burroughs, Ginsberg, and Kerouac, respec-
tively, but all six broke free to experiment and let the play element
in through unconventional doors. Ginsberg stripping at a reading,
Burroughs delving deeply into addiction, Cassady channeling holy

terror by driving countless stolen cars with otherworldly speed and abandon—the distinction between player and artist is gone poof who needs it this is what transformation transcendence liberation freedom sweet release looks like smack smack SMACK!

So this blend of art and play, of bohemianism and the underground, of jazz and literature, all together—but happening in a hostile environment, melding how, how you gonna be an innocent child (a Beat) when your parents (straight America) are so threatened they can't wait to beat you? You get cool, boy!

What is cool, and what explains it? Cool is an attitude, a subtle sanction of what is hip, in the know, the good stuff. Cool is what you have to know to be "in." Everything else is square, and such unplayful exclusivity is the most difficult part of accommodating Beat culture as a play exponent. Once you got in, all was playful, but cool carried a foreknowing protectiveness of play's fragility and that the beauty and play of a Charlie Parker solo, a Ginsberg riffing poem, or a great Neal Cassady life episode would not survive the glare of middle America's scrutiny.

Coolness may have African origins, by way of the strong link between the Beats and the predominantly black bebop and cool jazz players.[18] *Itutu*, or coolness, is the complex Yoruba trait of grace under pressure, that play is engaged through sealed lips and a composed and serious stance. Cool is ". . . a part of character . . . fully realizing the spark of creative goodness God endowed us with. . . . Art returns the idea of heaven to mankind."[19] Art opens the way for the gods to bestow their gifts, and the practitioner of *itutu* in turn shows generosity and gentleness of character.[20]

---

[18] For a thorough exploration of cool and hip, see J. Leland, *Hip: the history* (New York: Harper Perennial, 2005).

[19] Robert Farris Thompson, Flash of the Spirit: African & Afro-American Art & Philosophy (New York: Vintage, 1983), 16.

[20] A diluted Beat form walks among us in the early twenty-first century, a pose with no play or generosity beneath it, only insecure emptiness. Young musicians and actors from Justin Bieber to Keanu Reeves, Bruno Mars to Paris Hilton, affect a faux coolness that shields no particular divine gift.

Jazz improvisation bloomed in the cool of the forties and fifties and conjured the communal spirit that the dadas floundered about to find. The automatism of Huelsenbeck, Tzara, and Janco performing a *poème simultané* may have set the stage for John Cage, Yoko Ono, or other art music with elements of chance, but what the dadas sought was to connect people to each other and to a moment that released play.

Original play's most defining feature is belongingness, and Beat accessories—denim or flannel shirt; dark glasses; natty dress; jazz bebop cool music; free, bisexual, ardent sex; hobo New York underworld slang; free verse, experimental, gutty, forbidden literature and poetry—signaled identification and belongingness to the clan.[21]

And a cool clan is somewhat exclusive. But the belongingness of original play is not. Anyone who understands the non-hurting ground rules of play is welcome. To posit play publicly in the midst of a society that represses, or at best belittles play in lieu of status and ranking, requires the protection of cool to survive the non-playing dominant culture. Cool is the armor that allows the child's seed of joy to be on the front lines and somehow be lived in a real world that cannot welcome it.

The poetry, novels, and prose of Beat writers reveal the joy and vulnerability beneath the anger, suffering, and protective cool gear. As does the bebop jazz. Play cannot coexist with fear, and a society based upon fear or fight/flight will not readily accept playful community. Therefore, cool.

The trumpet of the impenetrable Miles Davis, the godfather of cool jazz, is described in the liner notes of one of his albums as making the sound of a small child who has been locked out, standing wistfully at the door, hoping to be let in.

But penetrate the cool, and all the other features that define play ring true. Beat broke, actually ignored, the establishment's rules. Beat created an opportunity to make new rules, break them, and if one so chose, make them again. This is the make-believe aspect of play.

---

[21] J. Leland, *Hip: the history* (New York: Harper Perennial, 2005), 123-136.

For example, the temporary state of play found analogue in the Beat "career." A conventional career is a logically built game with rules, climbing a career ladder. For a Beat, a job is something you do for a while to put together some cash to finance the next adventure. Play with that most Protestant of admonitions to "make something of yourself." This Beat revolution lives on in young American wayfarers and adventurers—the rucksack revolution realized.

Make no mistake, Beats were not free of the neurotic imprints, flaws, and wounds already on their personalities. William Burroughs once took poultry shears and cut off the tip of one of his fingers, because he wanted to see what it would feel like. This ability to experiment—taken to a radical extreme by the likes of Burroughs and other Beats—is a hallmark of play. But think of it as a new form emerging from underworld muck. Some of the muck is going to stick. They were not role models.

So what was the difference between the disruptive play of the dadas and that of the Beats? The dadas probed the organic process of how culture is created and arrested it at the amoeba stage by throwing the petri dish in society's face again and again, so that we could see where we went wrong, where we left play. BEGIN again and again and again. The Beats wanted to make a little bread, get some yeast going. So behind protective cool, they created time and space to cook, grow their cultures. And in this case, a rebel culture that was broadly accessible and appealing.

[The Beat Generation is] "a cultural revolution in progress, made by a post-World War II generation of disaffiliated young people coming of age into a Cold War world without spiritual values they could honor. Instead of obeying authority and conforming to traditional middle-class materialistic aspirations, these young people dealt

as best they could with their will to believe, even in the face
of an inability to do so in conventional terms.[22]

Jack Kerouac's books chronicled the lives of dharma bums and Beats
who spotted encroaching consumerism and took to the road to sound a
Paul Revere warning. They responded to consumer culture by forging
alternative, liberated lives. The Beat proposition lived up to dada's
challenge to normalcy: live your life as art.

These serious writers and their jazz contemporaries obliged themselves into Buddhist pursuits: "The proper move," said Allen Ginsberg, "would be to . . . look for wisdom, and also experience a different
culture than the Western culture, which . . . was perhaps exhausted
of inspiration . . . . It was time for a second religiousness."[23] Serious
because they directly challenged the mainstream, committing the
most daring actions one could expect or hope for, short of a political revolution. The conflict with the Establishment was, at its core,
painful, and the dark side of cool so allover inside and out, that the
play element was not always obvious.

The Beats refused to compromise and settle for the deadening
options society offered. They saw the vanilla and repressed gray-flannel-
suit mentality and redoubled their commitment to reckless adventure.
No, they were certainly not role models. More like human sacrifices.

## Adolescents and Beat

Angry adolescents feel like they have been "had" by mainstream culture.
It is this wrenching away from childhood and into adult reality teens
so rightly and keenly perceive as troubling that informs a great deal
of youth music, poetry, behavioral styles, and creative activities.

Instinctively, many sense the loss of the earth-bond and the tight-
ening grip of a surrogate culture.[24] But youths still have a strong

---

[22] A quote by Beat writer John Clellon Holmes, in *The Portable Beat Reader*, ed. Ann Charters (New York: Penguin Books, 1992), xx.

[23] Allen Ginsberg, "The Vomit of a Mad Tyger," *Shambhala Sun*, July 1994, 16.

[24] Pearce, *Magical Child*.

memory of the ideal world of play, thus they poignantly feel their lives crashing onto the rocks of the "real" world—work, taxes, greed, social inequity, and somber adulthood. In disgust, they gravitate to marginal employment and sulky alienation.

And the players making a living at play have made tradeoffs as well. Commodification stunts the potential of social context by squeezing it into a commercial format: theater, arena, television, download, or other package. Commercialism corrupts; a potent artistic statement with transformative intent becomes the candy *du jour* of a bored elite. Even the commercial successes of Ginsberg, Kerouac, and Burroughs were, astonishingly, a compromise. They relied on the noncommercial, manic crashings of Cassady, Huncke, and Solomon.[25]

Allen Ginsberg comments, "As most people do, at the age of 15 to 19, whether it's punk or bohemia or grunge or whatever new vision adolescents have, there is always some kind of striving for understanding and transformation of the universe according to one's own subjective, poetic generational inspiration."[26] But instead of achieving that transformation, consumerist pleasures channel youth angst and multiply the (mal)functioning of society's compartmentalization.

In his analysis of delinquency, David Greenberg astutely summarizes how the dominant society absorbs Beat and other bohemianisms:

> The similarity between the subculture of delinquency and that of the leisurely affluent makes sense in view of the position of the delinquent *vis à vis* the school. Like the factory, the school frequently requires monotonous and meaningless work. Regimentation is the rule. Expres-

---

[25] The last great rock band Nirvana reacted so strongly against this co-optation that Cobain saw no way out but through suicide. And the jury is still out on whether the internet smashes compartments and liberates art or is actually the most sophisticated and unassailable compartment yet.

[26] Allen Ginsberg, "The Vomit of a Mad Tyger," *Shambhala Sun*, July 1994, 16.

sions of originality and spontaneity are not only discouraged, but may be punished. Students who reap no present rewards in return for subordinating themselves to the discipline of the school are free to cultivate the self-expressive traits which the school fails to reward. . . . They may come to regard adults who work as defeated and lifeless because of their submission to a routine that necessitates self-suppression, and hence try to avoid work because of the cost in self-alienation.[27]

As the twentieth century dawned, dadas illuminated the human treasure that is disruptive play. They did so from the vantage of lives that rejected war and the status quo of social adjustment. dadas were adults making a conscious decision to adopt the perspective of the child and challenge rationality through dada anti-art—magazines, exhibitions, performances, hoaxes. The Beats modernized this vision, and with the benefit of dada and anarchist inspiration, and through great sacrifice, changed the values of American culture. The Beats were not the first bohemians, but they launched bohemian values into mass culture. Their art was of a time when electronic media was coming of age. As Beat morphed into rock and roll and sixties culture, their free-living perspective reached an audience more vast than New York's Greenwich Village or San Francisco's North Beach.

Even though dada was an international sensation, their no-program bohemianism was difficult for a teenager in Kansas or even an intellectual in Los Angeles to grasp, let alone adopt. But Beat was accessible. Thus, mass culture's adoption of Beat crafted a mirrored lens that reflected and magnified the initial dada impulse.

[27] David F. Greenberg, "Delinquency and the Age Structure of Society," in *The Value of Youth*, ed. Arthur Pearl, Douglas Grant, and Ernst Wenk (Davis, CA: International Dialogue, 1978), 62-63.

Who "got it"? The kids. If Jack Kerouac were alive today, he would be in his nineties, but he will always be the twenty-five-year-old Sal Paradise of *On the Road,* and James Dean will always be the twenty-four-year-old rebel, validating the adolescent urge. The connection between Beat consciousness and teen angst is not coincidental. Many of the kids who were digging on Elvis dug the Beats.

Compare the habits that characterized the Beats in the forties and fifties to those of American youth since 1964. Beat musical affection was primarily bebop jazz, the most antiestablishment music. Beats liked drugs. Marijuana had been smoked for centuries, but because the Beats were a bridge from a heretofore submerged underground to mainstream urban culture, marijuana got its first foothold in suburban America. And so did black music. And so did sexual liberation. And so did Eastern religion.

Even before the widespread availability of birth control, Beats and kids took off looking for sexual liberation. Questions of fidelity, sexually transmitted diseases, sex roles, child-rearing, patrimony, love, and spirit were all there but not examined. They were brushed aside by the immediate good time. Play was the thing, and the Beats affection for the Buddhist "now" concept gave license to take full advantage of any opportunities, sexual or otherwise, that presented themselves.

This included a more powerful, less guilt-ridden exploration of homosexuality, which was fully closeted at the time, but which Ginsberg was not bashful about documenting.

As Beat became mainstream, was it selling out or was it a popular and successful revolution? That depends upon your point of view. Philip Roth comments:

> The attitude of the Beats (if such a phrase has meaning)
> is not in certain ways without appeal. The whole thing is a
> kind of joke. America, ha-ha. The only trouble is that such a

position doesn't put very much distance between Beatdom
and its sworn enemy, best-sellerdom—not much more, at
any rate, than what it takes to get from one side of a nickel
to the other: for what is America, ha-ha, but the simple
reverse of America, hoo-ray?[28]

Will Durant is said to have stated that the greatest tragedy that can
befall an ideal is its fulfillment. Does the Beat Generation represent
a social movement? Are we justified in extrapolating its values, its
play, to society? Or is Beat best left on the shelf as simply an interesting and important literary movement, dada as an interesting and
important art movement, but nothing more?

"Any genuine literature ultimately helps to shape the culture and
gives it some of its aspiration," Tytell tells us.[29] And Burroughs himself
saw the connection:

The alienation, the restlessness, the dissatisfaction were
already there waiting when Kerouac pointed out the
road. . . . Art exerts a profound influence on the style of
life, the mode, range and direction of perception. Art tells
us what we know and don't know that we know. Certainly
*On the Road* performed that function in 1957 to an extraordinary extent. There's no doubt that we're living in a freer
America as a result of the Beat literary movement, which is
an important part of the larger picture of cultural and political change in this country during the last forty years.[30]

Literature as cultural catalyst is necessary on more than one level.
People like Tytell and Ann Charters have done significant work in
bringing Beat literature the respect it deserves. While it is fine and

---

[28] Philip Roth, "Writing American Fiction," in *The Sense of the 60's,* ed. Edward Quinn and
Paul J. Dolan (New York: The Free Press, 1968), 451.

[29] Tytell, *Paradise Outlaws,* 64.

[30] William Burroughs at the Jack Kerouac Conference, University of Colorado, 1982, quoted
in *The Portable Beat Reader,* ed. Ann Charters (New York: Penguin, 1992), xxxi.

important that Beat literature gains in stature, something it did not have until the 1980s, its value lies more in what it awakens. Art is residue, living life artistically is the thing. So the central question is not whether their literature gains respect as literature, but whether their values, indeed their trickster take on the transitory quality of values, their visitation by the play energy, lives on.

Many bohemian values are commonplace in the hipster version of twenty-first-century America. Corporations are eco-sensitive and support the growth of human potential. More people try to live lightly on the planet and have adopted Beat Buddhism and moderated drug use. Politically, the Cold War is over and hopes for nuclear disarmament and peace are fervent. Beat is rich.

Yet racism is far from solved. Ultraright movements persist. Global heating is not abated. Warmongering is still invoked. The millennial phenomenon is a mixed bag, high in values and low in community. More contained than playful. Now that we have affected the goatees, the appreciation of jazz, of respect for the earth, of Eastern spirituality, of broadened sexuality, we must ask whether we have extracted parts and overlooked the whole. That is, have we dressed a Puritan in Beat clothing, or have we really learned to sing the body Beat, which is a body in play? The question remains relevant.

The sixties generation rode into town hot on Beat's heels. The tracks of the deliberately displaced dadas and the ambivalent Beats converged on the hippies, whose very child-rearing à la Dr. Spock was popular, popularized, and imbued with the child's perspective. Their predecessors had to make a conscious effort to recapture the child's original play perspective and import it into art and social action. The hippies were the first generation where that play element was a given and a part of their upbringing. Their play may have been distorted and neurotic, but it was undeniable.

This idea of embracing irrationality through play, of reevaluating the spiritual contribution and the political implications of childhood is neither far-fetched nor without precedent.

In other words, hippie philosophy.

Like the avant-garde Impressionists who preceded dada, the Beats laid down a rhythm that was picked up and reinterpreted by the counterculture that was to follow. As World War I gave dada its focus and proved its antiestablishmentarianism, so did the war in Vietnam stoke the potency and meaningfulness of the post-Beat sixties counterculture.

And it is no coincidence that Ginsberg, Burroughs, and Cassady, the great Beat players, linked to the sixties counterculture, participating and helping to lead both movements. And what a blessing that these leaders of Beat fiction, particularly Kerouac, and these leaders of jazz, particularly Charlie "Bird" Parker, were contemporaries. Kerouac critically connected leading-edge white bohemian literature to breaking developments in black American music.

Beat writer LeRoi Jones/Amira Baraka became a leader and founder of the Black Arts movement. Ginsberg's devotion to Buddhism signified an equally important connection. And relationships between Beats and Bob Dylan, the Grateful Dead, Richard Hell, Tom Waits, Laurie Anderson, and The Band sustained and amplified Beat energy. Later, Ginsberg would record with the Clash. Songwriters like Paul Simon and Van Morrison would write two of the over fifty rock songs inspired by Kerouac. Burroughs was a seminal influence on David Bowie, Lou Reed, Patti Smith, and Kurt Cobain. The rock genre "heavy metal" takes its name from *Naked Lunch*, as do the bands Steely Dan, Soft Machine, and Throbbing Gristle. For starters.

The flower children were the Beats' children. Considered together, this sustained effort to play going against the current of a contest-based society spanned twenty years, long enough to send some signals to the future, touching on what is possible, what playful existence may yet come to be.

# EIGHT

# The Counterculture Breaks on Through to the Other Side

*This is the sin of sins against an awkward power structure, the refusal to take it seriously.*

Phil Ochs[1]

## Cryptical Envelopment

NEAL CASSADY, Beat. Neal Cassady, proto-hippie. The mad driving of Neal Cassady. He drove Kerouac and Ginsberg, and then Kesey and the Merry Pranksters in the *Furthur* bus. With Bob Weir of the Grateful Dead, he'd been working on "(That's It for) The Other One," the apocryphal and quintessential Dead jam. "The Other One" summons the spirit that blesses and haunts Grateful Dead music. On February 4, 1968, Cassady died of unknown causes, falling into a coma in a freezing Mexican night while walking along the railroad tracks near San Miguel de Allende. On that same night, 2,200 miles away, Weir finally completed the playful, menacing, psychedelic tarantella.

> Escapin' through the lily fields
> I came across an empty space
> It trembled and exploded
> Left a bus stop in its place
> The bus came by and I got on

---

[1] Phil Ochs, "Have You Heard? The War is Over!" *The Village Voice*, November 23, 1967.

That's when it all began
There was cowboy Neal
At the wheel
Of a bus to never-ever land[2]

Perhaps Cassady was driving the Dead into the future. Weir testifies with great certitude that Cowboy Neal was with him that night.

Meanwhile, a historic civil rights movement attempted to save America from its original sin of slavery and racial discrimination. The Beatles and the British Invasion aroused hope in the depressed aftermath of President John F. Kennedy's 1963 assassination. The new urban subculture waved their freak flag high from Haight-Ashbury in San Francisco. The Monterey Pop Festival launched Hendrix, Joplin, and The Who—and the big rock concert—in 1967. Hundreds of thousands arm-banded protesters declared independence in the streets of Chicago in 1968. And hundreds of thousands of rainbow-colored fans rocked, rolled, lived, and loved for three days at Woodstock in 1969. Hundreds of thousands more protested the Vietnam War Moratorium in October that same year. African-American artists expressed their pride, crafted a liberated identity, and demanded forty acres and a mule—the reparations due them. The Rolling Stones' Altamont debacle of 1969, where security provided by the Hell's Angels motorcycle gang precipitated a murder at the concert, heralded a spiritual crash. A reborn feminism and identity politics rose up.

None of these events sufficiently describes the countercultural awakening that is identified by its decade, the sixties. But all of these events—and the synaptic sparks of dialogue, music, dance, protest, and rebellion that fed them—contained an element of play and stoked that fire. The sixties was play's most famous moment. Original play sprang forth and rang out the question that inspired this book: What if we didn't take everything so seriously and capitulate to the competitions of war and business? What if we let our utopian

---

[2] Grateful Dead, "That's It for the Other One," by Bob Weir, on *Anthem of the Sun*, Warner Brothers, 1968, vinyl recording.

dreams and desires out to play, out of the box? *What if we did more than talk about it and constellated our lives around play and art instead of work and commerce?*

## History Doesn't Repeat Itself, but It Does Rhyme

The Sixties movement bore some uncanny resemblance to the WWI era. Impressionism opened the door, and dada barged in. The Beats made the hippies[3] possible.

dada's insubordinate ethos challenged the sense and seriousness of art and existence and exploded the art world with the playfulness of the child as it posited café society. A newly liberalized sexuality entwined with rock and roll challenged the limits of the musical experience, and with its irreverent attitude, defied, mocked, and played with the repressive restraints of fifties America. Uninhibited and unself-conscious, rock and roll released an attitude that grew and eventually became the face of a movement. Both dada and rock raised social and political questions during an unpopular war. To wit:

| MODERN ART (EARLY TWENTIETH CENTURY) | ROCK AND ROLL (MID-TWENTIETH CENTURY) |
|---|---|
| Impressionism makes dada possible | Beats make hippies possible |
| The innovators: Voltaire, Delacroix, Miller, Courbet all toppled the old standards and went for common walks of life and international influences (instead of nobility and pastoral scenes) | The innovators: Elvis, Fats Domino, Little Richard, Chuck Berry all toppled the old standards and went for earlier blues influences (instead of sterile WASP-ish romantic fantasies) |

---

[3] There is no adequate term to describe participants in the 1960s counterculture because the movement was so widespread. The term "hippie" describes its most avid participants. It's inadequate, but because it is a broad *cultural* term, it at least touches on the political, spiritual, and sexual changes that occurred. The term thus overlays and overlaps and is used interchangeably with counterculture.

(continued)

| MODERN ART (EARLY TWENTIETH CENTURY) | ROCK AND ROLL (MID-TWENTIETH CENTURY) |
|---|---|
| Technological advances like photography and portable paint and easels gave innovators an expanding format to work with and a broader audience | Technological advances like the electric guitar, 45 rpm singles and regional radio gave innovators expanding opportunities and a national/international audience |
| You get Impressionism and an irrevocable advance in fine art | You get rock and roll and an irrevocable advance in popular music |
| As Impressionism led into dada, the spirit of innovation became about more than art; it became political and cultural | As Beat led into hippie counterculture, the spirit of innovation became about more than popular music; it became political and cultural |
| dada, beyond its playfulness and sense of absurdity, was antiwar and utopian. | The counterculture, beyond its playfulness and sense of absurdity, was antiwar and utopian. |
| Ultimately, play migrated from its political context and into the more introspective and psychologically minded Surrealist movement. | Ultimately, play migrated from its political context and into the more introspective and psychologically minded human potential and New Games movements. |

But the counterculture went beyond cult status and, armed with modern media and rock and roll, mushroomed where dada contracted, confronted where Beats swerved. And thus, the hippie experiment in playing drew a broader and more violent reaction. As a sustainable alternative, the counterculture failed. But as an influence on US culture since, its impact has been tremendous, its presence vibrantly with us still, and the ultimate outcome—in terms of a liberated and playful future—undecided. In that sense, the ideas, influence, and experimentation of the sixties represent an ongoing success.

What drove Cassady? What was Cassady driving? Lewis Carroll and Grace Slick would have you "go ask Alice, when she's ten feet tall."[4] "Never-ever land" was an idealistic vision of adulthood imbued with playfulness. Cassady's life was testimony to that possibility. He echoed the life of dada Arthur Cravan and was a major figure of the Beats **and** the hippies. The fact of Neal Cassady transcends whatever breaks free of any historic binding one may be tempted to attribute to these eras. There's something timeless going on here.

## Child is dada to the Man, The Quodlibet for Tenderfeet

The image of revolution is the image of the child. Not to disarm the opponent, but to disarm the struggle for dominance itself. That sixties revolutionary call is best conceptualized as disruptive play.

> Of course, children have always been sensitive to adult hypocrisy. And individual children have grown up to be artists, satirists, or prophets, puncturing the lies of social life. But rarely, if ever, has the better part of a generation tried to hold on to that childhood sensitivity and make it into a principle of adult conduct.[5]

In the sixties, the magic of play was rediscovered, as was the fallacy of man as an inevitable belligerent. But this outpouring of playfulness stirred up a lot of confusion. In rejecting the Establishment, hippie play fell prey to narcissism and impulsivity. Finding the way to playful maturity was a daunting challenge.

One major trait of the child, of play, and of the Trickster, is engaging in activity that has no purpose beyond that of having fun. Hippies finding love on a street called Haight—dancing, loving, communing, and letting go of all material concerns…this is a paramount example of an innocent (many would call naive) attempt at the Play Society. Gone in the blink of an eye, but there it stands as a point in history,

---

4  Jefferson Airplane, "White Rabbit," by Grace Slick, on *Surrealistic Pillow*, RCA, 1967, vinyl recording.

5  Annie Gottlieb, *Do You Believe in Magic: Bringing the 60s Back Home* (New York: Simon & Schuster, 1987), 27-28.

an experiment…acknowledging spiritual forces at work, letting go of schedule, agenda, property: we'll have fun, and forces will reveal themselves if we can just sustain a contest-free improvisatory environment.

Some sixties' spontaneous travelers took off on a journey not knowing where it would lead. While sending some off the grid of American reality, this revolution led many others to the center of US foreign policy and war machine.

## Politics and Play: The Faster We Go the Rounder We Get

For the first time since the 1930s, the sixties heralded a return of mass political consciousness in the US. There was a holistic questioning of the entire political realm and the way things got done. Folks gave themselves permission to think utopian thoughts and dream utopian dreams. Idealistic theories got play: ideas of utopian anarchism and creative thinking and analyses of where the advanced stages of capitalism and technology were taking us. Herbert Marcuse (philosopher, political theorist), Gary Snyder (Beat, poet, Buddhist, essayist, environmental activist), Theodore Roszak (academic and author of *The Making of a Counterculture,* coining the term in 1969), Noam Chomsky (linguist, philosopher, cognitive scientist, historian, social critic, and political activist), Marshall McLuhan (philosopher and public intellectual, wrote *The Medium is the Massage),* and many others were read and understood.

In her book on the sixties, Annie Gottlieb describes three strands of white revolutionary politics.[6] First was what she calls the "instant-con-

---

[6] The African–American experience is key to the sixties, key to all US history. In what might appear to be a paradox, African-American participation in the playful fun of hippie love was limited. Leaders like Martin Luther King, Jr., Malcolm X, Stokely Carmichael, the Black Panthers, et al. linked their domestic struggles more to the imperialist conflict in Vietnam than to the frolic and play of Haight-Ashbury. Despite the deep infusion of the West African trickster Èsù-Elegba throughout African-American culture—both immensely popular (soul, R&B, blues, comedy, theater, etc.) and sectarian (Vodun, Gospel, etc.)—the sixties bespoke the time to raise consciousness of racial oppression and to enlarge the civil rights movement. Serious stuff. *Original Play* cannot survive or thrive in a conflict, yet the African-American contribution to the capacity to lead a playful life is immense. That paradox and that contribution is so large and so important to this account, including the experience of the sixties, that this book cannot offer the fuller discussion it requires. I call attention to, but reserve for another forum, play and the African-American experience.

sciousness" revolution, led by Timothy Leary and Allen Ginsberg: that if everyone took LSD all at once, a transformation of power politics would occur, and we would solve most of our serious problems. We'll never know how that would've turned out, though urban legends persist and the CIA did investigate.[7]

Second was the more organized approach known as the New Left, represented by organizations like the Students for a Democratic Society (SDS) and given to sober analysis of the political establishment and strategies to shift political power. Though the New Left appeared to disintegrate in the late sixties, it schooled many of today's successful, and usually single-issue activists, some elected leaders, and legitimate challengers to the power structure, in environmental, trade, labor, and international and human rights issues. From this group emerged disciplined and persistent activists, some of whom function well in the halls of power and have sustained struggles for progressive policies and if not the dissolution of power, at least a more equitable distribution of it. This is the least playful approach; it's serious, and these activists are not known for telling good jokes, dancing, or play.

Third, Gottlieb recognizes the Yippies, the Diggers, and the White Panthers:

> These groups combined expanded consciousness with small-c communism, playfulness with disruption. "Everything free" was their main idea, as articulated by White Panther Party founder John Sinclair: free sex, free dope, free music, free schools, free land for all comers at Morningstar Ranch, free money fluttering from the balcony of the New York Stock Exchange, free food ladled out daily by the Diggers in Golden Gate Park, free political prisoners Huey Newton and Bobby Seale. Abbie Hoffman proclaimed "the birth of FREE AMERICA in our own time . . . We demand the Politics of Ecstasy!"

---

[7] Andy Roberts, "Reservoir Drugs: The Enduring Myth of LSD in the Water Supply, *Psychedelic Press UK*, April 24, 2018, http://psypressuk.com/2014/03/12/reservoir-drugs-the-enduring-myth-of-lsd-in-the-water-supply/.

Not since World War I and dada had such bold ideals been so publicly expressed.

> The anarchism was sexy, the generosity was bold and sweet—a powerful symbol of love made material—but it had a fatal flaw. It depended unconsciously on the flood of affluence issuing from the warmaking capitalist machine. Yippies and Diggers played at the redistribution of wealth the way little kids play house with food from Mommy's kitchen: they never began to confront the realities of power. And that made their synthesis of culture and politics creative, but hopelessly romantic. In fact, it wasn't really politics at all: it was art.[8]

Now it's getting interesting, and the criticism—that Yippies and Diggers played like little kids and what they made was more art than politics—could be considered praise. Blurring that line is exactly what trickster politics are all about. The "instant consciousness" activists, Gottlieb's first strand, ignored the power structure. The New Left theorists/activists accepted it and chose to engage on power's terms. But the Yippies, Diggers, and White Panthers actively mocked power and sought to discredit it. This might be perceived as juvenile or "hopelessly romantic," yet it is the North Star of utopian politics, it is the vision, no matter how far-fetched it may seem. The Yippies were just such tricksters, intent on bringing redemption.

And what is wrong with repurposing the flood of affluence that issues from the capitalist machine? Presidential blowjobs, exploding smartphones, divorcing celebrities, *The Apprentice,* viral-yet-idiotic Facebook posts, watching OTHER people play online video games, Fidget Spinners—all confirm that something small and chipped off of the block of US wealth can have magnified impact, redirect the flow of capital, and even spread a germ of political consciousness.

The Yippies understood this, and while they were disparaged as "manipulators of the media," they were simply using what Madison

---

[8]  Gottlieb, *Do You Believe in Magic,* 126.

Avenue taught, except with the purpose of deflating, rather than per-
petuating, capitalist exploitation. The redirection of technologically
produced wealth is exactly what Marshall McLuhan recommended,
what culture jammers like Adbusters[9] and Anonymous employ:

> With the extension of the nervous system in electric tech-
> nology, information not only moves in much greater quan-
> tity than ever before, but at very much greater speed than
> ever before. Paradoxically, the acceleration of information
> movement restores us to the habit of mythical and inclusive
> perception. . . . The electric circuit has restored us to the
> world of pattern recognition and to an understanding of the
> life of forms which had been denied to all but the artists of
> the now receding mechanical age. Our main concern today
> is with the patterns of the . . . processes of creativity. . . .
> The elimination of the job in the work process means a
> return to the depth involvement in role-playing formerly
> associated only with arts and crafts. But now in the Age
> of Information the work process and the learning process
> become interfused.[10]

And the irreverent, the supposedly degenerate Yippies provide exactly
the (a)moral compass you want to take with you to keep from getting
lost in the woods of McLuhan's electric technology, what we today call
the cyberworld, where you face thickets of stimulation, ungrounded
fantasy, and vacuous consumption. Ethical use of the internet poses
a major challenge. Truth is fluid in an untethered world.

Yippies grasp for ungraspable fun. The basic Yippie tool, a dada
vision, the McLuhanesque convergence of electric media and social
change—is easily demonstrated. For example, when a criminal successfully poisons a small lot of an over-the-counter drug, the ensuing
media hysteria and fear can bring a multibillion-dollar company to
its knees. An unfortunate series of plane crashes that might otherwise enter the pile of annual statistics—or the rude eviction of an

---

[9] https://adbusters.org

[10] Marshall McLuhan, "Culture and Technology," in *The Sense of the 60's*, ed. Edward Quinn
and Paul J. Dolan (New York: The Free Press, 1968), 494.

airline passenger—can, given poor timing and certain media attention, drive an airline into bankruptcy. And hackers can create untold bedlam: the 2016 US elections, 4Chan, massive identity theft, character assassination, the Sony hack, etc.

In theater, timing is everything. A petty but nefarious crime of breaking into a political party's headquarters—Watergate—could in one cultural climate be all but overlooked, and in another, cause a president to resign. One president can get a blowjob and get impeached. Another can be exposed as a sexual predator during his campaign and still be elected.

And a single African-American woman insisting on her right to sit where she wants on a public bus can spark a civil rights movement.

A showcase trial of movement leaders—in this case, the Chicago Eight—can infuriate the Establishment and extend the shelf life of that movement. Gagging and then separating out the one black defendant confirmed our racist heritage and gave rein to the chaos which today is the water in which we all swim. The US had "…gone from being a country in which Americans looked to their government to confront and solve the social ills facing it, to one in which Americans put little faith or trust in their government to do either."[11]

So we need serious and deeply informed political activists who engage the power structure and win battles for environmental balance, civil rights and liberties, and fair distribution of wealth, goods, and labor. But we also need cosmic cowboys and cowgirls who take risks and imagine the fantastic: disruptive players who encourage and envision the demise of power, who, with a sense of theater and of timing, can make art that moves the political needle.

The sixties countercultural movement stands out in part because of its great diversity, which, when it reached a critical mass, allowed for spoilsports, tricksters, pranksters, and the like to find a role and introduce play. Play that refuses to fight according to any rules of

---

[11] Jules Witcover, *The Year the Dream Died: Revisiting 1968 in America* (New York: Warner Books, 1997), 507.

engagement. This is "fight the power." In play, there is no place for conflict. Yet young idealistic hippies, Yippies, and the like jumped into dangerous conflict with the message of "stop the conflict": stop fighting war, stop oppressing minorities and people of color, stop dictating what I can and can't do in my private life.

This kind of disruptive play explains much of the sixties. Almost every action was couched in conflict—antiwar and civil rights movements—or attracted conflict by provocation—drugs, music, sex. At the conclusion of the popular art film *Easy Rider*, the do-no-harm antiheros are senselessly murdered . . . just for being different.

Some believe that the mistake of the sixties was the way it shunned power, that its ideals diverted it from being effective. Though the complete dissolution of power does not seem realistic in the immediate future, what appeared as a failed sixties experiment was in fact . . . correct! Naive hippies were everywhere shouting . . .

> "The entire money system has to end. A society of free goods, freely produced, freely distributed. You take what you need, you give what you can. The world is yours to love and work for. No state, no police, no money, no barter, no borders, no property. Time and disposition to seek good, seek one another, to take trips deep into the mind, and to feel, to find out what it is to have a body, and to begin to use and make joy with it."[12]

How could supposedly intelligent leaders be spouting such silly idealism? Yet they were, and it was oft-repeated, and it endures as a historical signpost. The duplicity of the social contract, the proposition of perpetual war, was intuitively and intellectually recognized and exposed by the sixties counterculturalists, what Abbie Hoffman dubbed "Woodstock Nation." These artists, clowns, tricksters, and idealists sought outright transformation and refused to take power seriously.

---

[12] Julian Beck, *The Life of the Theater: Notes Toward a Statement on Anarchism and Theatre* (San Francisco: City Lights, 1972), 30.

When such mockery occurs, it can go one of two ways. It can escalate matters, as refusing to fight often infuriates the adversary. Or it can defuse it. Putting flowers in the barrels of guns, running a pig (sow) for president, levitating the Pentagon, guerilla theater, satiric parade puppets, acts of civil disobedience that also bring the carnival spirit into play. The sixties overflowed with examples of disruptive play.

In the very heat of a possible riot—with armed kids serving in the National Guard; Marxist-Leninists and FBI infiltrators alike itching for a violent confrontation; and masses of people excited, agitated, and hyped up for or against an ugly war in Southeast Asia—disruptive play aspired to the role of a magical solvent. A special, albeit fleeting, miracle.

Recall how play frequently has an "as-if" quality defined by the marking off of a "sacred circle" or playground that all the players understand: for example, when pretending that a cardboard box is a car or when dogs pretend to growl and bite but do not harm. Players in such circumstances recognize when playing has ceased.[13]

There is some magic here. In many antiwar demonstrations, when demonstrators would confront the state's power—police and National Guard—they would invert the play definition and "pretend" that we were all just people trying to get along and not so different from each other. Which was the "as-if" truth. The pretense of power is a fantasy made solid but still unreal. Thus, even in a tense confrontation, there is an element of the "as-if" quality creating a temporary and fragile play space. And when the guns went off at Kent State on May 4, 1970, and four students were killed, all recognized that playing had ceased.

## The Aftermath: We Leave The Castle

Since then, the Persian Gulf War, WTO meetings, the 2016 presidential election, etc. all galvanized political action networks. This is

---

[13] See Introduction.

good stuff, but it confines activity to reaction, a form of contest, not play. Activists enter a struggle intent on winning, or at least highlighting conflict. But disruptive players look for opportunities to replace win/lose conflict with play.

Like with guerrilla theater. Theater creates a temporary alternate reality, and theater has a potency film cannot match—real people playing parts and interacting in real time with a real audience. If theater presents an alternative means of interacting, or if it exposes the irrationality of so-called reality, it can catalyze change. Theater capitalizes on and suggests the "as if" quality of play. Improvisational theater comes closer, and theater as disruptive play, closer still.

Take as an example People's Park, a discarded plot of land owned by UC Berkeley[14] that was liberated spontaneously by an ad hoc group of community activists in April of 1969. As much an act of theater as occupation, the people who liberated People's Park carved out a small utopian space. They laid sod, planted flowers, built benches and swings, and inhabited the space, primarily for the fun of it. It was real, the lives lived in that space for a few short weeks were real, but it was theater; it was a symbolic gesture. It was an attempt to disruptively play without the provocation of a demonstration or other antiwar action. It was simply for life.

The University violently evicted of the citizens of People's Park and reclaimed the space for . . . a parking lot. The antihierarchical position of the counterculture was immediately recognized by the power structure as threatening. Even peaceful actions drew an ugly and forceful reaction. Even a symbolic gesture of play and antihierarchy could not be allowed to stand. People's Park dances at the crossroads of theater and politics, a concerted and collective instance of disruptive play.

---

[14] Sure, UC owned the land and the occupation/liberation could be considered a provocation. But the property could just as easily have been given over to the activists. Was the original conflict the "liberation" of property owned by someone else, or was the very concept of property the original provocation?

Play is belongingness, and at its best, sixties radicalism extended that. SDS, Black Panthers, White Panthers, Yippies, socialists, Trotskyists, Leninists, women's groups, gay groups, single-issue community groups . . . all had different agendas and missions, but it was pretty easy to contribute to and be accepted in them all.

And activists sought to extend that belongingness globally. Despite the superficiality of a white middle-class protester claiming solidarity with Vietnamese peasants, other oppressed people of the Global South,[15] and African-Americans, the intentions were sincere and of unprecedented energy and scale. Adopting the words "sisters and brothers" bespoke a felt bond and a hope that went beyond rhetoric.

The antiwar movement successfully included the playful disrespect of the trickster element, and such disruptive play befuddled and infuriated the power structure and did help stop the Vietnam War.

But the sixties revolution as insurrection was not going to succeed. It was a mite compared to US police and military might. American society could not be transformed by a *coup d'état*. The anarchists/Yippies/White Panthers/Diggers correctly assessed that any "them" and "us" conflict was doomed to just continue power struggles, not to transcend them.

Antiwar demonstrations animated a complex gestalt. Some would focus on how brutal the police were, others on how restrained they were; some on the antics of just a few troublemakers, others on the unified message of the crowd. Some on the wise words of the speakers, others on the raw sensuality of confrontation. Some on conflicts that arose between individuals, others on the connection to issues and events halfway around the world.

> It was a sense that something primitive was forcing its way up from beneath, something destructive and creative that would not stop short of total transformation. In part it was the accumulated rage of blacks, racing through Ameri-

---

[15] "Global South" has replaced "Third World" as a more appropriate term.

can streets in the form of fire. But it was more. It was the relentless removal of controls until, finally, all that the old America had repressed would erupt into the open—violence and chaos, femaleness and instinct, the irrational, the ecstatic, the sexual, the mystical.[16]

Consciousness was changing. In this complex mix of the struggle to resolve age-old wrongs, an emerging multiculturalism, utopian possibility, and justice sought in all corners of human existence and suffering, along came drugs and music and play.

---

[16] Gottlieb, *Do You Believe in Magic*, 39-40.

# NINE

# The Counterculture Breaks

*To get really high is to forget yourself. And to forget yourself is to see everything else. And to see everything else is to become an understanding molecule in evolution, a conscious tool of the universe. And I think every human being should be a conscious tool of the universe. That's why I think it's important to get high.*[1]

Jerry Garcia

## Drugs and Music and Play

Cartoons and music share playfulness, evoked in a world of rhythm that rubs elbows with irrationality. "Cartoons play out the nonhierarchical rule of rhythm. They give rhythm a look and meaning. . . . Cause and effect . . . gets left behind by cartoons' manic sprint. Rhythm, after all, starts anew—innocent, free—with each repeating downbeat."[2]

Sixties "lifestyle" activities of liberalized sex, recreational drugs, and rock and roll certainly incorporated play. But sexual missteps, addiction, and general narcissism swarmed around these activities.

Set aside for a moment all the bad stuff we know about what happens when you take drugs, or too many drugs, or the wrong kind of drugs. And in an attempt at objectivity, forget for a second all of the cul-

---

[1] Jerry Garcia, interviewed by Charles Reich and Jann Wenner on January 20, 1972, in *Garcia*, by the editors of *Rolling Stone* (Boston: Little, Brown, 1995), 95.

[2] J. Leland, *Hip: the history* (New York: Harper Perennial, 2004), 187-188.

tural teams that have lined up for and against the use of drugs, and discard the political contest surrounding drugs, in particular psychoactive drugs. And remember that the use of mind-altering substances is ancient. It was not invented in the sixties, but it did become more mainstream then, and in direct contrast to the alcohol-numbed 1950s.

One of the liberating effects of a drug that produces prolonged disassociation from conventional perception (a trip) is that it wrenches one free of the constraints of culture and commerce. In the best of circumstances, this creates conditions for play and creative experimentation . . . in thought, in art, in behavior.

Substantive ideas and lasting art require discipline. But the creativity that sparks them relies upon play, which psychoactive drugs can arouse and enhance. Drugs can play this role and did during the sixties.

Drugs in the sixties helped many people benefit from an expanded consciousness, that is, a *meta* approach to societal issues at least partially free of cultural norms. By this I mean that the disassociation produced by drugs can create an openness to other cultures and an awareness of archetypes that recur in them all: flood myths, trickster gods, rites of passage, culture-free child-like play—goodies ready to fill the vacuum left by the antiseptic culture of the fifties.

The ancient met with the emergent in the sixties, and drugs, for all the disparagement they receive, facilitated the process.

Fantastical drug experiences remind us that reality is relative and rationality temporal. Ultimately, the world is beyond rational systematizing, and living in a play state serves as a healthy reminder of that. We can touch that experience and need not be terrified by it. The drug adventures of the sixties brought greater sensitivity to playfulness and new perspectives on what we mean by "life, liberty and the pursuit of happiness."

The collapse into more dangerous drugs, addictions, and blasé abuse did not stem from the drugs or their evangelists. It became a nightmare in the US because US culture, unlike indigenous Latin American and African cultures, has no ancient grounding, no religious or cultural rituals to govern and guide their use. The first users of LSD were in awe of its powers but couldn't predict what dropping it into a secular society would ignite. Transported from a laboratory or a traditional culture to a secular one, psychedelic drug use is like giving Phaethon the sun chariot or Mickey Mouse the sorcerer's wand: more power than we know how to handle. And the intimidations of the police and straight culture didn't help.

Though the generation gap was a media-manufactured explanation of the rifts dividing US society in the sixties, youth and rebellion were undeniably connected. And it is here in this generational conflict that the case for play as a means of helping society become wiser and more mature gets entangled in the web of narcissistic arrest and indulgence. Whatever rift, whatever rejection there was of the customary rites of passage was necessary, for sixties youth could see the sexual repression, the Protestant work ethic, the manufactured seriousness of the Cold War all leading to the idiocy of the Vietnam War and a straitjacketed life. But such rejection also meant risking a free fall (even if a psychedelic free fall) until new rites could emerge, which would take at least a generation. And in that time, technology and consumerism, the highly capable partners of Narcissus, were only too happy to step in and fill the void.

So the sixties generation wielded the sword of its new ideals but was insufficient to the task of resisting a technologically pleasant environment. The very technologies and innovations that initially liberated—food, sex, music, film, drugs, "the driving experience," international travel that sanitizes and seals off the traveler—eventually numbed. In 2000, David Brooks described the deal struck and dubbed the new hipsters *bobo's*, or bourgeois bohemians.[3] The psychedelic advantage—a decoupling from culture—was also a vulnerability. Yet from that tender opening sprouted a popular art and a progressive social vision.

---

[3] David Brooks, *Bobos in Paradise: The New Upper Class and How They Got There* (New York: Simon & Schuster, 2000).

## And Music and Play and Politics: Sixties Art and Satire

The boisterous idiom of rock and roll, after a late fifties lull, found new release through the Beatles and the Rolling Stones. Just add drugs and watch the experimentation grow. Check out Jimi Hendrix, The Who, the Grateful Dead and the San Francisco rock bands, the Doors and the L.A. bands, Lou Reed and the New York bands, etc. Drugs expanded the form, expanded the content and the possibilities for playfulness. By taking musical risks and letting go, artists can connect with the vibrations that take us into a play state.

Modern artistic revolutions had languished as cults and failed to shake any hips, let alone governments. Radicalism connected with art only on the fringes. *Fin de siècle* anarchism was too extreme, the Spanish Civil War too distant, the Cold War too unreal and removed from American daily life. In other words, dada was not Pop popular. The Lost Generation was just that, expatriated to Europe. And while 50s rock and film were undoubtedly connected to fear of nuclear annihilation and American racism, they did not have the kind of connection or synergy with a large political movement that sixties rock did.

The sixties convergence of art and life could make your heart pound. Music and politics engendered and energized each other. Rock and roll gave youth courage to act and to act politically, and political upheaval paid it back, informing music with rebel energy. Musicians addressed culture wars, Vietnam, race, conformity, and more.

The composer who best conveys play is the dada and musical graffiti artist Erik Satie (1866-1925). When other composers were dedicating themselves to making serious music that either enshrined the nineteenth century (Mahler, Wagner, etc.) or announced the twentieth (Stravinsky, Bartók, Schoenberg, etc.), Satie would match their harmonic and rhythmic and melodic sophistication with musical jokes that were at once gorgeous and mocking. The Beats had an intimate, synergistic relationship with bebop jazz,[4] and out of that brew came

---

[4] Leland, *Hip: the history*, 111-136.

the man-child genius Thelonious Monk, whose music is virtually synonymous with play. Monk started with the pinnacle of jazz innovation of his time and took it from there, making jazz his playground; he'd romp and skylark with melodic angles that poked the funny bone. In sixties rock, the play element diffused, but it was everywhere.

Rock reigned as the most influential creative musical genre from 1954 until roughly 1994.[5] In that era, rock and roll artists challenged the conventional boundaries of music performance: light shows, the sexual/satirical antics of Frank Zappa (he did unspeakable things to a jelly-filled effigy), endless jams, protopunk (The Velvet Underground, garage rock, Monks, The Sonics and MC5, Iggy Pop and The Stooges), the lascivious bravado of Jim Morrison and Mick Jagger, Bob Dylan taking folk music electric, and the ritual smashing of instruments by The Who and Jimi Hendrix. Fifties rock had rebelled against the sterility of suburban life, planting a bomb. Sixties rock detonated it in a search of a new and playful way of living.

The musical arsenal was fully loaded. Folk traditions tracing back centuries informed communal excitement and identity. Harry Smith's *Anthology of American Folk Music* (1952), the world's first mixtape, comprised eighty-four previously released and seminal folk recordings from 1926-1932. For many sixties musicians, it was their bible.

These influences were charged up by the increasing reach of mass media and a burgeoning music industry: from the introduction of sheet music to records and radio, 33⅓ rpm albums, television and FM radio. The finishing touch was quality concert amplification, gelling a new critical mass where traces of community and a visceral collective feeling for music could be experienced en masse. Electric folk music.

Rock stars had an irrepressible playfulness about them. As bold and upsetting as this new music was, it refused to be taken too seri-

---

[5] The rock and roll era dates from Elvis Presley's "That's Alright Mama" (1954) to the death of Nirvana's Kurt Cobain (1994). This era also saw output from enormously creative, though less popular, composers such as Karlheinz Stockhausen, Olivier Messiaen, Krzysztof Penderecki, György Ligeti, Andrzej Panufnik, Steve Reich, John Cage, Philip Glass, Terry Riley, etc., as well as jazz giants like John Coltrane, Miles Davis, Thelonious Monk, Bill Evans, Charles Mingus, Cecil Taylor, Ornette Coleman, Eric Dolphy and more.

ously. Chuck Berry set the tone and invented modern rock by writing lyrics that related directly to carefree adolescence. The blues sources for guitar style and rock that Berry built on—T-Bone Walker, Lonnie Johnson, Carl Hogan, Muddy Waters, Howlin' Wolf, etc.—were "adult" lyrics about lives of suffering and sex that middle-class American teens could fantasize about, but not relate to seriously. Berry brought playfulness into that blues form with lyrics that could be a little bit silly and a lot of fun:

> Yeah, I'm doing all right in school.
>> They ain't said I've broke no rule.
>> I ain't never been in Dutch.
>> I don't browse around too much.
>> Don't bother me, leave me alone.
>> Anyway I'm almost grown.[6]

And:

> New Jersey Turnpike in the wee wee hours,
>> I was rollin' slowly 'cause of drizzlin' showers.
>> Here come a flat-top, he was movin' up with me,
>> Then come wavin' by me in a little old souped-up jitney.
>> I put my foot on my tank, and I began to roll.
>> Moanin' siren, 'twas the state patrol.
>> So I let out my wings, and then I blew my horn.
>> Bye, bye New Jersey, I've become airborne.
>
> Now you can't catch me, baby you can't catch me;
>> 'cause if you get too close, you know I'm gone like a cool breeze.[7]

And sixties rock was playful and rebellious. From the highly sophisticated yet whimsical compositions of Brian Wilson and the Beach Boys to the sharp irreverence of the Fugs and Frank Zappa's Mothers

---

[6] Chuck Berry, "Almost Grown," by Chuck Berry, Chuck Berry Is on Top, Chess Records, 1959, vinyl recording.

[7] Chuck Berry, "You Can't Catch Me," by Chuck Berry, on After School Session, Chess Records, 1957, vinyl recording.

of Invention to the psychedelic experimentation of Pink Floyd, playing with sounds, words, and meanings was the thing. Country Joe and the Fish could even make fun of white fear by portraying Harlem as a tourist destination,[8] and they ridiculed American involvement in Vietnam through a rousing cheer that intimated what fun it would be to fight in a meaningless war.[9] Bands competed to see who would be the first to get the word "motherfucker" played on the air.

And what about play's intrinsic irrationality, its single most defining feature? Bob Dylan sang beautiful songs, fun to listen to, and he reached an apex of the absurd and irrational in his lyrics, bringing a literary playfulness to an enormous audience. Even in a song as somber as "Desolation Row,"[10] Dylan's knack for unexpected juxtaposition brings a playful perspective on mournful themes:

> They're selling postcards of the hanging
> They're painting the passports brown
> The beauty parlor is filled with sailors
> The circus is in town
> Here comes the blind commissioner
> They've got him in a trance
> One hand is tied to the tightrope walker
> The other is in his pants
> And the riot squad they're restless
> They need somewhere to go
> As lady and I look out tonight
> From Desolation Row.[11]

A key component of play is the transience of competence; one cannot become too good for too long at any measurable skill in

---

[8] Country Joe and the Fish, "The Harlem Song," by Joe McDonald, on Together, Vanguard Records, 1968, vinyl recording.

[9] Country Joe and the Fish, "The Fish Cheer/I-Feel-Like-I'm-Fixin'-To-Die Rag" by Joe McDonald, on I-Feel-Like -I'm-Fixin'-To-Die, Vanguard Records, 1967, vinyl recording.

[10] It's speculated that the use of the word "desolation" in the title is borrowed from Jack Kerouac's novel Desolation Angels.

[11] Bob Dylan, "Desolation Row," by Bob Dylan, on Highway 61 Revisited, Columbia Records, 1965, vinyl recording.

order to remain in the play state. Satire brings playfulness to serious subjects and pokes fun at institutions (competence piled high and deep) whose accumulations of experts have made them arrogant, power-based, and status-seeking.

Enter Frank Zappa in the US and the Bonzo Dog Doo-Dah Band in England, who satirized society in general and the youth culture in particular. The Kinks, Captain Beefheart, Jefferson Airplane, The Who, The Turtles, Country Joe and the Fish, the Fugs; many of the folkies like Dylan, Dave Van Ronk, Phil Ochs; and even the musical theater satirist Tom Lehrer churned out self-effacing and society-mocking satire.[12]

Satire disarms its subjects like hip style ("I think my hair's getting good in the back," Zappa), war ("I-Feel-Like-I'm-Fixin'-to-Die Rag," Country Joe and the Fish), revolution ("Revolution #1," *The Beatles*), romance (Zappa's Mothers of Invention as Ruben and the Jets), empty conversation ("My Pink Half of the Drainpipe," Bonzo Dog Band), and white privilege (*Young and Rich*, The Tubes), in a perspective that cuts imposed and phony values down to a size where they no longer intimidate and can thus become playthings.

And if this sense of the absurd and satire in rock tested the margins of mainstream music, it was front and center in sixties literature and art. Carlos Castaneda's Mexican sorcerer Don Juan declared that nothing is more important than anything else,[13] which is the truth of play. Pop artists depicted the trivia of society—soup cans and comic strips—on huge canvases. Novelists killed the buzz and predicted the demise of sixties idealism but, through their existential processes, made the case for play. In *The Sense of the 60's*, Edward Quinn and Paul J. Dolan comment:

---

[12] This tradition was continued by The Tubes, Devo, Sparks, and Pink Floyd in the midseventies and eighties, and Weird Al Yankovic and Nirvana since then, but such ironic satire in contemporary popular music is conspicuous in its absence. We've become more sullen and less satirical.

[13] Carlos Castaneda, *The Teachings of Don Juan: A Yaqui Way of Knowledge* (New York: Washington Square Press, 1968).

Many of the young writers, having absorbed or developed a vision of human life as absurd, found the traditional demarcations between the serious and the light, the magnificent and the trivial, to be arbitrary and unreal. A world in which life is largely irrational and meaningless is a world in which tragedy and comedy are one. The tragedy of life in fact arises from the awareness that life is a farce, a vast cosmic joke. . . . John Barth and Philip Roth . . . affirm the possibility of transcending absurdity by the comic defiance of the individual.[14]

Such prescience is useful but limited as a social catalyst. Roth, for example, comments matter-of-factly that the American writer has no respect, no status, and no audience. The place where an audience could play-along and play-with was the rock concert, not the novel. Here, in increasing numbers, youth came to live the fantasies the music was spinning. They sought an identity different from their parents', and in the free-for-all atmosphere of play-infused music, revolution in the air, mind-altering drugs, and relaxed sexual mores, something new was bound to emerge.

In live music, there was a clear celebratory release, and as elusive as it was, the anarchic/utopian ethos that prevailed corresponded to the definition of play: a sense of belonging; no one gets hurt; embrace but do not kick, bite, or grab. Dance, smile, love. Great hopes came along with America's teens to the rock concerts.

For many, these late sixties years were an adolescent phase of experimentation that ended with the persistent assertion of economic necessity and family rearing. But the case example remains, indelibly etched into history. In the quasi-utopian and temporary social context of a rock concert, a substantial subculture tasted the possibilities.[15]

---

[14] Edward Quinn and Paul J. Dolan, eds., *The Sense of the 60's* (New York: The Free Press, 1968), 433.

[15] One could make the case that the blanketing of America and much of the world with megaconcerts and festivals is an attempt to spread that consciousness. One could just as easily argue that the commercialization of concerts represents the defeat of that dream.

## Musical Improvisation and Playfulness

The joyous and noisy spirit of play could infect live music. The jazz tradition established an improvisational style of sensitive interplay, from the very earliest Dixieland to the seminal jazz performances of Louis Armstrong and Earl "Fatha" Hines to the great ensembles of Miles, Monk, Coltrane, Bill Evans and more. In bluegrass as well, "the instruments talk to each other."[16] To reach this level of ensemble playing takes an extraordinary amount of musical talent and competence. That is, the practiced ability to express musical ideas fluidly and the hours of time together in a band to become familiar with how fellow musicians play.

Adult skills put in service to the journey back to the child state create great art, great writing, great theater. With the added element of right-stuff attitude and simpatico audiences, the best ensemble musical improvisation re-creates the play of animals and infants. This musical playfulness can be experienced by listeners and dancers and connects with the Trickster archetype and with play.

In this case, the play concept of "transient competence" translates into the transience of a musical idea, not the transient competence of a musician (though that was part of what defined garage and punk rock). In musical play, no idea is allowed to dominate for too long. In the best jams—jazz, rock, and otherwise—ideas sit around for a little while, and after they've been played with, experimented on, and exhausted, the musicians move on to another corner of the playground. In other words, the musical *ideas* are playing with each other in a similar way that animals and infants do.

Play, in this complex and sympathetic form, best describes what the Grateful Dead were able to manifest on a regular basis for thirty years. At their concerts, the interaction, or play, between audience and musicians was intense, tangible, and archetypal.

---

[16] Jerry Garcia in *Red and White, Blue Suede Shoes*, by Eric Pooley, in notes to *Grateful Dead: So Many Roads (1965-1995)*, Grateful Dead Records, 1999, CD, 9.

The Dead had observed the hazards of the star-making machinery and resolved to avoid them and sustain their lifeblood, the live show. They drew their own community around them, maintained an ideological distance from their record company, and held an aversion, intended or not, to overnight popularity. By building their audience gradually through live performance and avoiding pop wars for domination that require image-building and combative ambition (like any capitalist enterprise),[17] they were able to cultivate an approach to song, improvisation, and mutual musical response that nurtured and sustained play in their music. They had their ups and downs, and even broke up for a short time, but overall, they invoked the carnival, "a band beyond description . . . a rainbow full of sound . . . fireworks, calliopes, and clowns.[18] Their legendary longevity was held aloft on the breath of the musical playfulness that ebbed and flowed at their live shows. By some counts, they hold the record for most live performances of any band.[19]

A lay explanation of the collective Grateful Dead experience is that the listener enters an abstract cognitive state that sequences in a manner fully correspondent and rhythmically responsive to the live music. Wordless music listening, but on a more sensitized and interactive plane.

I can share a not-so-subtle example. Sometime around 1969, I attended a Dead concert at San Francisco's Winterland Ballroom with some friends; we were all about sixteen. The place was packed. The dance floor was ringed with a few rows of church pews where, along with the balcony, one could sit instead of stand or dance. Miraculously,

---

[17] The Dead pioneered this independence from the commerce of the music industry, and they stuck to it throughout their career. They became incredibly popular and built one of the most loyal fan bases ever, despite traditional commercial success. Pearl Jam's approach with their fans and their independence follows in the Dead's footsteps.

[18] Grateful Dead, "The Music Never Stopped," by John Perry Barlow and Bob Weir, on *Blues for Allah*, Grateful Dead Records, 1975, vinyl recording.

[19] "The 1998 edition of the Guinness Book of World Records recognized them with a listing under the heading, 'most rock concerts performed' (2,318 concerts). They played to an estimated total of 25 million people, more than any other band, with audiences of up to 80,000 attending a single show." Quote is from "Grateful Dead," *Wikipedia*, accessed July 16, 2016, https://en.wikipedia.org/wiki/Grateful_Dead#Live_performances.

we found an empty row and occupied it, but there were still lots of empty seats to my left, and my mates and I couldn't figure out why. Until we looked down. There on the floor was a couple making love: a slightly embarrassing feast for our virgin eyes, but a scene we definitely took in. The music and drugs were good too. Until the security guards came to separate the couple. Both of the participants were clearly enjoying themselves, but the security pegged the male as an instigator/perpetrator, even rapist. They quickly covered the woman in a blanket and took her away, and they handcuffed the guy, hitting him with their nightsticks as they pulled him up and held him standing in front of the clearly distracted crowd. He showed no shame or remorse, he stood proud. And naked.

Now despite the color and drama of this event, it would be hard to tell what was happening from the stage. We were all towards the back of the hall, and it was loud, and the band was playing rollicking rock and roll. But there in the middle of the concert, in the middle of a song, the Dead stopped playing. Cold. Just stopped. How could they know? What did they know? Did an audience member tell them? How could they shout above the music and interrupt the band if they did?

After the guy was led away and the hubbub subsided, the Dead started playing again, but they changed the song from what they had been playing to "The Same Thing," first performed in the 1920s by Bo Carter but later credited to Willie Dixon and popularized by Muddy Waters. Here are the lyrics the Dead's blues leader Pigpen sang that night:

> What make a man go crazy
> when a woman wears her dress so tight? (repeat)
> You know it's that the same thing
> that make a tom cat fight every night.

> Chorus:
> And it's that old same thing.
> It's that old same old thing.
> Now tell me who's to blame?

The whole world's fighting about
that old same thing.
Yes it is.

And why all of these men
trying to run a big legged woman down? (repeat)
It's got to be that same old thing
that make a bulldog hug a hound.

Chorus

What make you feel so good
when your baby get a dressing gown? (repeat)
It got to be the same old thing
That makes a preacher lay his bible down.

Yes it is.

Coincidence? Perhaps. But dial down this melodramatic example of musician-audience interaction and response, and you find innumerable smaller moments where the musicians and the audience respond to each other in subtler, perhaps even telepathic ways. Through dance, selection of notes and songs, dynamics, rhythms, and inflections, the Dead shared a special relationship with their audience. Fans called it the *groupmind*.[20]

The career of the Beatles arced in a unique parallel to that of the Grateful Dead. Both bands were formed by particularly talented musicians with a fondness for traditional American and English music. In the US, the Dead grew out of a bluegrass and jug band; in Liverpool, the Beatles started out playing skiffle, English and American folk tunes. Both bands had a strong affection for rhythm and blues and for great rock originators like Chuck Berry and Buddy Holly. Both bands emerged from local followings of extremely loyal fans, honing their improvisational and ensemble skills by night-after-night

---

[20] Expressed in the science fiction novel by John Wyndham, *The Chrysalids* (London: Penguin Books, 1955).

playing to those enthusiastic fans, cultivating a special rapport and connection with them.[21]

The Beatles, especially Lennon, were known and loved for their flip attitude with the press and their wry sense of humor. They orchestrated their saga and their art on a mythos of being at play. But the endless hype and promotion, the intrusiveness of the press, the inability to form intimate relationships, and the stress on existing relationships were all real, and enough to thwart less capable artists. But the Beatles, right up until their final act, even when they no longer played live, were able to sustain the image of four boys eternally at play in the world. Every album sparkles with playfulness. Their consistent message was that life's main purpose was to love and to have fun. To play. Despite the percentage of this that was hype, it could not have sold so well if there were not a resonant truth behind it.

The Beatles dealt with a mixed blessing, inverse to that of the Dead: their marketability was discovered early in their careers. The commercial potential, their ability to reach and excite huge numbers of white teens, was the sweetest candy the entertainment industry had ever tasted. And it exploited them for much more than a taste.

The band's playful attitude was evident in their press conferences, movies—in particular, *A Hard Day's Night*—and stage presence. They created playful caricatures of themselves: Paul's mugging, Ringo's sad sack, George's more solitary deep play, and John's droll humor. They experimented playfully with their image, cartooning in *Yellow Submarine* and outraging with the US "butcher" cover for *Yesterday and Today*.[22] But despite their hardy constitutions and determination to continuously grow and be creative, as a band they were overwhelmed by their media-hyped popularity and the screaming audiences. They

---

[21] I've written an article ("Musical Improvisation and Play: Dead Beatles") that compares the playfulness of the Beatles to the playfulness of the Grateful Dead. You can read it on my website, www.shepherdsiegel.com.

[22] The Beatles, *Yesterday and Today*, Capitol Records, 1966, vinyl recording.

were forced to stop performing live—any intimacy or chance at growth through live performance was lost.[23] John Lennon confirms:

> We were performers . . . in Liverpool, Hamburg and other dance halls and what we generated was fantastic, where we played straight rock, and there was nobody to touch us in Britain. As soon as we made it, we made it, but the edges were knocked off. Brian put us in suits and all that and we made it very, very big. But we sold out, you know. The music was dead before we even went on the theatre tour of Britain. We were feeling shit already because we had to reduce an hour or two hours playing, which we were glad about in one way, to twenty minutes and go on and repeat the same twenty minutes every night. The Beatles' music died then as musicians. . . . We always missed the club dates because that's when we were playing music. And then later on we became technically efficient recording artists, which was another thing.[24]

That the teen frenzy the Beatles touched off was so extreme is possible testimony to the intensity of the 1950s repressions of celebratory, carnival energy.[25] Regardless, it drove them to retreat from live performing in 1966.[26] That same year the Grateful Dead fully assembled their sound. Their creative juices were just beginning to flow. The pop stardom that accompanied Top 40 hit singles eluded the Dead, and in the shadows of cult-level popularity, they were able to nurture a special relationship with their audience and continually refine their

---

[23] The Beatles' popularity created the need for the folks who do the sound for live bands and all the sophisticated amplifiers, speakers, boards and, technology that were yet to come. The Beatles had no such luxury of modern rock amplification, and they could not be heard over the screamers in the audience. This as well put an end to their live performing days.

[24] John Lennon and Jann Wenner, *Lennon Remembers* (New York: Popular Library, 1971), 45-46.

[25] Peter Stallybrass and Allon White, *The Politics and Poetics of Transgression* (Ithaca, NY: Cornell University Press, 1986), 1-44.

[26] As it did Bob Dylan. Dylan himself shared the recognition of the potential and value of live performance, and he was fortunate enough to be able to return to it in 1974. And since 1987, he has performed almost continuously, in the Never Ending Tour.

"playing together" ability. The Grateful Dead could play live and also inspire live play.

Though the incessant and maddening leviathan of Beatlemania deprived them of the live performance's dynamics, the Beatles creativity and playfulness were irrepressible. As Lennon said, "Whatever media you put us in we can produce something worthwhile."[27] The studio, not the concert hall, became their playground.

And just as Dylan's playfulness was more in his lyrics than his live shows, the Beatles imbued their alternate outlets—songs, records, film, drawing, painting, and other experiences (the Maharishi, the bed-in, Apple Corps, etc.)—with play. They never lost a beat.

One of the most stunning Beatles triumphs of playfulness was the *Magical Mystery Tour* album and movie. An echo of the Merry Pranksters' *Furthur* adventure (the bus toured America with Ken Kesey and Neal Cassady in 1964), this one-hour film is about a mystery tour. Mystery tours were a common form of inexpensive tourism in England. You would bundle up the kids and get on the bus, which would tour you to destinations unknown, somewhere in the nostalgically venerated English countryside.[28] The film, which takes place in a world shared with David Lynch, Monty Python, Salvador Dali, and Federico Fellini, includes the surreal masterpiece "I Am the Walrus," with Dylan- and Lewis Carroll-level lyrical phantasms and the most sophisticated composition and orchestration of any Beatles song. It includes John's most obscure yet evocative lyrics. It boasts the Beatles' signature pop-rock swagger in a gorgeous pop setting, with wailing backgrounds, rock 'cellos, psychedelic interludes going out of rhythm and leading perfectly into the bridge, music *concrète* set in the background. "Revolution #9" went too far for most listeners. "Walrus" is the "Revolution #9" that worked beyond John's wildest

[27] Lennon and Wenner, *Lennon Remembers*, 46.

[28] Nick Baxter-Moore, "'This Is Where I Belong'—Identity, Social Class, and the Nostalgic Englishness of Ray Davies and the Kinks," *Popular Music and Society*, 29, no. 2 (May 2006): 156-158.

dreams. In fact, this was his wildest dream. The lyrics are a slice of playful psychedelic pie:

> I am he as you are he as you are me
>> And we are all together
>> See how they run like pigs from a gun
>> See how they fly
>> I'm crying

> Sitting on a cornflake
>> Waiting for the van to come
>> Corporation T-shirt, stupid bloody Tuesday
>> Man you've been a naughty boy
>> You let your face grow long . . .

> Yellow matter custard
>> Dripping from a dead dog's eye
>> Crabalocker fishwife, pornographic priestess
>> Boy, you've been a naughty girl
>> You let your knickers down . . .

As *coup d'édada*, the penultimate song in the *Magical Mystery Tour* film is "Death Cab for Cutie,"[29] performed by the Bonzo Dog Doo-Dah Band, England's answer to Frank Zappa and the Mothers of Invention. The Bonzos perform as the house band in a strip club and a lovely stripper accompanies the tune. Satyrs of satire!

This underappreciated piece of Beatles art had to be censored (the stripper completes her dance) and was a commercial flop. From the mountain of spaghetti shoveled by waiter John Lennon onto the plate of Ringo's distraught and sobbing aunt to the Victor Spinetti military vocalizations of unmistakable tone and undecipherable meaning, *Magical Mystery Tour* stands with *The White Album* as the most avant-garde and uninhibited piece of Beatles art—they dared to be playful in darker tones. And while the Beatles were deprived of that ability to develop the live show and reestablish rapport with

---

[29] The song, which also appears on the Bonzo's *Gorilla* album, lent its name to Ben Gibbard when he formed his indie rock band in 1997. Bonzo Dog Doo-Dah Band "Death Cab for Cutie, by Vivian Stanshall, *Gorilla*, Liberty Records, 1967.

a live audience, these two albums pushed the limits of playfulness in the studio. (We can try anything . . . and we will!)

But as sure as dada liberated the Trickster in Western society and that the Trickster archetype is an antiwar figure, it is just as certain that John Lennon was a Trickster figure. Besides his poetry and painting, and his role in the satiric antiwar film *How I Won the War*, all playful, he connected his soul to dada when he married its most talented prodigy and standard-bearer, Yoko Ono.

This is what it looks like when playfulness sustains into adulthood and the Trickster archetype holds forth: Lennon and Ono's 1969 bed-in for peace.

They knew that anything they did in public would be mobbed by the media, so they decided to make that relationship an opportunity for play, an opportunity for peace. On their honeymoon, they celebrated their sexual love and voiced their opposition to the Vietnam War by stripping down to their pajamas, getting into bed, and inviting the press into their Amsterdam hotel room . . . for two weeks. Totally hippie, totally dada, totally trickster, totally play, and nothing less than the beatific union of Yoko Ono's and John Lennon's art.

The possibility unveiled is a life that gets its bearings from an alternate reality: namely, one where play in its many forms is given greater license. Thus, despite the media-monster's absorption and glorification of rock and roll excess, the original acts of play still reverberate. A baton has been passed (rock is dead, long live hip-hop!), but somewhere, the idea is still in the air.

## Play for the Rest of Us

Themes that have dominated the cultural landscape might include: a slapdash idealistic vision (The sixties and its aftermath) pushed aside by a world of high competence and materialism (The eighties and its aftermath) that hopefully led to some new visions,[30] to a social

---

[30] Witness all the recent books on play besides this one: *Beyond Love and Work*, by Lenore Terr; *Deep Play*, by Diane Ackerman; *Serious Play*, by Michael Schrage; *The Reinvention of Work*, by Matthew Fox; *Rejuvenile*, by Christopher Noxon; etc.

media troll version of reality, a primordial amoral soup (the twenty-first century to date). We went from an avid exploration of play to a renewed suppression of it in the interest of high achievement, to atomized and technologized deadening pleasures, only to beckon play's reemergence.

But play that is mediated through consumerism and commerce is probably not play. Authentic play is free, and no one seems to have time for anything that doesn't cost anything.[31]

Towards the end of her chronicle of the sixties, Gottlieb provides some short biographies of visionaries who had successfully translated their sixties activism into meaningful work, at least into the eighties. We learn about an author, a neo-pagan, an architect, the publisher of a literary review, and the leaders of a socially responsible investment firm. While there is some element of play in the work that each of these folks do, it comes as no surprise that there are no full-time tricksters in the bunch. There is some humor, perhaps, but it is ancillary. Society just doesn't support play, **pure play just doesn't make money**, and if it is dressed up as a commodity, commodification will eat at it until it's a phony facsimile.

The closest we come is through society's support of the arts, which is always in trouble. It will take the transformative might of all the sixties visionaries and their enlightened progeny to establish a societal canvas where whole communities can create and engage in play activities.[32]

A huge part of the countercultural response was a celebration of play in the midst of a painful war. But it drove a wedge into US culture. Though the play of sixties youth might well have been an appropriate response to the madness, it became a target for Americans whose pro-war nationalist stance was threatened. Play, in this instance, was strained and confounded by a painful cultural schism. Overcoming prejudice against play is key to that healing.

Rock and roll culture attracted both types.

---

[31] Jeremy Rifkin, *The Age of Access* (New York: Tarcher/Putnam, 2000).

[32] See Jeremy Rifkin, *The Age of Access* (New York: Tarcher/Putnam, 2000); and Joe Pine and Jim Gilmore, *The Experience Economy* (Cambridge: Harvard, 2000).

In fact, the countercultural movement had stubbed its toe on its own unique contradiction, caught between the extreme stereotypes of militant leftist politics and hippie spiritualism. John Lennon's journey from the Maharishi to activist politics in New York provides a metaphorical example. A common yearning for change had yielded two seemingly opposite forces. Was there any element of the counterculture that could hold both of these extremes?

Yes . . . play could.

Disruptive play transcends both political and spiritual extremes. As sure-footed as the leftie theorists and the Eastern-religion gurus may have considered themselves, neither resonated fully with the gestalt of the American teenager. The ancient yearning of youth to come of age, to be initiated and passaged into adulthood could not be accommodated by a new political theory, a new religion, or a culture that was shredding at the seams. Rock and roll amplified this voice and created some camaraderie, but only among peers of the same age, without sufficient elders. The media hype of a generation gap nullified any chance for authentic rites of passage.

David Riesman's seminal study, *The Lonely Crowd*, and Warren Susman's study of US culture, *Culture as History*, identify this shift from traditional values—a production-oriented culture—to values motivated by peers and consumption. This social reality demands personality over character.[33] Basically, we have traded one surrogate for earth connection—traditional Puritan values—for another, peer-approved personality.

If adulthood meant fighting in Vietnam, struggling in unhappy marriages, contributing to pollution, and succumbing to greed, many would choose to stay in the playpen instead. Brian Wilson of the Beach Boys did just that. He built a huge sandbox in his Los Angeles home

---

[33] David Riesman, with Nathan Glazer and Reuel Denney. *The Lonely Crowd: A Study of the Changing American Character*. Abridged edition. (New Haven, CT: Yale, 2000); and Warren I. Susman, *Culture as History: The Transformation of American Society in the Twentieth Century* (New York: Pantheon, 1984).

and stayed in it for a few years. John Lennon and Yoko Ono stayed in bed for weeks. Family dynamics played out on a big cultural stage.

What was gained in the sixties was that the artist's sensibility seeped into daily life and broke new ground, making a widespread connection between so-called normal life and play. However briefly, an alternative approach to the American life burst forth in big cities like San Francisco, Boston, Philadelphia, Chicago, and New York; college towns like Berkeley, Madison, Portland, and Ann Arbor; rural refuges like Big Sur, Taos, and Sedona—and spread throughout the nation. To play was to belong to this fresh movement.

And what makes this period crucial is its durability. The counter-culture rejected the country's secular rituals: consumerism, the American way, gray-flannel-suit-ism, woman as homemaker, etc. In its place, adventurous and oversure youth embarked on a journey to create new rituals that were more fun and that could ultimately lead to a redefinition of what a mature adult could become.

There is an age-old framework for viewing the universe, this from the Kabbalah: that we have force and that we have form, which limits force. We have paint and the painter's creative energy, and we have the canvas, which limits that energy but at the same time makes it visible and viable. Form is empty without force, and force disperses uselessly without form. Play is a force that, if it can find a form, a social context, seeks to stretch that context. And if a rhythm is established over the course of history, play—that force of life itself—can trace its shape on the form that is our society. In the sixties, it had its grandest moment. The next one is now.

## Postscript

Across the political landscape, play went underground by the midseventies. Play retreated from the overt social contexts of demonstrations and Yippie actions but would scamper about in theater, glam rock, and punk, and the emergent human potential and New Games movements. Politically minded playfulness was succeeded by a more psychologically oriented effort to change the world by changing one's self.

The broader political movement splintered into special interests fighting for the environment, consumer causes, civil rights, and sexual equality. They balkanized and became serious. The rich mix that had formed an alternative culture gave way to atomization. Play and humor—which might have been the glue that held a more diverse movement together—were left by the wayside or banished to the contained environment of manufactured entertainment. Many veterans of the counterculture retained their values and found meaningful work in the public, private, and nonprofit sectors, but play was largely absent from the specific agendas that emerged. One surviving enclave was activism on the college campuses,[34] yet it is an activism disturbingly bereft of humor and play. But before we leave the sixties, we delve deeply into the life of one of history's greatest tricksters, one who defined disruptive play.

---

[34] Paul Rogat Loeb has chronicled and spurred on twenty-first-century college campus activism in notable books like *Soul of a Citizen* and *The Impossible Will Take a Little While*.

# TEN

# Abbie Hoffman, Lone Warrior of Play

*The radical must not argue his innocence, for the trial is not of his making; he must argue his ideas.*

E.L. Doctorow[1]

*[The holy fool's] beautiful, and often romantic vision of virtue, love, and peace among people so central to his character causes the other, more realistic characters to despise him and either seek to manipulate the holy fool or kill the holy fool because of his convictions.*

theburkean[2]

IMAGINE WAKING UP with your morning coffee, opening the Saturday paper, and as you ease into that first sip, reading the following headline:

## REBELS INVADE DISNEYLAND
## HOLD TREASURE ISLAND FOR SIXTEEN HOURS

---

[1]  E.L. Doctorow, *The Book of Daniel* (New York: Random House, 1971), 184.

[2]  theburkean, "The Holy Fool," (blog), *Civilized Frontier*, accessed September 18, 2017, https://civilizedfrontier.wordpress.com/2014/02/06/the-holy-fool/.

Don't scald yourself. On August 6, 1970, that's exactly what happened. It's mellow Los Angeles, where smog walks hand in hand with somnambulate contentment. The Do Not Disturb sign had been hung out for years. What could possibly disrupt "the happiest place on earth," where we take our children, for heaven's sake? Yet on that sunny August day, in semiserious protest of Disneyland's "no long hair on men, no miniskirts on women" policy, twenty-five from a group of about three hundred self-proclaimed Yippies stormed the gates, "took" Treasure Island, and proceeded through the rituals of making a list of demands and challenging the Pirates of the Caribbean to a fight.

"Aaaarrrgh!"

After "capturing" Castle Rock on Treasure Island, raising the Viet Cong flag, and getting stoned, the Yippies marched down Main Street, harassed the Disneyland Marching Band, and sang the theme song to the Mickey Mouse Club as well as "We are marching to ~~Pretoria~~ Cambodia." They smoked pot in Adventures Thru Inner Space, climbed the mast of the Chicken of the Sea pirate ship, and caused a commotion outside the entrance gates, complaining about the policies. Other guests retaliated by singing "God Bless America." For the first time in park history, Disneyland closed five hours early.[3]

As theater that simultaneously mocks left-wing activism and the establishment response, it was priceless—one of the best, purest examples of disruptive play. Fight the power. Play as Huizinga describes it is cultural play, contest. Disruptive play, in this instance, is the play of the spoilsport who challenges the contest through mockery and a refusal to follow the rules. What would it look like to raise the stakes on the Disneyland invasion?

Well, three years previously, *The New York Times* reported:

---

[3] Jim Hill, "Yippie-Dee-Doo-Dah, Part 1: When the Yippies Invaded Disneyland," (website), The Huffington Post, Huffpost Entertainment, accessed August 4-6, 2011, https://www. huffingtonpost.com/jim-hill/yippies-disneyland_b_917731.html

### PENTAGON FOCUS OF MASS PROTEST

October 21, 1967 WASHINGTON———Flower power is also planned along with the demonstration. Some 2,200 flower children—the younger variety of hippies who like to wear flowers in their hair or draw them on their bodies—plan to surround the Pentagon amid cries of "Love, love, love."[4]

And

### NO LIVE TV COVERAGE OF PROTESTS IN CAPITAL

October 21, 1967 WASHINGTON———The three television networks will not present live coverage of today's peace demonstrations in Washington . . . they believe that the presence of large mobile units necessary for live coverage might induce demonstrators to "perform" for the cameras.[5]

As biased and inaccurate as the *Times* was at this event, certain truths—such as the bravado and willingness of the demonstrators to take risky actions—bled through. Even David Dellinger, representing the more calm and straitlaced side of the antiwar movement, let it be known that the usual rules of engagement were on tenterhooks: "Many demonstrators will not be content with 'government-approved protest activities' or with 'the ritualistic charade of merely stepping across a line and being arrested.'"[6] *We came to play*, he seemed to be saying.

Now do the math. The US is involved in a war, a bad war. Vietnam was a mistake and, had the US stayed out, hundreds of thousands of lives would have been saved and Vietnam would have the same government it has today, which it democratically chose in 1954.

Thousands of kids in the US could see the injustice of the Vietnam War and vehemently objected. They were motivated to act. The zeit-

---

4  *The New York Times*, October 21, 1967, 28.

5  *The New York Times*, October 21, 1967, 28.

6  *The New York Times*, October 21, 1967, 28.

geist of the times integrated liberation goals of fighting imperialism and racism with establishment "rationality," inspiring something more creative than armed insurrection. Yet, in these times, even peaceful protest provoked punishment. The Black Panthers took the brunt of it, their militant stand unleashing violent retribution from J. Edgar Hoover and the FBI, turning a brilliant cadre of heroes into ghosts.[7] Leftists who hoped to end the Vietnam War through the electoral process saw that possibility vanish with the assassination of Robert Kennedy. With no political revolution, no peacemaking electoral option, the crisis loomed, and the situation seemed grim.

So playful jesting emerged as a tactic that might catch the power structure off guard and also alert the world that all possible attempts would be made to spoil the game played by the warmongers of America's military-industrial complex.

The idea blossomed straight from the brains of the Beats—Gary Snyder shared it with Ed Sanders of the Fugs (which included Tuli Kupferberg, immortalized in Allen Ginsberg's *Howl)* and activist Keith Lampe, who in turn passed it on to cultural revolutionary Abbie Hoffman. Abbie saw the idea as a way to attract hippies and direct their religious mysticism towards a political goal. Abbie announced the ritual at the October 1967 press conference before the Washington, DC, demonstration that would draw more than one hundred and fifty thousand people. He sought a permit to levitate the Pentagon three hundred feet into the air.

What?

*He sought a permit to levitate the Pentagon three hundred feet into the air.*

Ever the savvy negotiator and showing his willingness to compromise, when the military denied him, he said that he would settle for a permit to raise it just ten feet off the ground. In the days leading up to the demonstration, Abbie and Marty Carey walked the perimeter of the building to calculate how many demonstrators it would take

---

[7] These losses—Huey Newton, Eldridge Cleaver, Bobby Seale, George Jackson, Fred Hampton, all imprisoned, killed, or exiled—created a dearth in black leadership, save for women leaders like Angela Davis and Ericka Huggins who the FBI spared death or prison.

to encircle it. His allies in New York held a benefit concert where a plywood model of the Pentagon was raised by piano wire amid smoke and Fugs rock.[8] At a press conference in his apartment, Abbie enlisted four couples who stripped and made love after he sprayed them with water, telling the reporters who were diligently taking notes that it was Lace, a compound of LSD and a skin-penetrating chemical. He said that if the police used Mace, he would have no choice but to retaliate with this potent love drug.[9]

On October 22, Norman Mailer was arrested in DC with hundreds of other demonstrators. His book *The Armies of the Night* documents the affair. The "flower children" were in fact the Yippies, who surrounded the Pentagon (the photographs of the event are amazing) in their (some say successful) attempt to lift the Pentagon inches off the ground through an exorcism rite.

*To lift the Pentagon inches off the ground through an exorcism rite.*
Right. What exactly is going on here?

The Vietnam War was the ultimate foil, energizing notions of play that are not contest. And the scale of the protest inspired the naive hope that this would be America's last binge of armed conflict. For the protests were unprecedented, pointing media instead of weapons, driven by a vague but commonly held utopian vision; the movement mounted a full-scale siege of idealism on the government and war policies.

The iconic import of the Pentagon levitation can get lost in the deluge of media events past and present that swirl around us, but absurdist performance art had never reached such a scale. The government had predicted twenty thousand protesters. Over one hundred and fifty thousand came. The networks refused to cover it live. Fifty thousand marched across the Potomac from the main demonstration at the Lincoln Memorial to the Pentagon. Only a few hundred of those made it to the exorcism. But through his mastery of media and myth

---

[8] This may have inspired the Stonehenge prank featured in the film *This is Spinal Tap*.

[9] Marty Jezer, *Abbie Hoffman: American Rebel* (New Brunswick, NJ: Rutgers, 1992), 114-118.

à la Marshall McLuhan, and despite media's efforts to avoid colluding with Abbie's script, the Pentagon exorcism lives on as a hallmark event that embodies the spirit of the times. Antiwar politics, hippie spiritualism, connecting the kids demonstrating and the kids in military uniform, media myth-making, comedy, performance art, theater . . . disruptive play.

Both Abbie Hoffman and the comedian/performance artist Andy Kaufman took it to heart, happened upon and were blown away by the power of disruptive play. In very different ways, they both vigorously challenged mainstream normalcy. Both were consummate players, and though they were exponents of subcultures that supported them, those subcultures ultimately could not protect or insulate them. They paid dearly for their commitments to exposing absurdity, charade, and the relative nature of normalcy. Both made a plaything of the rationality that the media establishment relies on for the version of reality it peddles.

## The First Yippie

The life of Abbie Hoffman—political activist, humorist, and anarchist—shows how one who can play in the political arena inevitably embodies trickster characteristics. And that disruptively playing with power threatens it. Power will seek to bind or destroy the trickster.

Besides the general leading the occupation of Disneyland, Abbie was: A teenage hoodlum expelled from high school for, among other things, declaring his atheism. Mentored by Herbert Marcuse in Marxist theory and Abraham Maslow in the psychology of self-actualization. An early participant in the Student Nonviolent Coordinating Committee. A fan and disseminator of the Diggers, a community action group that helped poor folks find cheap ways to exist in a city. An antiwar and anticapitalist puller of stunts. One of the Chicago Eight, tried for conspiracy because of his participation in the protests at the 1968 Democratic Convention. Author of several books and articles that detailed his political philosophy of action. An environmental activist. And ultimately a fugitive and a victim of suicide.

Along with Paul Krassner, Stew Albert, and Jerry Rubin, Abbie celebrated New Year's Eve 1967 by inventing the Youth International Party, the Yippies, a facade-myth of carnival energy that created playful irrationality too slippery for the media and mocked the seriousness of their leftie comrades as well. Were he involved at the time, I'm certain Andy would have been nominated as the spokesperson for the party. Comic Pat Paulsen echoed Yippie nonsensibility and played it well on the *Smothers Brothers Comedy Hour* by running for president himself as a comedy sketch, six times between 1968 and 1996.

Abbie brought a deeper understanding of the same limits that confounded Andy Kaufman and devised actions with the specific intent to cross them and unbox play. He performed his art on the political stage, though, which has boundaries that differ yet overlap with the entertainment world. Abbie orchestrated an interesting reversal. He let the media treat him as a wild-eyed radical. He knew that that was his assigned character in mainstream America's game show;[10] it merely served to get him on the air. The game he challenged was bigger than media; it was on the societal level, where boundaries were determined by government and enforced by police.

Abbie makes his case in the first paragraph of his first book, *Revolution for the Hell of It:*[11]

> Once one has experienced LSD, existential revolution,
> fought the intellectual game-playing of the individual in
> society, of one's identity, one realizes that action is the only
> reality; not only reality but morality as well.[12]

Abbie waves two bright crimson flags that mark him as a disruptive player and trickster. One, he fights the game. He is acutely aware

---

[10] Game shows being the precursor to reality TV, but we see an early version of politics as entertainment here.

[11] His actual first publication was *Fuck the System*, published under the pseudonym George Metesky, and *Revolution for the Hell of It* was published with "Free" as the author. *Fuck the System* was reprised in *Steal This Book*, and Abbie considered *Revolution for the Hell of It* his debut piece.

[12] Abbie Hoffman, *Revolution for the Hell of It* (New York: Dial, 1968), 8.

of contest and will play but won't compete. He is the ultimate spoil-sport, calling out the entire game of the establishment. Other proponents of play, like Fred Donaldson and Diane Ackerman, retreat from the public arena to find a safe place to play, either the protected classroom or day care center or the Grand Canyon or Antarctic.

Abbie chose the center of the Cold War on May 13, 1960. A brutal police sweep of students protesting the House Un-American Activities Committee (HUAC) hearings in San Francisco triggered his transformation from rebel hipster to rebel hipster political activist. The event clarified for Abbie how the capitalism versus communism contest was about producing an ideological rationality that justified a repressive war machine more than it was about the ideologies themselves.

The hearings were lessons in political theater. First, the HUAC used the trappings of legality to create public humiliation and suspicion that ruined careers and forced progressive voices underground. They would let right-wing vigilante groups help decide which liberals and leftists they should target and subpoena. They would pack the hearings with anticommunists, where witnesses were unwilling passive targets of accusations. Progressives brought before them could not question informants or challenge the validity of the committee's "facts." In 1960, the HUAC questioned witnesses about activities that went as far back as the 1930s. Their intimidating presence made people afraid to exercise basic civil rights like signing a petition, donating money, or walking a picket line. All this from a quasi-legal inquiry that did not have to make legal charges or prosecute suspects in order to wreck lives. In other words, Abbie saw how the HUAC used the power of theater as a fictitious game where they could fight and subdue and ruin the people they perceived as their enemy. By the time he wrote *Revolution for the Hell of It*, Abbie had figured out the power of theater to fight the game itself. [13]

---

[13] Marty Jezer, *Abbie Hoffman: American Rebel* (New Brunswick, NJ: Rutgers, 1992), 38-41.

His second bright red flag: "Action is the only reality." Don't talk about it, think it, wait for a triumph of ideas before acting. Act now. Play is action, and action is intelligence demonstrated, that begets more and greater intelligence. Abbie blended the influence of countercultural heroes Fidel Castro and Che Guevara with the self-actualization theories of Abraham Maslow and with the mind-altering powers of LSD. His stream-of-consciousness prose is reminiscent of Kerouac's. In the first three pages of *Revolution for the Hell of It*, Abbie steals kernels of meaning from *The Wizard of Oz*, Black Power, the biblical story of Abraham and Isaac, LSD, Billy the Kid, Castro, and Bonnie and Clyde.

Kerouac himself occasionally stumbles across the line of his subculture and makes commentary on its contrast to the mainstream—he takes on consumerism and extols spontaneous living not wedded to career—but he was averse to political analysis. Abbie, on the other hand, imbued every comment with the electrons of political awareness. While Kerouac avoided politics, Abbie brought it out onto the dance floor, but stayed clear of its sluggish dogmatizing.

The cool-protected Beats cultivated the buds that were to flower in the sixties. They predicted the inevitable clash between an alternative Beat style and the Puritan military-industrial complex, but no one foresaw the multiplying effect of rock and roll plus drugs plus a vital mass political movement. No one could predict the scale that clash would reach and the ideals it would birth. And key to the idealism of the sixties was the revolution in psychology led in part by Abbie's mentor and professor at Brandeis University, Abraham Maslow.

## Abbie as a Maslovian

Part of Maslow's challenge to established psychology is that humans have the potential to experience higher and higher planes of existence. Mix that with the melee of the sixties and his star pupil, Abbie Hoffman. Maslow advanced the concept of self-actualization, that of a human being fully experiencing life and all of its richest possibilities.

At one point, he defines it as having the creativeness of a happy and secure child: "spontaneous, effortless, innocent, easy, a kind of freedom from stereotypes and clichés."[14] Maslow's exemplars were people in their fifties and sixties who had retained or regained aspects of childlikeness, what he called being non-rubricizing—or open to experience—and being easily spontaneous and expressive. "Their innocence of perceptions and expressiveness was combined with sophisticated minds."[15]

Maslow built humanistic psychology on a hierarchy of needs. People must first satisfy basic needs like survival, safety, and security. Then they can seek out belongingness and affection; respect and self-respect; and ultimately self-actualization.[16]

Abbie intellectually and instinctively embraced the hierarchy of needs. At Woodstock, Abbie responded to the needs of people who had been injured, or more frequently, had ingested bad drugs. This need for life, safety, and health—even in the midst of a Woodstock celebration and a reach towards mass self-actualization—took precedence. Abbie worked to take over tent space, coordinate doctors' efforts, and get accurate information announced from the stage about what not to swallow or smoke and where to get help if you did.[17]

And at the next rung, belongingness, lives play. It comes in fairly early and is basic to this hierarchy. On the individual and societal level, then, when the needs for belongingness and play are satisfied, it opens the door for respect and self-respect and for self-actualization. Many in our society have met the needs on Maslow's first two rungs, though current realities reek of backsliding. To reach a critical mass of feeding, clothing, and sheltering all, and to ensure that all will be able to live their lives with adequate safety and health, is to make human progress.

---

[14] Abraham H. Maslow, *Toward a Psychology of Being*, 2nd ed. (New York: Van Nostrand Reinhold, 1968), 138.

[15] Maslow, *Toward a Psychology of Being*, 138.

[16] Maslow, *Toward a Psychology of Being*, 3; and Abraham Maslow, *The Farther Reaches of Human Nature* (New York: Viking, 1971).

[17] Jonah Raskin, *For the Hell of It: The Life and Times of Abbie Hoffman* (Berkeley: University of California Press, 1998), 195-197.

These stages of individual growth touted by Maslow and the human potential movement can be applied on a societal level. This is key to understanding Abbie's politics. For example, he transposed the Freudian versus Maslovian models to the antiwar movement. If a Freudian analysis concluded that war was a disease,[18] then research, discussion, and treatment would focus on curing the disease by fighting it as one. Hoffman and Maslow[19] would instead say that we need to reach for a healthy organism—person, community, society—where war is not possible. It's a critical distinction that explains the quantum leap between getting in the game to win the fight against the war in Vietnam—which was the standard New Left agenda—versus fighting the game that allowed such a war to even be considered, which was the hippie-inspired Yippie position Abbie represented.[20]

Maslow was aware of social context and stated that the labels of mental health and sickness were often relative. "Certainly it seems more and more clear that what we call 'normal' in psychology is really a psychopathology of the average, so undramatic and so widely spread that we don't even notice it ordinarily."[21] His views have gained widespread support. Thomas Szasz, Paul Goodman, Rollo May, Ashley Montagu, Lewis Mumford, David Riesman, Carl Rogers, Eric Fromm, Ernest Becker, Paul Tillich, and others worked with Maslow to create the humanistic psychology school of thought and practice.

---

[18] Or one could just as easily find that the war was a necessary reality to which the neurotic must adjust.

[19] Even though Maslow did not support Abbie's methods.

[20] Indeed, in 1999, the NATO actions in Kosovo sought a turning point. Bronislaw Geremek, the foreign minister of Poland, called the combat in Kosovo "the first signal of the coming century . . . [that] human rights will be the fundamental basis for defining international relations. Relations between the states can no longer be founded on respect for sovereignty—they must be founded on respect for human rights." (The Washington Post, June 6, 1999, p. A20) http://www.washingtonpost.com/wp-srv/inatl/longterm/balkans/stories/moral060699. htm Tricky business that, but it could signal a global shift to power politics that recognize that Maslow's second rung of safety and security takes precedence over any national privilege to tyrannize. The outspreading of activities to fulfill the third rung of belongingness and affection ought not be far behind; we should prepare for it. Or do we prepare for permanent war, as Iraq, then Afghanistan, and Syria entrench us in a perpetual game of death?

[21] Maslow, *Toward a Psychology of Being*, 7-8, 16.

These thinkers would interpret what might be called abnormal behavior as actually a healthy response to social conditions. "Even the behavior problem boy is being looked upon with new tolerance. *Why* is he delinquent? . . . Occasionally it is for good reasons and the boy is simply resisting exploitation, domination, neglect, contempt, and trampling upon."[22]

Yet we resist the task of making our society healthy, we persist in applying these psychological principles inward to clinical settings or isolated alternative communities rather than outward to society itself. Until Abbie came along and tried to do shock gestalt therapy on all of America, all at once, in public. The media stage was the couch. He bit off more than any mortal could chew, but his antics tested society's tolerance for an activism creed comprised of McLuhan + Maslow + the social conscience of the sixties + guerrilla theater.

## Abbie as The Mythic Player and Revolutionary

One of the most commonly accepted games in our society is the exchange of money and the expectation that one accumulates as much as possible and shares it in a controlled and prescribed manner. And one of Abbie's cleanest Zen-politics acts was to give money away, to refuse to play that game.

He made it part of his daily life—drawing inspiration and experience from Haight-Ashbury's Diggers, community anarchists who from 1966 to 1968 opened stores which gave away their stock; provided free food, medical care, and temporary housing; and organized free concerts. But Abbie pulled his most famous caper with his troupe at the New York Stock Exchange in August of 1967. They convinced the guards that they were tourists, got on the guided tour, and tossed several hundred one-dollar bills over the gallery railing. The brokers cheered and scrambled over each other for their piece of the action. One of the real tourists was mightily amused: "I've been throwing away money in New York for five days now. This is sure a hell of a lot

---

22 Maslow, *Toward a Psychology of Being*, 8.

quicker and more fun."[23] The guards anxiously tried to prevent it. The media, who were not allowed to observe, concocted their own versions—Was it Monopoly money? Torn-up dollar bills? —both were reported. Abbie called out the money game, made a myth in the process, and raised consciousness around worship of the dollar bill.

The prank had a precedent. Remember Johannes Baader invading the Weimar Diet and hurling down leaflets, declaring himself "President of the Globe?"[24]

This is disruptive play. When exponents of a counterculture challenge the money game, they are not pop psychologists or expensive leadership trainers who play with dolphins or consult with corporations on how to make their workforce a more fun place to accrue profit. The motivation of a disruptive player is to remind people that the point of a good economic system is not money. It is to free us from our obsession with money and to provide the time and space to elevate the quality of our lives and our relationships.[25]

The sixties were a time for great risk-takers, including and especially Abbie. But as we shall see in the next chapter, the star-making machinery that hypes celebrity makes risk-taking possible, desirable, even recommended, but only within certain limits. Go too far and if the law can't get its hands on you, the media will find ways to crush you. Abbie's writings, and even more so his actions, testify to his intent on going too far, on finding the ecstasy behind the game. By giving away money, he challenged the system of ownership and private property; the sources of class difference, of oppression; or in the present argument, harmful contest. But the New York Stock Exchange prank, more than an attack on materialism, was pulled to shock people to a place beyond contest, not to make them wrong but to make them change. Performance art, monkey theater, humanistic psychology, public therapy.

[23] Abbie Hoffman, *The Best of Abbie Hoffman: Selections from Revolution for the Hell of It, Woodstock Nation, Steal This Book and New Writings* (New York: Four Walls Eight Windows: New York, 1989), 21-22

[24] Robert Short, *Dada and Surrealism* (Secaucus, NJ: Chartwell Books, 1980), 38.

[25] Russell Jacoby, "Utopia-Phobia," *Tikkun* 14, no. 3 (May/June 1999): 51.

In retrospect, was such a revolutionary stance productive? Did Abbie create a mass revolution that undid the anti-play economic order? Yes and no. Certainly, the money game is alive and well, with more people playing it through the stock market and more bankers gambling with our general welfare than ever. But to find a way to redistribute labor and goods and create a great society, we need a history worth studying. Abbie left explicit and unambiguous markers. He took a fairly vague utopian spirit that was floating around the media, the streets, the music, the movement, and the hippie communities—oversimplified and disdained in the establishment press—and translated it into clean, clear actions that are permanently etched in history. We know that in a Play Society, to play well and often means to work less on winning and accumulating.

Actions are intelligence expressed, and Abbie was able to take influences like Fidel Castro and translate what were effective revolutionary actions in Cuba into actions that could make revolution in the media-drenched United States.

Reading Abbie's chronicles, one begins to realize how consistently and hard he worked to communicate the irrational. He fought rationality; he played. Why? Because he saw a media that had appointed itself the sense-maker of our culture. He objected to anyone's claim to telling "the truth." He believed in myth. Media dictated a rationality and claimed the "last word," and that needed questioning. Rather than engage in a contest and try to invoke his rationality, Abbie dispensed with the game altogether and trumped the media with myth. Convincing the public that he had organized a levitation of the Pentagon was a fabulous myth put together with pocket change and a loud voice. It served to deflate a US government that was spending millions to perpetuate a countermyth that we were winning the war in Vietnam.

That the security guards would not allow the press to directly cover the stock exchange performance could be made into an advantage.[26]

---

[26] Hoffman, *Revolution for the Hell of It*, 32-33.

Dispense "false" information, not to mislead people but to lead them beyond the filter of the media to greater archetypal myths. Like the levitation of the Pentagon. Like the myth of Lace. Like the rumor that Abbie was Judge Julius Hoffman's (the judge at the Chicago Eight trial) illegitimate son. Like his testimony at that trial, his greatest opportunity to act out ideas of politics as theater by challenging the enforced rationality of the courtroom:

Defense Attorney
Weinglass: Will you please identify yourself for the record.

Hoffman: My name is Abbie. I am an orphan of America . . .

Weinglass: Where do you reside?

Hoffman: I live in Woodstock Nation.

Weinglass: Will you tell the Court and jury where it is?

Hoffman: Yes. It is a nation of alienated young people. We carry it around with us as a state of mind in the same way the Sioux Indians carried the Sioux nation around with them. It's a nation dedicated to cooperation versus competition, to the idea that people should have better means of exchange than property and money, that there should be some other basis for human interaction, it is a nation dedicated to—

Judge
Hoffman: Just where it is, that is all.

Hoffman: It is in my mind and in the minds of my brothers and sisters. It does not consist of property or material but, rather, of ideas and certain values . . .

Judge
Hoffman: No, we want the place of residence, if he has one, place of doing business, if you have a business. Nothing about

> philosophy or India, sir. Just where you live, if you have a place to live. Now, you said Woodstock. In what state is Woodstock?

Hoffman: It is in the state of mind, in the mind of myself and my brothers and sisters . . .

Weinglass: Can you tell the court and jury your present age?

Hoffman: My age is 33. I am a child of the 60s.

Weinglass: When were you born?

Hoffman: Psychologically, 1960. . . .

Weinglass: Can you tell the Court and jury what is your present occupation?

Hoffman: I am a cultural revolutionary. Well, I am really a defendant—full-time.[27]

In the play of children and animals, competence is transitory. Thus, in interviews with himself, what some may interpret as intellectual laziness or theoretical weakness is in fact intellectual play. Abbie never

---

[27] Marty Jezer, *Abbie Hoffman: American Rebel* (New Brunswick, NJ: Rutgers, 1992), 204-205. Jezer is quoting from David Dellinger's *Conspiracy Trial*.

And in the E.L. Doctorow novel, *The Book of Daniel*, finds a kindred mind:

"The difference between Socrates and Jesus is that no one has ever been put to death in Socrates' name. And that is because Socrates' ideas were never made law.

Law, in whatever name, protects privilege. I speak of the law of any state that has not achieved socialism. The sole authority of the law is in its capacity to enforce itself. That capacity expresses itself in Trial. There could be no law without trial. Trial is the point of the law. And punishment is the point of the trial—you can't try someone unless you assume the power to punish him. All the corruption and hypocritical self-service of the law is brought to the point of the point in the verdict of the court. It is a sharp point, an unbelievably sharp point. But there is fascination for the race in the agony of the condemned. That is a law, a real law, that rulers can never overcome—it is fixed and immutable as a law of physics.

"Therefore the radical wastes his opportunity if he seriously considers the issues of his trial. If he is found guilty it is the ruling power's decision that he cannot be tolerated. If he is found innocent it is the ruling power's decision that he need not be feared. *The radical must not argue his innocence, for the trial is not of his making; he must argue his ideas.*" (emphasis mine)

E.L. Doctorow, *The Book of Daniel* (New York: Random House, 1971), 184.

strays so far down an intellectual path that more people can't join into his dialogue. He is not exclusive, that inclusive belongingness is the essence of original play, and in Abbie's guide to guerilla theater:

> This reluctance to define ourselves gives us glorious freedom in which to fuck with the system. . . . We are dynamiting brain cells. We are putting people through changes. The key to the puzzle lies in theater. We are theater in the streets: total and committed. We aim to involve people and use (unlike other movements locked in ideology) any weapon (prop) we can find. The aim is not to earn the respect, admiration, and love of everybody—it's to get people to do, to participate, whether positively or negatively. All is relevant, only "the play's the thing."
>
> . . . Theater also has some advantages. It is involving for those people that are ready for it while at the same time dismissed as nonthreatening by those that could potentially wreck the stage. It's dynamite. By allowing all: loving, cheating, anger, violence, stealing, trading, you become situation-oriented and as such become more effective.
>
> . . . Don't rely on words. Words are the absolute in horseshit. Rely on doing—go all the way every time. Move fast. If you spend too long on one play, it becomes boring to you and the audience. When they get bored, they are turned off. They are not receiving information. Get their attention, leave a few clues and vanish.
>
> . . . Get ready for a big event at the Democratic National Convention in Chicago next August. How about a truly open convention? Thousands of VOTE FOR ME buttons, everybody prints his own campaign literature and distributes pictures of themselves. Then we all rush the convention, get to the rostrum and nominate ourselves.[28]

And in an interview with himself:

> **. . .America: the land of the free. Free means you don't pay, doesn't it**
> Yes, I guess so.

---

[28] Hoffman, *The Best of Abbie Hoffman*, 3, 17, 18-19, 24, and 33.

**Do you mean all the goods and services would be free?**
Precisely. That's what the technological revolution would
produce if we let it run unchecked. If we stopped trying to
control it.

**Who controls it?**
The profit incentive, I guess. Property hang-ups. One task
we have is to separate the concept of productivity from
work. Work is money. Work is postponement of pleasure.
Work is always done for someone else: the boss, the kids,
the guy next door. Work is competition. Work was linked
to productivity to serve the Industrial Revolution. We must
separate the two. We must abolish work and all the drudgery it represents . . .

**Don't you think competition leads to productivity?**
Well, I think it did during the Industrial Revolution, but
it won't do for the future. Competition also leads to war.
Cooperation will be the motivating factor in a free society.
I think cooperation is more akin to the human spirit.
Competition is grafted on by institutions, by a capital-
ist economy, by religion, by schools. Every institution I can
think of in this country promotes competition.[29]

Fresh from Marcuse's and Maslow's classroom, perched atop the
wave of a newly born radicalism, Abbie's comments are nothing
less than a manifesto for bringing original play to the center of our
culture and its arrangements of power, which would mean rearrang-
ing power right out of existence.

During the Vietnam War, the rational media, playing the game by
the rules, would frame the domestic distress as a conflict, a contest. They
would seek out rational spokespeople from the antiwar movement.
They always came from leftist groups, usually formed around socialist principles or a New Left ideology, ready to respond to the reporter's call with a rationally arrived-at statement and ready to make an
effort to educate the American public about the economic and ideological forces that duped us into fighting an unjust war in Vietnam.

---

[29] Hoffman, *The Best of Abbie Hoffman*, 37-38.

Fine. But these folks didn't really speak for the mass movement that was a much more chaotic carnival and, for better or ill, much less intellectual or theoretically grounded than Tom Hayden, eloquent as he was, would have the media believe.

The Democratic National Convention in Chicago 1968 was an experiment in manipulating the media, as were most of Abbie's metapranks. The Yippies at the convention bled Vietnam into broader and diverse issues. And they just plain bled. It was a sacrificial affair. In the tense wake of the assassinations of Martin Luther King, Jr. and Robert Kennedy, the party chicanery gave the nomination to Hubert Humphrey, stoking the protest. Chicago's Mayor Richard Daley unleashed a police and National Guard riot. Twenty-three thousand police and guardsmen took on ten thousand demonstrators, spraying mace and teargas and beating them. The police assault in front of the Hilton Hotel became the most famous image, televised live. The crowd shouted the now legendary slogan, "The whole world is watching."[30]

Daley and his minions were convinced that the rebellion of play, of the antiwar movement, could, with a few smacks, be put back into its box. The Kent State killings were two years away, but Daley gave notice that whatever tolerance America had for dissent had been expended. The experiment in civil rights—true democracy opens the door for play and the end of the game—would give way to the master-slave dynamic, and he was "the man" in charge of that game. Fighting contest on the stage with the world's leading superpower is going to hurt.

As with players like Alfred Jarry, as with dada, with the Beats, the play element in Western culture is an elusive, often momentary flash. Chicago and the trial to follow were its last gasps—big, honkin', fart-sized, in-your-face, funny gasps—but the system's dogged persecution of players would ultimately slap down Abbie and the Yippies and political exuberance.

---

[30] Todd Gitlin, *The Sixties: Years of Hope, Days of Rage* (Toronto: Bantam Books, 1987), 332.

## Abbie the Trailblazer

Whether conscious of it or not, spin doctors and media public relations folk owe a huge debt to Abbie who elevated the strategy (art form?) of gauging political action to a predictable media reaction. His inspiration can be found anywhere from Greenpeace harassing whalers to the Christian Coalition staging rallies at abortion clinics, from Donald Trump's presidential show to Bill Clinton playing saxophone on Jay Leno's show to Saddam Hussein posturing before CNN. And from the Yes Men—posing as WTO officials or executives from Dow Chemical offering reparations to Bhopal victims—to Andy Kaufman refusing to perform a skit.

Abbie realized the power of commercials, describing them in terms of figure-ground relations. In a one-hour television show, ten minutes of advertising are more valuable to the advertiser than twenty because the ratio of figure to ground makes the television show itself background for the ads. He reasoned that when coverage of the Democratic Convention included ten minutes on the demonstrations outside to fifty minutes on the convention itself, they'd more or less hit the golden ratio. "We were an advertisement for revolution."[31] People were staying tuned in to the convention to wait for the precious minutes when the chaos outside would be televised.

The Democratic Convention of 1968 was a bloody, confusing mess. Abbie claimed victory because it guaranteed that a pig would win the presidency in '68.[32] The demonstrations achieved the goal of polarization: not Democrats against Republicans but rebels against the duopoly that ensured that the war in Vietnam would end no time soon. As an example of disruptive play, this episode was a warning of the high level of destructive power that can be unleashed when play really pisses off the establishment, in this case Daley and the Chicago police.

---

[31] Hoffman, *The Best of Abbie Hoffman*, 75.

[32] Abbie and his crew had performed a spoof where they nominated a pig (actually a sow) for president.

Abbie's story is an able chronicle of the farthest reaches of the sixties revolution. He was a cultural revolutionary, not a political one. Yet he muscled himself into the face of the political leadership. For better or ill, he made it clear to them that the revolution was not going to follow any communist textbook rules; the democratic exercise of the Bill of Rights, LSD, television, rock and roll, and the A-bomb (and eventually technocracy and the internet) had blown too many holes into theories built on nineteenth-century paradigms. And to the dropped-out, zonked-out hippies, Abbie was an equally irritating reminder that there are no bystanders. Their actions, regardless of how safely removed from mainstream America they may have intended them, had political impact.

For example, society's dropouts who build a contest-free communal life must eventually reenter the mainstream as an idea or movement catches on or fails. Current notions of urban cohousing and food cooperatives are outgrowths of the commune movement. Abbie's political metabolism would not allow him to wait twenty-five years to see it, thus to witness alternative culture out of mainstream context was at the time frustrating and diminished of import. But he knew that there was latent value in "safe" social experiment. He describes a visit to Antioch University in Ohio:

> I coughed all the way to Antioch explaining that my lungs were not accustomed to fresh air. It didn't take long to figure out where Antioch's head was at. There are lots of progressive nursery schools, but there the kiddies are so big!

> Most issues that are being fought for at other schools were won at Antioch ten years ago. Perhaps won is not the right word, they were liberally given. Like the big sheet of paper over the men's pissing stall for graffiti. . . . No ROTC, close teacher-student community relations, people turn on and fuck everywhere, naked swim-ins in the gym pool, a black dorm, nice woods, coed dorms, Sunday tourists who drive through to stare at the commie-hippies, and so much love and identity-searching. It was all "Who am I?" stuff. Every-

thing was so beautiful, I was completely bored after three hours. The school lacked the energy that comes from struggle. When I was leaving the next day Eric remarked, "You know surveys show that 55 per cent of us end up in corporations." What "Hair" is to Broadway, Antioch is to the universities. That's not really a put-down. If you can't fuck you might as well jerk off. Antioch is the best play going, that is, if you've got about $25,000 for an orchestra seat.[33]

## Abbie's Endgame

Abbie's first and primary written contributions, *Revolution for the Hell of It* and *Woodstock Nation*, cover events leading up to the exorcising of the Pentagon (March 1967) to Woodstock (July 1969) and the aftermath. The rapidity of change in those two years is jolting. His reportage shifts from the proclamation of a new nation and exciting, free relationships formed amongst brothers and sisters—Maslow's influence is most apparent in the earliest pages—to a heeding of how quickly corporate America moved in to sell the revolution back to us, to make it a commodity. *Woodstock Nation* was really more of a postmortem than a manifesto.

In retrospect, this was inevitable. What is incredible is that, like bebop and punk, for a brief period, say 1966 through 1970, an entire cultural movement—not just music, fashion, and lifestyle but the full commitment of thousands of kids' lives—dumbfounded and bewildered mainstream commerce. But it was more than kids making their own music; it was folks making their own lives, discarding the values that had been fed to them. How the hell you gonna sell that?

At first the efforts may have been awkward. Abbie cites a two-day training that JCPenney gave to its merchandising executives who listened first to a child psychologist and then to a seventeen-year-old who put out an underground newspaper; they visited a disc jockey and a far-out clothing store and had dinner at Max's Kansas City. Their

---

[33] Hoffman, *The Best of Abbie Hoffman*, 117.

home-study kits included multicolored bags containing a kaleido-scope, a water pistol, a yo-yo, a poster of a nude girl with flowers in her hair, a Rascals LP, underground and aboveground youth newspapers and magazines, incense, an empty stash box, and a small mirror.

Such a huge youth market could not be ignored. In 1970, almost one out of every three Americans were under the age of twenty-five. The machineries of marketing to this demographic plowed ahead at full steam. The meaningful core of the sixties effort was quickly made into purchasable commodity. Capitalism, like strong whiskey after a failed relationship, helped us to forget that the Woodstock Nation was about building a new culture. *See, it was just another fad after all, just the next phase of rock and roll. Let's get on with style; the war is over.*

There is the whole cloud of stupidity surrounding Abbie's arrest for selling cocaine and then his flight, but it happened at a crossroads. He had taken his own myth of himself, based partly on Beat heroes like William Burroughs and Neal Cassady and the fiction of Jack Kerouac, and in a romantic delusion, he figured that he could get away with outrageous drugging and even trafficking, like some character in a Burroughs novel. But Abbie had consciously politicized the Beat ethos, taken it to the streets and put it in terms that the kids and J. Edgar Hoover could understand, confirmed the fears that the youth revolution was more than style, that it did threaten the power structure. Burroughs, Lenny Bruce, and Ginsberg had a bad enough time with the law. Abbie didn't stand a chance. That his escapades, escapes, and escalations lasted as long as they did is a modern miracle. He lost relevance and was mislabeled as a dinosaur during his time underground, which began when he ran from the drug charges in 1974. And he was ostracized by the media after his reemergence in 1980, not because he had fallen behind but because there was no way the movement could have kept up with him, and because Western institutions are built to bind and marginalize the trickster.

As such, he was at the crossroads (or in the crosshairs) of America, where the Protestant work ethic was to be revived in the service of political correctness . . . to fight fire with fire. If you were going to take on the corporate establishment, if you were going to fight toxic pollution, military buildup, racism, or nuclear power, you had to specialize. Specialization is one of the defining characteristics of the Protestant work ethic. This meant sacrificing some of the pleasures of the revolution—mainly holism but also psychedelic or other drugs—for the struggle that had been engaged: pursuing a lawsuit, attending endless meetings, etc. It had become very serious, and the government, which had been practicing on Lenny Bruce and Hurricane Carter, was now ready for full battle. Abbie, in his later persona of Barry Freed, realized this, but only after the major stumble of getting nailed for selling cocaine.

Abbie did regain media attention and respect after his reemergence, lecturing audiences about CIA covert activities and garnering respect, if not action, from a new generation of college students.

So why, on April 12, 1989, did Abbie kill himself?

Understanding the pivotal role of play in his life may provide some clues. The Abbie Hoffman of the sixties was ceaselessly committed to fighting the contest, to playing on the biggest stage he could find. His actions carried many of the noncompetitive characteristics of original play. His was a golden moment of disruptive play, but only a moment, a hiccup between phases of capitalism that was just big enough to hold the idea that a revolution was not trading one power base for another, it was trading in power altogether. And Abbie was not the sole creator. He was reflecting the times, feeding off its energy. He was just very, very fast. When the sixties moment passed, like everyone, he reconsidered his positions, and though the latter part of his career warrants attention, something was lost.

Compare examples of Abbie's previous 1968 excerpts to these from a piece he wrote for *Parade* magazine in 1984 on how to organize around local issues:

**Begin with the proper state of mind.** You must feel strongly that, if you put time and energy into a thought-out campaign, you will prevail.

**Get into the fight as early as possible.** . . . At the earliest stage, you might even be able to go on the offensive.

**Think in terms of team sports or war.** Shifting from analysis to action means changing roles from that of a detective to that of a coach or general. By mapping out allies, potential allies and the opposition, by scanning the field repeatedly for strengths and weaknesses on both sides, you are making abstract ideas concrete. Many people have a philosophical resistance to creating a 'them" and an "us," to seeing things in black and white. Such an attitude of "oneness" might feel good, but not when you are challenging the process of decision-making.

Notice the dramatic shift to the language of contest and the military analogy. Could this be the same guy? Abbie was able to hold many of the ideals of the sixties in his head, heart, and soul and subsequently commit to pursuing the utopia that they suggested. And Abbie was not the only person magnetized to such a dream. But living with life in the US as it progressed through the seventies and eighties had to be difficult.

The dream was over. That moment was a vision and a prophecy, a historical bookmark if you will, but not the era itself. It is testament to the toughness of Abbie's soul that he lasted as long as he did.

When the movement splintered and dispersed into special interest political groups, corporate rock, dropout human potential communities, and some wrecked people besides, there was no place for Abbie to roost. Ever conscious that he was a public figure, even when in hiding, he made the compromise of choosing a special issue he considered important—the environment—and dedicated his considerable skills to winning battles that would preserve and improve it.[34] He could have done a lot worse; and in the final analysis, he was a *mensch.*

He was painfully aware that he had made a Maslovian retreat to the first two rungs of the hierarchy. That was his nature and his training, as previously witnessed at Woodstock. But this exercise would be protracted. His contribution had to be confined to reshaping one piece of the puzzle. While a fugitive, he adopted the identity of Barry Freed. He organized *Save The Rivers,* successfully stopping winter navigation of the St. Lawrence Seaway and thus reducing environmental risks.

The historical moment of the Yippies cannot be wiped away, and it stands as a beacon. We can see that the spirit of play reemerges in some gay activism and political puppet theater.[35] We can see play in new theater forms, in some dimensions of the WTO demonstrations of 1999, the Occupy movement a decade later, antics of The Yes Men, Anonymous, and the reemergence of socialist idealism. Some folks have in fact found their way into the system, have not forgotten the lessons of the sixties, and are opening doors to a more playful world and a less contest-based society. Those gains aspire to the viability that would support a soul as bright, vulnerable, and demanding as Abbie's.

As Abbie closes *Woodstock Nation,* we get a peek at his emerging maturity and realizations that the transformation may not come so quickly or so soon. It is incredibly brave and risky to be laying claim to an accurate analysis of America and making a call to action when you are high on LSD. In such a setting, Abbie is often dismissed. But better to realize that here was an exceptional mind, soul, and heart sent into the eye of a cultural hurricane. This man brought a powerful lens to the possibilities of the sixties revolution; he was a reporter from that frontier. But he was also a cultural crowbar, leveraging events to maximum consciousness so that we could all glimpse

---

[34] Jezer, *Abbie Hoffman, American Rebel,* 267-270.

[35] Clive Thompson, *"Free the Puppets!" Raygun,* June 2000, 79-83.

that vision and move a step closer to it. With a warm and a fierce heart, Abbie entered the biggest contests in the world and refused to compete; he challenged the contestants to stop the game and start playing. For one brief moment, the national stage let Yippies yap and play and be grand spoilsports. As disruptive players, they shocked the system, and the system doesn't absorb such shocks, especially when hurled by individuals. It devours these punk spoilsports.

Movements produce leaders, and leaders are credited with being able to understand the deeper issues at the core of those movements. But movements witness and attract other individuals who also possess deeper understanding. They do not necessarily emerge as leaders but are ubiquitous spoilsports. If they break the spell of a game that everyone else has agreed to play, they are spoilsports who play the valued and martyred trickster role of raising consciousness. Not necessarily anarchists representing no order, but they do open the door to alternative orders through play. Under certain circumstances, the role is a sacrificial one. And as Huizinga stated, they could be heretics or prophets . . . or both.

In social movements, such innovators do need to have a following. The strength of their numbers and the ability of the group to win elections at the polls or concessions from the government—for example, the environmental movement—determines that group's ability to influence. If they are far out on the limb of a radical vision, they will either alter society or be driven into exile and perish. Such is the case of Abbie Hoffman.

In the arts, such innovators do not initially need to be leaders with followers. They are striking out in a new direction that other artists may or may not follow. Ultimately, the marketplace and its ability to deliver their art to their audience will determine whether the artist develops a following. The development of a network of radio stations, field and studio recordings, and record distribution of the music that made rock 'n' roll so successful is a good example. Muddy Waters and Elvis made it. Hundreds we have never heard of did not.

If they are far out on the limb of innovation, either they will become foundations of a new art movement or the limb will break and they will crash. In the analogous entertainment industry, such is the case of Andy Kaufman.

Abbie was a classic spoilsport, a trickster too far out to have survived. That he was prophetic in his revelations of the potential for disruptive play makes his life no less painful, but we will be grateful for generations to come for his contributions. Abbie brought theater to politics in unprecedented style and scale. In strange analogy, Andy Kaufman challenged masses to question the premises of entertainment and the implied social contracts between audience and performer. And so we migrate from the political stage to the comedic one and meet up with this other lone warrior, a holy fool.

# ELEVEN

# Andy Kaufman, Holy Fool

*It is curious to note how much more lenient society is to the cheat than to the spoil-sport. This is because the spoil-sport shatters the play-world itself. By withdrawing from the game he reveals the relativity and fragility of the play-world in which he had temporarily shut himself with others. He robs play of its illusion. . . Therefore he must be cast out, for he threatens the existence of the play-community.*

*The spoil-sport breaks the magic world, therefore he is a coward and must be ejected. In the world of high seriousness, too, the cheat and the hypocrite have always had an easier time of it than the spoil-sports, here called apostates, heretics, innovators, prophets, conscientious objectors, etc. It sometimes happens, however, that the spoil-sports in their turn make a new community with rules of its own. The outlaw, the revolutionary, the cabbalist or member of a secret society, indeed heretics of all kinds are of a highly associative if not sociable disposition, and a certain element of play is prominent in all their doings.*

*Johan Huizinga*[1]

*I never told a joke in my life.*

*Andy Kaufman*

---

[1] Johan Huizinga, *Homo Ludens: A Study of the Play Element in Culture* (Boston: Beacon Press, 1955), 11-12.

WHERE IS THE LINE between entertainment and guerilla theater? Does performance art have to direct us to political action, or can we be provoked to question even more general assumptions about life? Is there value in provocation for its own sake, the trickster at work, in it for the laughs, no purpose necessary?

Andy's behavior seemed to ask us these questions. We remember him as a comic, but he described himself as" a song and dance man."[2] In his first television appearance in 1972, he did a convincing Elvis Presley impersonation, lip-syncing "Blue Suede Shoes." For the follow-up interview on *Kennedy at Night*, Andy answered questions as Elvis. Staying in character was one of his hallmarks, essential to his performance discipline but always an impediment to connection.

Three years later, Andy was featured in the very first season of *Saturday Night Live*, often playing Foreign Man from the fictional island of Caspiar. ABC picked him up, and in the character's variation as Latka Gravas, he became a star of the sitcom *Taxi* from 1978-1983. He went on to expend this fame through trickster capers that challenged our assumptions about comedy, performance, and cultural possibility. His appearances always meant an opportunity to embrace the irrational.

In the short-lived career of the network sketch-comedy show *Fridays*, Andy appeared as a guest on February 20, 1981. He conspired with Michael Richards—who was to go on to fame as Kramer in *Seinfeld*—to break out of a sketch. The sketch had two couples at dinner sneaking away to the bathroom to smoke marijuana. But in the middle of the televised live performance, Andy refused to perform. Richards grabbed the cue cards and threw them down on the table in front of Andy, who responded by throwing a glass of water on Richards. Pandemonium broke out with fist fights and shoving on the set. Since the show was broadcast live, home viewers saw most

---

[2] Ron Givens, "Andy Kaufman Recalled as Bizarre, Gifted," *New York Daily News*, December 23, 1999, accessed August 6, 2016, http://www.nydailynews.com/archives/nydn-features/andy-tales-kaufman-family-friends-colleagues-remember-performer-man-moon-article-1.854317.

of these events transpire until the network cut the cameras. In the news stories that appeared later that week, it was never made clear whether the entire prank was a put-on or whether the cast members were truly taken aback, angered, and aghast. Where did the put-on end and reality begin? This is the stuff of myths . . . and the question Andy consistently posed and just as consistently refused to answer.

## Andy's Shtick

His most offensive character was Tony Clifton, the garish Las Vegas entertainer whose insults made Don Rickles or Andrew Dice Clay look like sweet grandmas. Andy shrouded this character in mystery, claiming to not be him and having his writer, Bob Zmuda, occasionally take the role to deepen the mystery. Clifton is eerily like a late twentieth-century version of Alfred Jarry's *Père Ubu*, pure id, shed of all considerations save feeding his own need for attention, sex, food, etc. His unabashed cruelty can be hilarious, like when he asks the management to have the audience extinguish their smokes because of his sensitive lungs and then comes on stage chain-smoking.

Andy's message was unwavering, from his Mighty Mouse routine to his sham as a professional wrestler: *What are YOU the audience doing there, expecting to be entertained, expecting ME the entertainer to leave you with a whole package so that you can take my routine, know its beginning, its middle, its end? When I'm putting you on and when I'm not? If I do these things, then I am making sense to you. I refuse to do those things. I refuse to make sense.* And in this respect, Andy brings huge doses of irrationality to his art, an essential element of play.

Andy refused to entertain people in the way they were accustomed. His shortcoming was that he had nothing more than an unshackling of expectations to offer his followers once he convinced them to enter his unique play-world. As an entertainer, he had no obligation to lead his audience to social action or to an alternative life. But as a cultural revolutionary challenging the boundaries of entertainment, he entered the arena of social context whether he liked it or not (he didn't seem to like it). In this new territory, one must be careful and thoughtful and have some vision of where people might go if you are lucky (or unlucky) enough to have them follow you.

Andy instinctively knew that there was value in crossing the boundaries of entertainment and that there was more than entertainment value at stake when he would challenge people's expectations. To use a worn phrase in the most powerful sense, he took people out of their comfort zone, often to the point of ire. He would stand nervously by his record player waiting for the cue to lip-sync "Here I come to save the day!" on the theme song of Mighty Mouse; that was the entire routine. He would come on stage in turban and underpants, play the conga, and sing nonsense syllables in a foreign-sounding language derivative of nothing; that was the entire routine. He would play the stern schoolmaster and begin to read F. Scott Fitzgerald's *The Great Gatsby* until the audience would boo him off the stage. He would sit on stage and eat. Do his laundry. You get the idea.

He had the power to transport an audience, creating wacky and different reference points. It's attractive; we want to "get it" and join in the new reality. But like Icarus or Phaethon, he really didn't know what to do with this awesome power once he had unleashed it. Even when he could see the train wreck up ahead, he just kept on charging; once in character, he lacked the mobility to take the situation to the next level—to consciously address the new social context he had created—or to make a graceful exit.

He did relate to his audiences. The *Gatsby* routine could not succeed if it did not provoke. He played with them. When he had his very own show at Carnegie Hall, Andy rented buses that took the audience out for milk and cookies afterwards to celebrate. This is perhaps the most joyful and positive example of his performance art, his playing with typical expectations. I know it sounds silly (good!) but going out for milk and cookies en masse represents Andy's best attempt to parlay his boundary-crossing comedy into a new reality that his audience could experience with him.

And it was extremely positive. He sought a symbolic link to childhood—milk and cookies—that would viscerally remind the audience of their own childhood and play. When, in an effort to quell the after-show party, Andy invited the audience to continue with him the next day on the Staten Island Ferry, three hundred of the original audience actually showed up. Play, when we give it a chance, catches on.

But kids who seek attention don't care if it is positive or negative. There is no such thing as bad press. So Andy's provocations, with the wonderful exception of the Carnegie milk-and-cookies treat, tended to elicit the negative.

His tricksterism had a chance of going somewhere. Suppose he toured the country, and after every performance, the audience would share milk and cookies. It could catch on. Laugh *with* me—it could change our society.

How do comedians get laughs? They establish a common understanding with us, and because we share the same culture, they are able to lead us logically towards an obvious resolution to a problem or situation. Then, before arriving at the solution, they do the unexpected, and it is this shift in expectations, this minor tampering with the rules of the game, that causes us to laugh—it's fun to break the rules. In this respect, Andy was no different than any other comedian. Most comics break the rules of logic through simple narration, or the rules of kinesthetics through slapstick. Andy broke the rules of comedy itself, reaching for new levels of scale, setting, and bravura that distinguished him from other comics. He went further in daring the constraints of the art and of the society that makes the rules under which that art is performed. He crossed boundaries, as all comedy does, but he did it in unconventional directions—metacomedy: the joke was on us, on his employers, on comedy itself, on society at large.

Most artists perform for the love of their art but seek compensation and fame and will act to protect their careers. Often, the development of a career in the arts is accelerated by the artist's ability to get away with the outrageous. Witness The Who and Jimi Hendrix smashing their instruments, Beyoncé highlighting Black Panthers and Black Lives Matter during Super Bowl 50's halftime show, Bob Dylan going electric at the Newport Folk Festival, Picasso's consistent assault on the standards of art, the nudity of *Hair*, Stravinsky's *Le Sacre du Printemps*, Charlie "Bird" Parker's bebop innovations, and Johnny Rotten's Sex Pistols. The list could go on, but all of these artists risked their careers on an innovation that they were committed to and that, at the time, was outrageous to an established view on how their art should be performed.

Andy emphatically fit these descriptors. But because his outrageousness so violated the rules of the game—as performance art does—the jury is still out as to whether his innovations become the norm in comedy in quite the manner Picasso, Bird, and Hendrix permanently changed the face of their art forms. Andy probably didn't, precisely because he was pursuing social change or a change in consciousness more than he was pursuing a new form of comedy. That is, he went so far out that the art form could not follow his lead without ceasing to be that very form. dada posed the same challenge. Picasso, Bird, and Hendrix all made social comment, but their first allegiance was to their art. Taken to heart, Andy's innovations would destroy comedy as we know it and pave the way for a new level of ceremonial wackiness. He challenged the meaning of people coming together for entertainment and spoiled the norms of the entertainment ritual. More than celebrity, fame, money, or career, Andy wanted the juice of the reaction, the provocation.

I went to a Dan Hicks concert once, in Santa Cruz, California, in the late 1970s. The promoter had rented the Del Mar movie theater for the Sunday summer afternoon event. Hicks was performing his songs solo on the guitar . . . or so the audience thought. But he would play the first few bars of a song and then say, "Naw, I don't feel like playing that one today," or something to that effect, and then banter with the audience, just talking, but incredibly funny shtick. At first it was tolerated; the audience was amused; the jokes were funny. Then he would do it again. Ultimately, he didn't play a single song the entire concert. Despite his hilarious repartee, much of the audience booed and walked out. I was entertained, tickled, and utterly transfixed by this trickster with the unmitigated nerve to play with the audience's expectations so provocatively.

Other tales of Hicks's hijinks abound. He must have been a real spoilsport. Whatever he did to raise ire and refuse rules, the record companies blackballed him for much of the 1970s and '80s, blunting his career. And this is the stuff of real suffering, when spoilsporting is carried to the extreme, threatens the social contract of commerce, and is performed by individuals unsupported by a cohesive community.

The most profound example of spoilsporting would be Andy's career as, first, the Intergender Wrestling Champion of the World and, later, as a professional wrestler taking on the audience of Memphis, Tennessee. He was doing something that had huge market potential, but it was based on the enormity of the negative response.

Sometimes this works. A rock manager Shep Gordon saw Alice Cooper perform and get booed off stage at a concert in Phoenix. After the show, Gordon rushed backstage and signed Cooper to a contract immediately. He said that anyone who could get such a strong reaction must have something going, and he proved to be right. Gordon helped Cooper find his audience and build a successful career. But Alice was selective in which rules he broke, and his rebellion was only offensive to the *parents* of his market. He used grotesque and death-tinged imagery, a stylistic device which has since become commonplace, from Nirvana to Marilyn Manson to Black Sabbath/Ozzy Osbourne to Tool to the entire goth and death-metal genres. And his medium was a very good heavy metal band, with very simple rules of musical form. And Alice was not a spoilsport. Stretching the rules is qualitatively different from breaking them.

Andy's most successful successor, Sacha Baron Cohen (aka Ali G, Borat Sagdiyev, Brüno Gehard, and Admiral General Aladeen), would seem to be coasting less painfully through some very radical pranks, put-ons, and controversial film and TV. In the middle phase of his career, he would seem to have departed from his prankster role and has been successful as a more conventional actor (appearing in *Madagascar, Hugo, Sweeny Todd,* and *Les Misérables*). I would suggest that Cohen is benefitting from a more niched and diverse entertainment universe that lets him steal the spotlight periodically but then steal away from it . . . and this may sustain him. He has a significant audience, but they're also busying themselves with a larger multitude of celebrities. Andy had an audience who loved him, but he couldn't hook up with their support for any length of time. His artistic drive would compulsively repel.

Huizinga sees comedy and tragedy as play only to the extent that there was competition amongst writers, artists, comics, and comedians for audience appreciation and money. But he missed the play element that is intrinsic to comedy as exposed during a comedian's performance. Like the original play of animals and young children, comedy thrives on transient competence. Indeed, it defines it. I am telling you something, and it is true it is true it is true it is true until I deliver the punch line that makes it suddenly not true. This is the very nature of original play, where contest and competence and even the rules of play are flexible and transitory. Play is fun in the same underlying rhythm and for the same reason that jokes are funny.

So comics are natural players, and comedy in and of itself is not competitive. What happens when the *original play* (non)sensibilities of a comic invade the *cultural play* (non?)sensibilities of amateur and professional wrestling?

Andy's career predated the internet and its power to amplify and taint reputations, yet he predicted so many things. He did Elvis impersonations—really good Elvis impersonations—before it was hip or common, before Elvis died. When he got in trouble with NBC, he threatened to buy the network (how many puffed-up billionaires typically flirt with that idea) and take it to twenty-four-hour programming (a radical and untried notion at the time). And, most prescient of all, Andy sniffed out the primal energy that was building up around professional wrestling in the US as the ultimate mass entertainment and perhaps the modern world's most garish exhibition of the elements of contest or *cultural play*. In choosing to lampoon wrestling, Andy sensed that this was where the ravenous American hunger for ever more raw entertainment was being sated. And he pounced.

## Andy As The Intergender Wrestling Champion of the World

Andy had established a pattern of zaniness and the unexpected through eight previous appearances on *Saturday Night Live:* Old MacDonald sing-alongs, *Great Gatsby* readings, Elvis impersonations, the Mighty Mouse routine. But on an October 1979 show, he declared himself the World Intergender Wrestling Champion, and offered $500 to any woman who could come on stage and pin him in a three-minute round of wrestling. He had been throwing out the challenge to audiences on his live tours for a while already, but this was nationally broadcast TV. Andy likened this act as a riff on the old carnival wrestlers who would challenge the locals. The trick was that Andy was playing the trick, but his intention was to set himself up as the loser, as the one tricked. He never lost a match, but many believe that the stunt cost him his career.

Wrestling at the millennium was a sport where the athletic skill of the contestants is almost irrelevant. The masterminds of the industry have instead done a superb job of amplifying all the other trimmings of contest so that professional wrestling would reign supreme as entertainment.

It also conforms to our definition of play. Every match has special drama to it, and the aura of a temporary reality is unmistakable. The rituals are many and are mimicked and immortalized in video games. It is satisfying unto itself. It has an order and a beauty of its own. Play is not a moral activity and only the most guileless individual would take the ethical and moral struggles of these comic book characters beyond the face value of entertainment. These are not role models. The costuming is unparalleled. There are intense secret society qualities and special agreements amongst wrestlers and between them and their fans. The boundaries of when play has begun and ended are a little blurry but are kept within limits, and testing that boundary adds to the drama. Were he alive today, Huizinga might point to professional wrestling as the best modern example we have of cultural play. For Andy to have made it his target was a stroke of genius.

Andy did a months-long stint challenging women to wrestling matches and boasting of how it proves the superiority of men. This social comedy lays bare the preposterous arguments that rank the sexes. And he chooses wrestling, the silliest sport, for his parody, wearing long underwear as his costume. In this case, we have the happy juxtaposition of a very silly man making a parody of two ubiquitous social phenomena. Of course, neither of these pursuits are silly unto themselves, the silliness comes in when proponents of any cultural activity, in politics or sports or whatever, take themselves too seriously. Seriousness was the target, wrestling and feminism merely vehicles. But endemic to Andy bits was the Andy backfire.

For many of his acts, but particularly the wrestling bit, Andy received thousands of hate mail letters, posthumously compiled in *Dear Andy Kaufman, I Hate Your Guts!* [3] Among the unamused was a professional wrestler named Jerry Lawler, a local hero in Memphis. Realizing a childhood fantasy, Andy took the opportunity to get in the ring with

---

[3] Lynn Margulies and Bob Zmuda, *Dear Andy Kaufman, I Hate Your Guts!* (Los Angeles: Process Publishing, 2009).

Lawler. Lawler was capable of casting out this spoilsport who threatened the existence of the wrestling play-community. Throughout their feud, the stakes proposed by Lawler were that if Andy lost, he would leave the wrestling profession. Lawler himself cheated—the cheat is tolerated more than the spoilsport—and used an illegal move that sent Andy to the hospital.[4] Lawler now claims he was in on prank all along. If so, all the better. That shows that Andy fully understood how the cheat would be preferred to the spoilsport.

Andy leapt from taunting women to taunting Memphians. When he stepped into the ring to take on Lawler, the hoax had transfigured from Andy the chauvinist vs. Women to Andy the Hollywood snob vs. hillbilly Memphis. He played videos showing residents how to use soap. He made speeches attacking them. He staged an injury (or exaggerated a minor injury) to get more material for assaulting the failings of Memphis society. The final insult was to return to his Intergender status, and in a challenge at Memphis's Mid-South Coliseum, he announced that the woman who pinned him would get to marry him. All of this was staged, but that nuance was lost on the Memphis crowds, and much bile was spewed on Andy, to the chagrin of his manager, George Shapiro, who found booking Andy becoming increasingly difficult.

But the challenge was too irresistible to Andy. Of course he was kidding, and mocking Hollywood snobs as much as Memphis hicks. Memphians were enraged and calling for his head. And many believe that it was at this point that Andy lost track of when he was doing a routine and when he was living his real life. But one might also contend that we will never know. He never tipped his hand. Even when it seemed like he did, you were never sure.

Yet with the wrestling venture, he took a fantasy event and exploded it outwards from the unreal world of media entertainment into the real

---

[4] Andy had sought a TV appearance with World Wrestling Federation but was rebuffed by CEO Vince McMahon. The challenge from Lawler was the next best thing.

world. The routine got so big, crossed so many boundaries and rules set by the entertainment and hype industry, that it became his life.

Simply put, he was mocking the good people of Memphis, and they were vaguely aware of this and incensed. Consciously or not, this is where Andy had been heading all along. Well, if not brilliant, it was an edifying debacle that revealed the dangers of play injected into unfamiliar and hostile contexts, cultural or political. Andy would not be sharing milk and cookies with the fans of Memphis.

Andy was a spoilsport in the purest sense. By posturing and deal making between matches, he would brazenly switch loyalties for money, just to expose that practice. He was the Johnny Rotten of wrestling, a true punk thrashing at the unholy alter of staged wrestling—fantasy entertainment that, on a regular schedule, explodes into the so-called personal lives of the fighters and their girlfriends.[5]

Andy defiled a space that the Memphis fans held sacred. As the more heroic brand of spoilsport, he might have devised an opportunity to transcend with the people of Memphis and create a greater game. The nature of Andy's insulting challenge and his track record as a provocateur made that near impossible. But it did demonstrate his uncanny ability to sniff out a game ripe for exposure and produce wild and unpredictable publicity and energy. To do so in the interest of making social progress means having at least an inkling of where to go when the old game is spoiled. But once drawn into his liberating world, the audience had nowhere to go. What was left to them, then, was the anger and disappointment in having had their expectations unmet, not unlike the Dan Hicks audience.

## Andy the Trickster Untethered

Though laid to waste by the forces he unleashed, Andy (like many contemporary artists) had no vision of where the power of his antics

---

[5] One could make that case that, as Jarry predicted dada, Andy blazed the trail for the spectacles of WrestleMania, Royal Rumble, Summer Slam, Survivor Series, and the like.

might lead. Lacking a sense of the potential for collective interaction, forces compelled Andy into the death trap set for any fully eccentric individual who steps outside the carefully drawn boundaries of America's media-fed pop culture and still tries to bite from the apple of celebrity: like Jim Morrison, Kurt Cobain, Sandra Bernhard, Pee-wee Herman (Paul Reubens), Charlie Chaplin, Jane Fonda, Sarah Silverman, Miley Cyrus, Joaquin Phoenix, Charlie Sheen, Robin Williams, Lenny Bruce, Roman Polanski, and Woody Allen.

There are others who are fully intent on playing with their artistic medium and have dedicated themselves to the task. They let their art speak for itself, and shun commentary, interview, or other publicity. They take measures to protect their creations above all else and survive by insisting on very private, almost reclusive lives: Meryl Streep, Stanley Kubrick, Alfred Hitchcock, Kate Winslet, Miles Davis, John Coltrane, Greta Garbo, Bob Dylan, Johnny Depp, even Joe DiMaggio and Sandy Koufax. Those who successfully ride the crests and inundations of celebrity show a deep respect for the rules.

For example, Madonna was the outrageous poster girl for the avant-garde movement you just missed. Her entire career was carefully calculated to be on the cutting edge of pop music, but no farther. She may have pushed boundaries with her latest musical style or by being highly sexual on stage or even by dating notorious figures, but she never crossed them. She was a classic entertainer always intent on being the biggest but never getting too far ahead of popular culture's current standards. David Bowie, Rihanna, Jim Carrey, Nicki Minaj, Mick Jagger, Kanye West, Bill Murray, and Lady Gaga are other good examples. And for all the wildness and seeming rule-breaking it celebrates, professional wrestling is a contained phenomenon as well.

Going after Elvis was an obvious target for Andy. As an icon of pop culture, Elvis is as huge as it gets. This was prophetic as well; Elvis impersonators were just coming onto the scene. Perhaps Andy hoped to provoke a reaction from the King or his fans—would the mockery incite like it did the wrestling fans, or would it be treated as sacred homage? Most likely it was simply an apt demonstration of Andy's mimetic powers. As a highly popular and accessible showstopper, the Elvis bit sustained some of the radical notions of his other routines, buying him time and moving his career along.

Andy was made tragic by his intuitive trickster capacity. Media thrust that pranksterism into social context, and Andy just cheered it along and stoked the fire all the way. While he copped a great buzz from it, he did not know, and perhaps did not care, about how to give people an alternate means of seeking, processing, and responding to such consciousness-raising entertainment. In analyzing French fairy tales, where the trickster plays a key role, Robert Darnton comments:

> Tricksterism is a kind of holding pattern. . . . It expressed an orientation to the world rather than a latent strain of radicalism. It provided a way of coping with a harsh society instead of a formula for overthrowing it."[6]

The one defining criterion of play that Andy's behavior does not meet is that all players know when they are playing and, thus, know when playing has ceased. The little boy who cries wolf runs into a problem here. From the middle to the end of his career, Andy had to plead with his audiences to take him seriously when he would describe his physical injuries and the legal and competitive battles with Jerry Lawler and the wrestling fans of Memphis. With Andy, you really couldn't tell when playing had ceased. Once he'd moved his play world into his real life, the spell was cast, and it swallowed him whole.

Perhaps his final routine as a professional wrestler is a comment on celebrity itself and makes a mockery of all the stars who believe their own press and lose track of who they really are. But clearly Andy walked a dangerous path. Like other tricksters, he had followers but was not a leader. He was a consciousness-raising spoilsport.

---

[6] Robert Darnton, *The Great Cat Massacre and Other Episodes in French Cultural History* (New York: Vintage, 1985), 59.

Rather than rely upon or wait for an individual to successfully lead a culture into a more playful space (a possible definition of messiah), people can form groups that provide a safer means for cultivating public play on an incrementally larger scale. Of course, taking the social context by surprise, i.e., playing where no one expects you to play, is more than half the fun.

We learn at least two great lessons from Andy. Firstly, he gave us the ultimate demonstration of the limitations of an individual's ability to provide omniscient leadership; opening a new door must be seen as just that. It's up to the audience and a collective intelligence to pursue the means of walking through that door and entering a new time. Secondly, he exposed the limitations of entertainment itself as experienced in our culture. We are bound and restrained by art that consistently reaches for and points the way to a higher (play)ground, but the boundaries of commerce, duration, space, and behavior keep play in its box and inhibit its potential for altering culture.

Andy's soulmate, sixties activist and Yippie Abbie Hoffman, combined Andy's boundary-crossing bravery with a deeper analysis and a political mission. We are all better off for having witnessed their performances and their lives. Beyond Andy's contribution, Abbie also gave us a glimpse of the Play Society. And to that end (really, to that beginning), we return to the broader themes of play beyond tricksterism and find that it is in the arts, in cartoons in fact, that the incursion of playfulness into mainstream culture, the seeds of the Play Society, are sown.

# Presently in the Past

# TWELVE

# Bart and Lisa, *Simpsons Libertas*

*And terror all at once replaced by total trust*
*Rainer Maria Rilke, Childhood[1]*

**WE'VE OBSERVED THE FOLKTALES** of Native Americans, Africans, and Europeans and the antics of dada and the disrupters of the mid-twentieth century, trickster individuals all. These are not the stories of historical liberation movements but of individual prophets, pranksters, and heretics. The dadas certainly were collective in spirit. The progenitors of dada, the *Cabaret Voltaire*, operated in a collective fashion. And although Abbie Hoffman was an exponent of a huge counterculture and himself an organizer, what he, Andy Kaufman, Marcel Duchamp, and Alfred Jarry accomplished was generally through individual effort, performance, art, and action.

Such stories show that an individual can shine a light on the potential for liberation and the Play Society, but it will take collective action to get there. To restore and then replenish original play in our lives broadly is a social endeavor. To challenge cultural play, what Huizinga says is the basis of all society, is to engage in disruptive play.

Here's a riddle: How can you play in a public arena, not on stage, in a way that is not contest? The answer is that, with few exceptions,

---

[1] Rainer Maria Rilke, *Selected Poems of Rainer Maria Rilke, A Translation from the German*, trans. Robert Bly (New York: Harper & Row, 1981), 73.

you can't, not without creating disruption. The following story is a striking illustration of this dynamic, showing all the ways play and contest bang up against each other, and it's a great example of disruptive play. This story affirms children's stewardship of play, yet illuminates its connections across ages, in particular with our elders.

## Wild Barts Can't Be Broken

The folks who put out *The Simpsons* are some of today's most powerful storytellers, and they cracked a hole in the universe when the Fox Network aired episode 214, *Wild Barts Can't Be Broken*, on January 17, 1999. In a stellar performance of grit and American pathos, Matt Groening's quintessential American family and the townspeople of Springfield made it painfully clear to everyone that play is a valuable, viable, and formidable means of effecting social change. Join Homer and Marge, Bart, and Lisa, as they set out to once again raise America's consciousness to new heights. Here's how it went down:

The set-up plot revolves around baseball, America's most revered contest, featuring Springfield's hapless minor league team, the Isotopes. Homer leaves after the first pitch, bemoaning their incompetence, and he waits outside in the car with the motor running for the rest of the game. On the ride home, Homer condemns the team to eternal ineptitude. Lisa, reviewing the statistics, predicts that with some middle relief pitching, they *could* make the playoffs.

Six months later, Homer is shocked to learn that the Isotopes are in fact in the playoffs (with a little help from a sniper at the all-star game), and he jumps as hard and as fast as he can onto the bandwagon. Watching the final game at Moe's, the local tavern, Homer gets featured in the news feigning constant loyalty to the team. They win the championship. The crowd goes wild. Homer and his gang head out in his car to continue boozing and carousing.

In the pitch-black night, the celebrants go wild. They physically beat on each other. They drive onto the Springfield Elementary School campus, first ravaging the baseball diamond, then driving down the hallways of the school. The hallway cruise turns nasty when one of Homer's cronies releases a fire extinguisher in the car. They smash up lockers, walls, and doors. They end their rampage in the shower, singing "We Are the Champions."

Cut to the next morning. Homer tries in vain to remember anything from the night before. The TV news comes on, and the vandalism is reported. Bart cheers, "Yes! Someone trashed the school!" With no suspects, Police Chief Wiggum assuredly states that "we're jumping to the conclusion that this was the work of no-good punk kids," and he imposes a curfew: "Any kid caught on the street after dark will be shot . . . or returned to their parents, as the situation may warrant."

Bart and Lisa try to argue for their rights, but Homer and Marge just laugh them off. "But it's not fair. Adults always blame kids for everything," protests Lisa. Homer reasons that everything bad is named after kids: acting childish, kidnapping, child abuse. "What about adultery?" asks Bart. "Not until you're older, son," counsels Homer.

In the next scene, we hear the opening strains of Beethoven's Pastoral Symphony as the neighborhood children play and then gleefully rush to welcome the ice cream truck. But just as it pulls up, Chief Wiggum cuts it off, breaks up the party, and sends all the children home: "Achtung, babies! Curfew is in effect. Return to your homes immediately." The awful reality sets in:

Bart and Lisa drearily look out the living room window at the beautiful evening they cannot go outdoors to enjoy. In an effort to cheer the kids up, Marge pulls out the old board games. Bart morosely suggests going to bed instead—at 5:30. (Homer, who is exempt from the curfew, takes off for the carnival that is in town.)

The next day at school, Milhouse complains that he spent the evening listening to his mother talk about her problems. "Adults blow," surmises Bart.

Chief Wiggum puts up a big, scary billboard of himself drinking coffee, that says, "WE'RE WATCHING YOU KIDS, COPS NEVER SLEEP." Bart and Lisa fly a kite indoors with an electric fan.

Driven to distraction, Lisa turns on the television. Just as Bart is about to throw a bowling ball into the set, Lisa stops him: "Wait, there's a commercial!" So there is, and it's for a B-horror flick. *The Bloodening* is advertised as being so scary that a registered nurse is posted at the theater for each showing. Bart hatches a plot to break curfew, get into the drive-in, and see *The Bloodening*.

Our intrepid band of kids sneak in and are mesmerized by the mainly black-and-white thriller about otherworldly goth children endowed with the power to make their eyes glow blue and read the minds of the adult villagers who would banish them. They confound the adults by exposing their secret scandals—pilfering the poor box, sneaking puddings, and committing adultery. Tracked down and cornered by a mob, the supernatural demon-children fight back and triumph by telepathically compelling the mob to self-flagellate. Bart and his friends are sitting on the drive-in asphalt cheering them on.

All of a sudden, the film stops, the lights go up, and Chief Wiggum busts the band of lawbreakers. "Listen up, punks!" he intones, "The moral of the story is, the adults always win!" Wiggum is loading the delinquents into his paddy wagon, but then he freaks and screams when the kids' eyes glow blue. It turns out that Eddie the cop was shining his flashlight to create the scary effect. He quietly chuckles when the Chief tells him to knock it off.

The little criminals, outfitted in orange coverall prison garb, are forced to scrub the hated billboard. The chief admonishes, "And let this be a lesson to you. Kids never learn," as he drives off and splatters the billboard with more mud. Now the kids are really angry and determined to fight back. Milhouse wishes they had the glowing-eye power of the kids in the movie, but Lisa helps the group to realize that they already know all of the adults' embarrassing secrets, and she organizes the kids to a guerrilla theater action. Milhouse suggests that they put the information on the internet. "No," reasons Bart, "We have to reach people whose opinions actually matter."

An elaborate plan takes shape. After collecting all the hardware and equipment needed to pull their caper off, we see the group, with a dog, exiting stage right through a fence hole in an homage to *Our Gang*, the spotlight narrowing on the winking dog.

Homer and Marge are at home deciding which program to watch. Homer goes along with Marge's choice—"Okay, whatever takes my mind off my life." But Lisa enters with Grandpa's old radio and turns the TV off. "Oh, wouldn't it be grand to gather 'round and have a listen?"

"Well, turn SOMETHING on," pleads Homer, "I'm starting to think!"

As she is going through stations, programming is interrupted for a very special presentation, "We Know All Your Secrets," complete with Bart's scary voice.

They expose Chief Wiggum as a transvestite, Mrs. Krabappel as a pilferer of cafeteria supplies, and Homer Simpson, who eats out of the neighbor's garbage ("I have a problem," he quietly whines). This is but the first installment. They promise more.

The Mayor calls a town meeting that is interrupted by the next episode of "We Know All Your Secrets," where divorcée Luann Van Houten's infidelity to her boyfriend is revealed. In the middle of the broadcast, the Chief and the town scientist track the pirate radio station down, behind the reviled billboard, whose moving parts power the radio transmitter. Harsh words are exchanged:

Wiggum:   All right you kids, come down now. We promise we won't kill you.

Homer:   Speak for yourself. Bart, get down here! I'm gonna spank you back to the Stone Age.

Bart: You can't make us come down.

Nelson: You adults are always giving us orders.

The
Reverend: You kids are always disobeying them.

Milhouse: Adults treat kids like children.

Mr.
Van Houten: Kids treat adults like cash machines.

Kids: Adults.

Adults: Kids.

Kids: Adults.

Enter Broadway fanfare, and we get a musical version of a form of cultural play from ancient times, a "slanging-match," or more recently "dozens," where each group creatively trash-talks the other.[2] *The Simpsons'* version is based on the tune "Kids" from *Bye Bye Birdie*. (Adults: Kids. You bum my smokes and don't say thank you; Kids: You adults strut around like your farts don't stink.) In the third verse, the seniors of Springfield, who can't stand the noise, break up the hostilities.

Grampa Simpson promises to teach everyone a lesson. Homer says, "O yeah, what can you OLD folks teach us." Everyone bristles and rants at the elders. But a vote is taken, and by one vote (Lisa reminds the family how seniors always turn out for elections; Marge reminds Homer that perhaps he should have voted), a curfew is imposed for anyone under the age of seventy. Grampa Simpson shines a flashlight into the family's living room declaring lights out for the entire family of punk kids.

---

[2] Evidence of slanging matches date to pre-Islamic Arabic, Germanic, Greek, and Old Norse literature. Johan Huizinga, *Homo Ludens: A Study of the Play Element in Culture* (Boston: Beacon Press, 1955), 68-70.

Grampa Simpson exults, "Hooray! We took back the night!" Beethoven's Pastoral Symphony returns full force, and we are treated to a scene where the post-seventy citizens of Springfield are playing in the parks and neighborhoods, rediscovering the joys of their youth. The episode closes with the sounds of seniors playing Kick the Can (referencing a *Twilight Zone* episode[3] where by playing such games, elders are able to return to their childhoods), ringing bicycle bells, and playing in the Springfield night air.

## Lisa and Bart and Disruptive play

Could it be any better explained? This parable drips with insight. It depicts the very conflict of play versus contest. On the one hand, we have the children and their energy of play, their natural activities, which are not harmful. Then we have the model of the grownups, adversaries who would rashly blame an act of destruction on the kids and, more ominously, associate that vandalism with the nonharmful aspects of children's play. The moment blame enters, we are beset by conflict and play evaporates.

We are regaled with an impressive array of all the tainted and more alienated forms of enjoyment that we turn to when we have no outlet for authentic play. The set-up plot takes place at a baseball game, a contest. The event around which the plot revolves was wanton vandalism rendered by drunken fools celebrating a contest victory. The first night of the curfew, Homer takes off to be entertained by the carnival. He avoids thinking about his life by watching TV. Since the kids can't go outside and play, their mom suggests they divert their energy with board games. The adults engage in transvestitism, adultery, and pilfering, and as vagabonds. The police chief is a dangerous sadist.

---

[3] *The Twilight Zone*, Season 3, episode 21, "Kick the Can," directed by Lamont Johnson, written by George Clayton Johnson and Rod Serling, February 9, 1962, CBS.

Not all of the above are damnable acts or necessarily even bad. Some take our need for pleasure too far, others are perfectly acceptable. But all of them can be thought of as something adults (or kids) do instead of simply playing, which is denied us by the rules of cultural play, of adult contest society. This is the lesson of the elders in the final scene, as they capture the adult means of making rules and use them to create an arena for *them* to just play. They are reconnecting with an energy that had been pent-up throughout their adult lives.

Homer is a sucker for all alienated pleasures, from phony loyalty to a baseball team (an ancient one) to booze (also ancient), carnage, television, the carnival—he loves 'em all. Police Chief Wiggum, on the other hand, plays an extremely loathsome part in this script; he is strictly anti-play in all its forms. It is no coincidence that the purest form of authority, the police chief (as opposed to parents, mayor, minister, or school principal) lands this role.

Wiggum represents the pure exercise of power, and he directs it in an effort to do more than punish the children. His sensibilities of law and order are so transgressed by the crimes he alleges that his actions verge on calling for the extermination of kids, certainly the energy they represent. It is Wiggum who declares the curfew, who seeks to prevent play on the first evening after, who incessantly hunts the kids down, who devises cruel punishments. He is obsessed with seeing them pay for their supposed crimes, and his true character is revealed in his immediate willingness to rush to judgment. In a power-grab reminiscent of tyranny, he uses the school vandalism to justify a campaign against all he dislikes about kids, mainly their desire to play. His day has come, and he exploits one incident to justify punishing all that is kid-like and playful.

This is no joke. Wiggum has no humane vision for what life, for children and adults alike, might be like. He only knows how to use police power to restore law and order. Whereas Homer, in this episode, is a frustrated, stupid, and helpless parent seeking perhaps unwise retribution upon his son, Wiggum has clearly declared an all-out war upon the children. Larry Doyle, the writer of this episode, has presented us with a pure and undiluted example of the essence of not-play energy, based solely upon the exercise of power and authority.

Whether or not we side with the kids, the stark madness, cruelty and stupidity of Wiggum's campaign gnaws at the viewer and the citizens of Springfield as well. Chestnuts like "We're jumping to the conclusion that this was the work of no-good punk kids," "Any kid caught on the street after dark will be shot," "Kids never learn," and "Adults always win" just can't sit right with anyone, human or 'toon. And Doyle gives us a bona fide example of subversion, from right within Wiggum's ranks, as one of his officers "accidentally" casts his flashlight on the rounded-up little curfew-violators, scaring his despotic boss.

But what makes *The Simpsons* so valuable as a communicator of big ideas is that they take us beyond the grim depiction of our social reality and its injustices. Thanks to Lisa Simpson, the shining hope for millions, there is vision, there is intelligence, and there is a plan. When the kids have had enough and they're not going to take it anymore, she rallies them to action that is well-conceived and effective. Beyond irony, the actions led by Lisa and her accomplices use play—in this case, guerrilla theater through scandal exposé, and years before WikiLeaks—as a political weapon to expose the secrets upon which power structures are built. The spirit and substance of just that type of action and its potential for social change are the central themes of play extended into a social context. For example, imagine protesting a "no long hair on males" policy at Disneyland by organizing a fantasy army of Yippies to invade the theme park and "liberate" Treasure Island. That kind of thing could only happen in a cartoon, right?[4]

---

[4] *The New York Times*, October 21, 1967, 28.

The kids' plan to avenge themselves, to restore their rights and their space for being kids, is risky indeed. For what they do is take the energy of their play and engage it in the political arena; they use play to fight back. But instead of the oppressive tactics of curfews and locking people up, the kids seek to embarrass the adults into retreat. John Roche, who was an aide in Lyndon Johnson's White House, once said that if someone had been able to pull Adolph Hitler's pants down at the right public moment, he would never have risen to power. Every time he tried one of those spectacular speeches the people would have just laughed at him because the image of "Mein Führer" with his pants down around his ankles would have been too much.[5] Fifty-five years later, Lisa and "Her [Our] Gang" (for their antics are inspired by the old series of comedy short films)[6] attempt to do just that. It is the idea of prank taken to the level of political action. It is the power of the image to expose the game and dissolve power.

Notice the exchange when publishing the town's secrets on the internet is first suggested. Bart nixes it; the information has to go to people whose opinions actually matter. Besides this humorous slight on bloggers, Bart makes a very strong point, with all due respect to Anonymous and other online activists. The prank has to be politically engaged, has to actually be directed to a power center. This is risky business indeed, as we shall see.

To a limited extent, the stratagem succeeds. The grownups quickly realize that the kids know all their secrets and that the success of adult society relies on our ability to keep our secrets, "mutual secrecy being one of the conditions of life upon this globe."[7] They panic, and the mayor calls a town meeting. Further exposure leads to a showdown at the billboard, trumped by the elders who ultimately take political power and make the world safe for play.

---

[5] Abbie Hoffman, *The Best of Abbie Hoffman: Selections from Revolution for the Hell of It, Woodstock Nation, Steal This Book and New Writings* ((New York: Four Walls Eight Windows, 1989), 20.

[6] *Our Gang*, produced by Hal Roach (Pathé Exchange, MGM, 1922-1944), series of movie shorts.

[7] E.M. Forster, *Aspects of the Novel* (London: Penguin, 1964, 55).

When the power of pranksterism, a means of mocking what is "serious" and "adult" is diverted into conventional arts, entertainment, and buffoonery, it depletes its potential for upsetting the serious, adult world and prevents it from making a crack in our universe and opening up ideas for a more playful world. People in power have depended upon this defanging of play for centuries. In the realm of seventeenth century European fairy tales, the heroes are sly pranksters, but given the opportunity to overwhelm their villains, they consistently stop short of total victory. Robert Darnton's study of fairy tales shows that when heroes overcame their opponents and were granted *whatever wish they wanted…*

> The clever weakling makes a fool of the strong oppressor by raising a chorus of laughter at his expense . . . but laughter . . . has limits. Once it subsides, the tables turn back again . . . the old order regains its hold on the revelers.[8]

The mischievous, playful instinct was intimidated from its full potential. Peasant fairy tale heroes, offered any wish possible, would simply seek a good meal or, at most, the temporary humiliation of the ruling class, not a reordering of power and class structures. But we've come a long way from Jack and the Beanstalk *(Petit Jean)* to Lisa and *The Simpsons.* As an emergent and transcendent power, play's early showing in Western history had to be humbly yet mischievously framed as nonthreatening.

By using play and pranks to create that opening, the great and necessary risk is that of injecting play into power struggles and engaging combat. A review of Henry James's *The Turn of the Screw* asks, "Can innocence react to adult corruption without being touched by it?"[9] Thus adulterated, disruptive play risks its magic. This is in fact what happens when the kids face off with the adults, and their contest is engaged in the form of a Broadway musical number. It turns into a

---

[8] Robert Darnton, *The Great Cat Massacre and Other Episodes in French Cultural History* (New York: Vintage, 1985), 33, 34, 59.

[9] Michael Upchurch, review of *Turn of the Screw* by Henry James, *The Seattle Times*, June 27, 1999.

slanging-match, and fittingly, it is the elders who take charge and restore an authentic community. Behold! It is one that embraces play. Perhaps the most important point of this episode is that it debunks the commonly accepted myth that play is only for children.

This final scene (Beethoven's Pastoral Symphony and the harmonious images it evokes is hilariously poignant) makes a few points. It is a glimpse of the pure play energy as conceived by *The Simpsons'* artists. One hopes that if the other grownups and the kids learn to stop bickering, they will be invited to join the elders. One hopes to challenge the base pleasures of our society—Homer Simpson being the quintessential consumer of them—with more authentic, playful pursuits. One hopes for a life that goes beyond the preoccupations of the rat race and consumerist distractions that can confound play.

Finally, can the value of child's play, under current arrangements, only be fully understood by (Springfield's) elders who have the perspective and the ability to compare what was good and right about their childhood with what they experienced as grownups, workers, citizens, and parents? Do our elders actually believe that message? And if so, might that also demonstrate that play need not burn up in the fires of adolescence—to be relegated and repressed into mere booze, baseball, and boinking as the "adult" means of reconnecting with the play state? *The Simpsons* raises these questions and more.

What the Simpsons episode suggests for its community on a regular basis is something we only glimpse when a contest society has designated periods for releasing energy pent up by oppressive seriousness. And whether it be Bart, Lisa, Bugs, or some rampant online avatar, playful, humorous fantasy inspires. In the next chapter, political consciousness meshes with fantasy, humor, and play. These cartoons are real.

# THIRTEEN

# Banksy, Anonymous, and the Yes Men

*The greatest crimes in the world are not commit-*
*ted by people breaking the rules but by people fol-*
*lowing the rules. It's people who follow orders that*
*drop bombs and massacre villages.[1]*

*Banksy*

PLAY IS DANGEROUS. I'm remembering *The Fight Club*[2] and how the film incorporates some aspects of a play revolution but mixed in with serious notions about masculinity and featuring graphic, bone-crunching violence. *The Fight Club* does a double reverse on conflict and fighting. No one wins each one-on-one fist-fight. Men strive to fight off the emasculating pressures of rampant consumerism. It amps up their rebellious play to the level of violence. Frolic and playfulness are now cloaked in a violent search for authentic masculinity. Is that noncompetitive play? The movie, completed just a couple of years before 9/11, concludes with eerie prescience: the destruction of the skyscrapers of credit card companies. The enemy is not an economic system or tyrant or foreign power per se, it's consumerism run amok.

---

[1] Banksy, *Wall and Piece* (London: Century, 2005), 51.

[2] *The Fight Club*, dir. David Fincher (Los Angeles, CA: Fox 2000 Pictures, 1999), film.

But there are other ways to resist hyperbolic commerce and encroaching consumerism. The playful child and the Trickster show the way. Art is a means.

## Banksy The Yippie Painter

Consider the following images: Monkeys with sandwich boards that say "Laugh now, one day we'll be in charge." Monkeys that upend an "intelligence test" in order to escape from it. Pretty little girls hugging bombs. Two English bobbies making out. A Royal Guard pissing on a wall. A Royal Guard drawing the sign for anarchy, ⊕. Armed riot police surreptitiously graffiti-painting the peace sign, ☮, on a wall. Hip-hop rats carrying a boom box. Rats in tuxedos gracing a red carpet into their rat portal. Rats as the livers and totems of urban culture, absorbing "junk food waste, ambient radiation and hardcore urban rap music, these creatures have evolved at an unprecedented rate.... one day they may be in charge."[3] An ATM machine spitting out cash. Fake English ten-pound notes with the motto "Trust no one." Photo opportunity spots marked with "This is not a photo opportunity." The Palestinian segregation wall adorned with pictures of natural beauty. A ladder that climbs up the Palestinian segregation wall.

The street artist covertly mounting art in the Louvre along with "the masters": a Mona Lisa with a smiley face smile instead of Mona's. Police restriction tape, spy cameras, and military helicopters on nineteenth-century classic pastoral oil paintings. More defaced nineteenth-century art: A naked baby Jesus with suicide bomb explosives taped around his belly. Mother Mary with an iPod.

A Burger King cardboard crown on the head of a starving African boy. The Queen of England with a gas mask on a postage stamp. Old folks lawn bowling with bombs. Armed riot cops with smiley faces. A little girl holding a portable TV set like it's her favorite doll, on the

---

[3] Banksy, *Wall and Piece*, 155.

screen is written "The End." Winston Churchill with a green Mohawk punk haircut stenciled on the wall.

Banksy disruptively placed all of the above images in public. Banksy has much to say about the state of the world, and as an artist, much to say about art. Unlike the mass market forces that determine the success of music, movies, and novels, "The Art we look at is made by only a select few. A small group create, promote, purchase, exhibit and decide the success of Art. Only a few hundred people in the world have any real say. When you go to an Art gallery you are simply a tourist looking at the trophy cabinet of a few millionaires."[4] Thus, in this case, Trickster remains bound. dada is back in the museums. Banksy is emphasizing the critical need to challenge art.

Banksy, the celebrated twenty-first-century street artist, wages war on war, consumerism, and commerce through graphic satire. Playfulness energizes Banksy as he appropriates corporate logos, images of monkeys, of rats, and paints any public surface. He poses questions that bespeak the amorality of true tricksterism—*we're in this for a good laugh, and potentially raised consciousness.*

And then he is co-opted by an intuitive wheeler-dealer. In true trickster fashion, Banksy is the butt of this joke, and he documents it brilliantly in his film *Exit Through the Gift Shop.*

Banksy's work brings in millions . . . but transient street art lives on apart from commerce. Banksy mounted fake graffiti from the "Post-Catatonic" era: a primitive man rolling a shopping cart (with a bull from the cave paintings of Lascaux in the background) . . . sure, political, anticonsumerist, but in it for the laughs. The earliest art wasn't art; it was graffiti.

We've seen that many individuals, fictional and real, Western and non-, can embody many Trickster characteristics. But any articulate and coherent social vision is not about celebrities, icons, or garden variety rogues and pranksters; it's about entire populations coming

---

[4] Banksy, *Wall and Piece,* 144.

to terms with Trickster in their own personalities and translating that into political and cultural action.

Thus Banksy, a collectively minded anonymous disruptive player, is anonymous in a way that invites people to identify with him (her?). And mass identification proceeds to mass movements, subversive and celebratory, all carnivalesque, that foretell the Play Society.

## Banksy and Graffiti

In Banksy, we have an artist who stakes out high moral ground, yet embodies numerous Trickster characteristics of amorality. He works through perhaps the most disruptively playful medium, graffiti:

> Graffiti is not the lowest form of art. Despite having to creep about at night and lie to your mum, it's actually the most honest artform available. There is no elitism or hype, it exhibits on some of the best walls a town has to offer, and nobody is put off by the price of admission. A wall has always been the best place to publish your work. The people who run our cities don't understand graffiti because they think nothing has the right to exist unless it makes a profit. But if you just value money then your opinion is worthless. . . . The people who truly deface our neighbourhoods are the companies that scrawl their giant slogans across buildings and buses trying to make us feel inadequate unless we buy their stuff. They expect to be able to shout their message in your face from every available surface but you're never allowed to answer back. Well, they started this fight and the wall is the weapon of choice to hit them back.[5]

Graffiti is playful because the artist is here and gone, and in many cases, so is the art . . . temporality. Playful because it is whimsical. Disruptively playful because it breaks the rules of language, breaks the rules of public property propriety; playful because it mocks, and in the case of Banksy, playful because it is satire of the highest order.

---

[5] Banksy, *Wall and Piece*, 8.

Sometimes Banksy is just in it for the laughs; frequently, Banksy is attacking war, sexism, consumerism, and apathy. A dada contradiction, his campaign against money and wealth and commerce has produced some of the most expensive contemporary works of art.

Banksy the subversive spars with art's endemic commerce. Banksy correctly sees advertising as an invasion of our space taken without our permission. He sees defacing, mocking, appropriation, and satire of such as our right.

> Any advert in public space that gives you no choice whether you see it or not is yours . . . to take, re-arrange and re-use. You can do whatever you like with it. Asking for permission is like asking to keep a rock someone just threw at your head. You owe the companies nothing. You especially don't owe them any courtesy. They have re-arranged the world to put themselves in front of you. They never asked for your permission, don't even start asking for theirs.[6]

We have drifted back and through the worlds of art and of politics. In most cases, we have examined artists like the dadas and the Beats who are able to connect the dots between what is artistically meaningful and what is politically just. We have examined political activists like the Yippies and Abbie Hoffman, and soon we'll check out the Yes Men who make full use of artistic talents to inform their protest and their platform. And because creativity is a main character in all the above, so is play, and so there are openings for tricksters and tricksterism.

Banksy demonstrates that the dada truth—art can neutralize the commerce system designed to contain it—is a point worth making again. And that rebellion against said commerce system can be extrapolated to the political realms of capitalism, exploitation, imperialism . . . and war. Art, the trickster, and play are all, if nothing else, antiwar.

Banksy does have a clear political program, and he bursts forth with a rediscovery of the potency of art to make a political point.

---

[6] Banksy, *Wall and Piece*, 160.

Banksy is a true dada and hippie in the consistent way that Banksy art promotes love, color, childhood, nature, and the sensibilities of being antiwar, antimilitary, anticommerce.

And Banksy is not alone. Banksy's images are part of a street art tradition dating as far back as WWII, when American GI's scribbled "Kilroy Was Here" on walls throughout liberated Europe. Cornbread, a Philadelphia high school student, is widely credited with starting the modern street art movement in 1967. The New York City graffiti boom of the 1960s and Bronx-centered subway train murals in the 1980s inspired Banksy. There are the conceptual works of Richard Hambleton, Keith Haring, AVANT, and Jean-Michel Basquiat.[7] Graffiti's refrains grew alongside punk rock's subversion and the 1901 quote, "We will destroy all the museums."[8] Recent notables include Shepard Fairey, Space Invader, Zeus, Seizer, Neckface, Sweet Toof and Cyclops, Ron English, Dotmasters, Swoon, Borf and Buff Monster.

## Banksy the Disappearing Movie Star

In one of our era's more deft misdirections, Banksy hijacked his own film about himself by making it about his most famous and successful imposter, Thierry Guetta. The film's title, *Exit Through the Gift Shop*, is itself a Banksy statement. Go view art, but then exit through the gift shop to go buy the jewelry, notecards, books, baubles, bangles, and beads that sustain the commerce connected to that art.

Banksy sets out to make a documentary or statement film about his art and in so doing relies upon a follower who has been capturing Banksy and his accomplices at work, getting some very excusive video, especially nighttime escapades, when all the best graffiti work is done. This supposed ally, Thierry, on one level has no idea what he's doing, as he compulsively films everything; he takes thousands of hours of video that overwhelm categorization, editing, or culling.

7  "Street Art," *Wikipedia*, accessed on June 23, 2017, https://en.wikipedia.org/wiki/Street_art#cite_note-:0-16.

8  Annalisa Zox-Weaver, "Institutional Guerilla Art," *Sculpture Review*, Summer 2015, 22–26.

But on another level, as a helper, he intuitively co-opts Banksy and his collaborators' techniques and begins to make millions in knock-offs of Banksy's works, appropriating the style but having no substance. Unlike Banksy, Thierry makes it very easy for patrons to buy his art. One of his most ubiquitous works is the cover of Madonna's 2009 retrospective anthology, *Celebration.*[9]

Is Thierry the unwitting trickster imparting wisdom to the more deliberate ones, Banksy in particular? Not necessarily. Thierry's theft and his unquenchable camera represent capitalism's devouring of art: start with something real and vital → get famous for it → commercialize it → cash in → undermine and defeat whatever change in consciousness was originally intended. What started as Banksy was anticommerce. What ended as Thierry was strictly commercial. The energies of art/play and capitalism ultimately cannot coexist.

Banksy on Thierry:

> He's kind the rightful heir to Andy Warhol, in a way. Andy Warhol made a statement by repeating famous icons until they became meaningless, but he was extremely iconic in the way that he did it. But then Thierry really made them meaningless.

Shepard Fairey:

> I do think that the whole phenomenon of Thierry's obsession with street art, becoming a street artist, a lot of suckers buying into his show, and him selling a lot of expensive art very quickly, it's—anthropologically, sociologically, it's a fascinating thing to observe, and maybe there's some things to be learned from it.

Bansky:

> I don't know what it means, Thierry's huge success and arrival in the art world. I mean, maybe Thierry was a genius

---

[9] Madonna, *Celebration*, Warner Brothers Records, 2009, CD.

all along. Maybe he got a bit lucky. Maybe it means art is a bit of a joke. . . . I don't think Thierry played by the rules, in some ways, but then, there aren't supposed to be any rules, so I don't really know what the moral is. I mean, I always used to encourage everyone I met to make art. I used to think everyone should do it. I don't really do that so much anymore.

Thierry:

> Some people, you know, might think that I'm a rabbit because I'm running around, and they think that I'm not organized. But I said, "Wait till the end of life, and you'll see if I'm a rabbit or a turtle."

Banksy, on giving Thierry full access to film him and his fellow street artists:

> "I guess Thierry showed up at a time when I realized that the reaction to this stuff was, you know, one of the most interesting things about it, because for me it's an important part of the job to run away as soon as we've done it, but at least with Thierry, we had someone hanging around afterwards who could capture some of it.[10]

## Banksy the Trickster, Graffiti and Play

"to run away as soon as we've done it." This is certainly a practical consideration, a required job skill even, for any graffiti artist who doesn't want to get caught. It also impels graffiti into the realm of play . . . the artists don't even have the spare moments to stop playing.

If one could summarize Banksy's art with one statement, it would be that it is visual satire intended to help the viewer connect the dots between commerce, war, and consumerism and how they co-opt authentic human creativity. His medium, graffiti . . . a form of disruptive play. In that sense, *Exit Through the Gift Shop*, from its title to its sleight of hand that makes it about an intuitive co-opter instead of

---

[10] *Exit through the Gift Shop*, directed by Banksy (East Melbourne, Victoria, Australia: Madman, 2010), DVD.

Banksy, continues to protect Banksy's anonymity. *If I resist the market's attempt to make me a celebrity, I can short-circuit the co-optation. Exit Through the Gift Shop* becomes a film consistent with Banksy's graffiti.

Rebels like Banksy and other street artists reassure us that the sealing off of public life by corporate interests is not complete and that real life can burst through and perforate the "Matrix" with messages of truth and resistance. Graffiti's live-and-in-person immediacy and the adventure of installing it and eliciting a public response make it attractive and vital. It revives connection, human connection on a common plane and a shared sensibility. Such appropriation of corporate logos and overall culture jamming helps to keep us free.

The internet is a less immediate and once-removed public commons. Think of it as a digital wall onto which millions are posting graffiti. It's not going away, and it is the next battlefield for our freedoms. Anonymous, the digital protest ensemble with a deliberately undefined membership—anyone can join, anyone can quit—prowls and protects. It's a space on the internet where individuals can choose to associate or not and, at times, build consensus for specific actions. Anonymous, the legion of online hacktivists, represents the discovery of the internet as an amoral soup cauldron and thus an intriguing, if not perfect, fit for the undifferentiated id-like trickster spirit. And the trickster pattern is played out when Anonymous runs into a legal challenge via Tom Cruise and Scientology. Morality rises from the soup.

## Anonymous: Prehistory

At the dawn of the twenty-first century, technology vomited out the internet, a decentralized institution that is nonetheless central. We asked, "What can go on the internet? What can you do with the internet?" The answer being "almost anything." We've come to recognize it as a virtual mirror of the world, distorted and incomplete, but certainly one that reflects and affects a lot more than anyone could have imagined in 1990 or even 2000. Just a few of the things that go on on the Web: commerce, intelligence (both the spy kind and stuff from smart people), free speech, harassment, air strikes, promotion, petition, protest, fame, theft, disgrace, games, communication, populism, relationships, and entertainment. And in a format distinctly different from the original, i.e., the written note versus the email; brick and mortar versus online shopping; the humble or arrogant or awkward ask for a date versus the screen swipe; the door-knocking and signature gathering versus the posted petition. The back-alley holdup versus identity theft. It's a black mirror of human activity.

And as a blank canvas, as a playground for folks of all stripes, the internet has hosted modern-day versions of human dramas from time immemorial. The story of Anonymous provides a rich example of how the Trickster dynamic (compulsive and dedicated boundary-crossing)[11] was replayed—specifically, how "[the Trickster, who] possesses no values, moral or social, is at the mercy of his passions and appetites, yet through his actions, all values come into being."[12] In other words, the multitude of boundaries that can be crossed, whether security to be hacked or tastes to be offended, made the internet a jackpot for those who are in it for the fun of it, to laugh out loud, *LOL*, in it for the *lulz*. One could barely have imagined a more potent arena for the Trickster, for disruptive play. This is hacker culture, which at its root, is about pranking and juvenile crime.

Hacker culture traces its origins to the Tech Model Railroad Club at MIT. It was formed in 1946 and is known for building elaborate and complex model electric train systems. It was also fertile ground for students who wanted to learn how things worked and to then

---

[11] Lewis Hyde, *Trickster Makes This World* (New York: Farrar, Straus and Giroux, 1998).

[12] Paul Radin, *The Trickster: A Study in American Indian Mythology* (New York: Schocken, 1956), xxiii–xxiv.

master them. And it was the origin, in 1959, of the motto "Information wants to be free." Here lie the first hackers, whose original public action was putting a Volkswagen bug on top of a building. This stunt and prank practice was continued by groups like the Cult of the Dead Cow (founded 1984 in Texas), who claimed to have caused Ronald Reagan's Alzheimer's disease (hoax!) and also helped the hacker group Hong Kong Blondes disrupt Chinese government websites. Another group, Lopht, founded in 1992 in Boston, used their skills to alert the public and Congress of security weaknesses and vulnerabilities in the internet. They considered themselves "gray hats," in the middle ground between the honorable and completely legal "white hat" hackers and the rebel outlaw black hats.

Like trickster Jacob stealing Esau's birthright, Bill Gates allegedly stole MS-DOS from another programmer. Steve Jobs and Steve Wozniak got tricky trying to find ways to get around paying their phone bills—their "blue boxes," which they sold, could bypass phone billing, like folks who latch on to cable TV illegally.

It is out of the ethos of this kind of mischief that early stage hackers figured out how to manipulate DDoS (distributed denial of services) attacks, whereby the attacker makes a website or other network unavailable by disrupting its connections to the internet. They usually accomplish this by flooding the target with superfluous requests in order to overload the system and prevent its intended functioning. In other words, DDoSs can make a site crash. These attacks quickly evolved from the acts of lone rogues to a collective movement.

People and information want to be free. The first phase is the glee of a prank. The second is the incipient morality that the internet should be free (a place of freedom, and sure, without cost) and uncensored, that everyone should have access to it; let's support people we like who are living under oppressive regimes, and let's attack people we don't like who are seeking to control people, freedoms, and information. The third phase can be defined as hacktivism: overt political activity in which technology assistance is used for human rights activism, usually within the purview of the law. The legal argument in defense of hacktivist actions that test the law, like DDoS, is that it is the legitimate migration of the sit-in protest from the brick and mortar to the cyber environment.

The first precedent for this, and a portent of what was to come, was set when the Electronic Disturbance Theater took down the Lufthansa Airlines website in 2001 because their planes were being used to deport immigrants from Germany. The German courts ruled that the action, accompanied by a sit-in at the company's headquarters, was a legal and legitimate form of protest and civil disobedience.

## Anonymous: History

Anonymous grew out of an unsupervised playground known as 4chan, which was the original blog, but one with no primary author; it's more accurately described as a bulletin board. An unassuming fifteen-year-old, Chris Poole, started 4Chan out of his love for Japanese anime and manga and his desire to share. An associated site, /b/, also grew out of 4chan, as its most obnoxious extension. It's a place where anything goes; horrible and wonderful stuff shows up: a cat meme with the words "I Can Has Cheezburger," viral spreading of Rick Astley videos, exposure of animal abusers, and Anonymous. Then uh oh, a hoax that Steve Jobs was dead, causing a 10 percent drop in Apple stock; an ill-intentioned hack of Trayvon Martin's email account; threats to bomb NFL games. Expression with absolutely no restrictions whatsoever. Vile, disgusting, and funny. How did the site get that way? Well, the object of the /b/ game is for your thread to stay up longer by attracting comments. Thus, there was a movement towards the grotesque, the sensational and the sensationally untrue, and the cultivation of the meme—a picture plus caption shorthand that is alternately funny, gross, insulting, or poignant—anything sure to draw fire or hee-haws.[13]

From there it was just a short leap to /trolls/, folks bent on making someone else as pissed off as possible . . . just for the *lulz*. And this all incorporates the Trickster archetype, a character who is in it for the laughs and whose pranks can fall on either side of the moral equation. It is as likely to be mean or stupid as it is to be just. And Anonymous, if one can make any generalizations, is strictly anticelebrity. Its network is set up to sustain anonymity, and narcissistic fame-seeking is immediately crushed. This ethos also grants Anonymous access to the shape-shifting world of the trickster.[14]

Anonymous got a first-hand dose of trickster alchemy in 2006. Values and morality emerged amongst the hacktivists as they battled Scientology.

At first, Anonymous "possesses no values, moral or social, is at the mercy of [their] passions and appetites."[15] This is a pithy and pretty accurate description of 4chan's amoral playground. But the fact that Anonymous and 4channers will fight back, fight for their right to say whatever they want, initiates the process that awakens values.

Right-wing and racist radio talk show host Hal Turner, who webcast his show from his home, stepped into the role of antagonist. In late 2006 and on into '07, Turner picked a fight with a 4channer, so the Anonymous legion coordinated DDoS attacks that shut down his site and cost him thousands of dollars. They had heavy industrial materials ordered and delivered to his home on large pallets. They procured escorts off Craigslist in his name. They publicized private and personal information about him. They ordered hundreds of pizzas and had them delivered to his home. Eventually, they destroyed his ability

---

[13] Check it out, just Google "famous memes."

[14] Gabriella Coleman, *Hacker, Hoaxer, Whistleblower, Spy: The Many Faces of Anonymous* (New York: Verso, 2015), 47-50.

[15] Adapted from Paul Radin, *The Trickster*, xxiii-xxiv.

to pay for his radio show, and he went off the air. Anonymous had flexed its muscles and discovered what they were capable of if they organized against a common target. The fact that he fought back with verbal slander and racist epithets only made his takedown more fun.

And it got a bit more interesting, as the hacking into Turner's private information revealed that he was an FBI informant. By making that fact more widely known, Turner lost his credibility as a white supremacist. And then he was convicted of threatening to kill three judges of the US Court of Appeals for the Seventh Circuit.

Despite those who wanted to maintain it as a nihilist, and often nasty, playground, this fable births the idea of Anonymous NOT as amoral but as an activist/hacktivist nation that can do good with a social justice agenda. What happened next was on an even grander scale.

In January 2008, the famous actor and Scientologist Tom Cruise put out a video on his Scientology beliefs. The monologue was intended to stay within the secretive and closed boundaries of true believer Scientologists, but it unintentionally leaked and was distributed widely by Gawker, Radar, and others. NBC was going to broadcast it but backed down. Scientology, known for their aggressive corps of lawyers hired to protect their secrecy and security, threatened various hackers and re-posters. They were very good at it, and the postings seemed to come down as fast as they went up. But the news site Gawker refused to take the video down. Anonymous entered the fray.

What Scientology considered blasphemy of their sacred rights—secrecy and control—was confronted as a blasphemy of rights sacred to Anonymous: openness and absence of control. Thus did a moral principle arise from the playground. The website Gawker refused to take the Cruise video down and entered into a free speech battle with Scientology.[16]

---

[16] In 2016, Hulk Hogan, aka Terry Bollea, won a $140 million lawsuit against Gawker for posting portions of a sex tape with him and Heather Clem, the wife of radio personality Bubba the Love Sponge. The lawsuit put Gawker out of business. It was financed by tech billionaire Peter Thiel, allegedly motivated by Gawker outing (and supporting) him as gay.

Scientology represents an almost cosmic opposite, a cultural inversion of Anonymous, and as such a foil, serves to define the Anonymous values:[17]

| SCIENTOLOGY | ANONYMOUS |
| --- | --- |
| Is based on a science fiction novel | Is based on science |
| Restricts playfulness and fun, though not always | Is playful and fun, but not always |
| Aggressively protects its intellectual property and asserts proprietary status | Believes information wants to be free and attacks claims to proprietary status |
| Requires obedience to a hierarchical order | Thrives on discourses about freedom |
| Uses technology to protect its insularity | Uses technology to break down barriers and expose secrets |
| Is based on secrecy and exclusivity | Is based on openness and inclusivity |

Besides making attempts throughout their network to post the Cruise video, Anon's jammed Scientology's 1-800 number and also deployed the pizza tactic. Another popular weapon was the Low Orbit Ion Cannon (its name taken from the video game *Red Alert*). The LOIC empowered individuals to enact a DDoS attack. Once loaded onto a computer and aimed at a site, it goes to that website and hits the refresh button hundreds of times every minute, thus crashing the site.

The antics of a few sites to post the Cruise video antagonized the Scientology lawyers, whose actions in turn created a viral phenomenon and energized Anonymous's struggle to get the video out, really

---

[17] This is perhaps comparable to how World War I provided much the same crucible to dada, or the Vietnam War to the hippies. Comparison is adapted from *Hacker, Hoaxer, Whistleblower, Spy: The Many Faces of Anonymous*, by Gabriella Coleman (New York: Verso, 2015).

just to piss off the Scientologists. Besides threatening to and eventually taking legal action, Scientology made online accusations and accountings that cast themselves as victims. As the debate raged, many Anons came to understand that Scientology offended values that they'd not realized they had, or at least hadn't thought about before. The censorship aspect especially struck them to their core.

The climactic effect, the transformative part of this episode, was that the war with Scientology got thousands of Anons out of their homes and away from their screens as they took their attack to the next level and organized protests around the world. From Australia to Israel to England to the US, Anons donned their Guy Fawkes masks and protested for real in front of Scientology offices/churches. People who had only known each other online were meeting in person for the first time, bringing new life to their online community and the fun of discovering real people behind those online conversations. These folks had built up voluminous common references via 4chan . . . so they had a lot to talk about. The event probably accelerated the love lives of a number of Anons. Also, these Anon-nerds included more women than one might have thought. No doubt the Scientology episode signaled a sea change.

And this sudden attack of morality drew a strong and expected reaction from the amoral trolls. These nascent crusaders— those who want to use Anonymous as a force for good—were name-called "white knights" and "moralfags." Trolls further reacted, for example, by hacking into a website for epileptics and creating a strobe effect that could induce seizure, a tactic that prompted some arrests and persists to this day. This contrasted strikingly with the emerging social justice and freedom of expression initiative, dividing the Anonymous crowd.

### Anonymous? WikiLeaks.

WikiLeaks was founded by an Australian hacker, Julian Assange, in 2006. But it did not garner much notice until 2010, when it provoked a major morality debate that grew and continues to this day. In April 2010, they released *Collateral Murder*, gunsight footage from a 2007 American airstrike in Baghdad where Iraqi journalists, civilians, and children were among those killed. In July, they released almost 77,000 documents related to the war in Afghanistan. In October, close to 400,000 documents pertaining to the Iraq War that mapped over 109,000 war dead, including 15,000 previously unreported fatalities. In November, in redacted form, US State Department cables. Then in April 2011, over 700 secret documents related to detained prisoners in Guantanamo Bay. These kinds of activities were not the kind of spontaneous trickster pranks pulled for the *lulz*, and they brought WikiLeaks significant attention and controversy.[18]

While vilified by some as wrong and unethical, WikiLeaks' own story positions themselves as a highly moral organization. "Information wants to be free" could be their somber motto, too, and their stated commitment is to get the truth to the public through the publication of original source material. Like 4chan and Anonymous, they make their stand on the nonnegotiability of the constitutional right to free speech. In 2010, Assange stated:

> [It is] not an ultimate freedom, however free speech is what regulates government and regulates law. That is why in the US Constitution the Bill of Rights says that Congress is to make no such law abridging the freedom of the press. It is to take the rights of the press outside the rights of the law because those rights are superior to the law because in fact they create the law. Every constitution, every bit of legislation is derived from the flow of information. Similarly, every government is elected as a result of people understanding things.[19]

---

[18] Due to some carelessness on her part, it also led to the arrest of the primary leaker, Chelsea Manning. In July 2013 she was convicted of violating the Espionage Act.

[19] Julian Assange, interview by Stephen Colbert, *The Colbert Report*, Comedy Central, April 12, 2010.

After VISA, MasterCard, and PayPal restricted WikiLeaks by suspending payment of donations, Anonymous initiated a DDoS campaign and shut MasterCard and PayPal down. Having a trove of pranks at your disposal means being able to fight back. Did Anonymous take a moral stand in support of WikiLeaks, or was it more a matter of taking a stand in support of anyone's freedom of speech? Or was it simply a fabulous opportunity to play—to do some really big pranking and mischief?

By January 2011, that question was answered. OpTunisia was an Anonymous initiative to support the Tunisian Jasmine Revolution, civil resistance and demonstrations that led to the ousting of President Zine Al Abidine Ben Ali. Anonymous played a critical role, keeping the internet up during the uprising and building solidarity with the people's movement.

In Egypt, Anonymous helped to disseminate information during the Arab Spring of that year. The Egyptian government tried to shut down the internet completely; Anonymous shared means and methods of going around them and turning it back on. And Anonymous shut down Egypt's government websites.

WikiLeaks reintroduced moral ambiguity into the arena. In September 2011, they released over a quarter million unredacted cables of diplomacy analysis that had been sent to the US State Department between 1966 and 2010. The reason for their actions is unclear. Was it carelessness? Or because critics were developing the argument and legal case for how people could get hurt or diplomatic projects compromised? Or was it because they might have already broken a law? Or because WikiLeaks' own security had been compromised, and they feared the collapse of their organization.

This huge release of information provoked the FBI to assume a link between Anonymous and WikiLeaks, and they started going after Anonymous hacktivists.

Chaos within the chaos-makers provided an opening for an entrepreneurial security firm, HBGary Federal, to come forward. They claimed to have infiltrated WikiLeaks and conceived a strategy to discredit them. Comedian Stephen Colbert likened their efforts to sticking your penis into a hornet's nest, and in fact, HBGary was virtually and promptly disposed of by Anonymous.

The devastating attack—Anonymous hacked HBGary's emails, deleted files and backups, gained access to CEO Aaron Barr's social media accounts and spread true and untrue stuff around, and allegedly wiped data from Barr's iPhone and iPad—changed Anonymous as dramatically as OpTunisia did. Occurring within two months of each other, these two events were formative for the collective. "OpTunisia is where it [Anonymous]got its moral compass and its sense that it could affect the world. HBGary is where it got its swagger."[20]

## The Rise of the Chaotic Actor: White Hat, Gray Hat, Black Hat

The Sony hack a couple of years later, though it's hacker is still unidentified (North Korea? Anonymous? The "GOP"/Guardians of Peace?), demonstrated just how much chaos hacktivism could wreak. To add to it, one hacker, Hector Monsegur, aka Sabu, managed to be a fifteen-minute hero among Anonymous in 2012 when he helped to found LulzSec, ran the hack of the Brazilian government, but then turned informant and led the FBI to eight hacktivist colleagues.

And we clearly see values emerging in Anonymous. They seized the rights of free expression and direct protest in the streets in reaction to a government bent on surveillance, rife with corruption, and constantly tempted to oppress and control its citizens.

LulzSec turned the volume up on Anonymous. It was a split-off "black hat" group that claimed to be the Final Boss of the internet and stood for freedom of speech and the end of censorship. They were rough tough outlaws, hooked on the thrill of transgression.

---

[20] Quinn Norton of *Wired* magazine, quoted in the Brain Knappenberger documentary film *We Are Legion: The Story of the Hacktivists* (Los Angeles, CA: Luminant Media, 2012).

THEY claimed to have done the Sony hack! And to have taken the CIA website down.

LulzSec was a group, mostly from Anonymous . . . *no rules, we're just going to make trouble; we play.* They tried to distance themselves from Anonymous, but folks weren't buying it. LulzSec's more militant approach created a lot of debate and infighting in Anonymous about morality and bombastic lawbreaking. Ultimately, LulzSec announced a "fifty days of lulz" rampage, hacking into government, corporate, and media websites: US banks, the US Senate, the CIA, and Arizona police departments were among their targets.

They simultaneously announced that it was a final act, stating "Our crew of six wishes you a happy 2011. So with those last thoughts, it's time to say *bon voyage*. . . . We hope, wish, even beg, that the movement manifests itself into a revolution that can continue on without us."[21]

Yet then a LulzSec hoax stating that Fox News' Rupert Murdoch was dead followed their self-demise. Ha!

In conclusion, it's fair to say that Anonymous in many ways is a major trickster character in the cyber-landscape of the twenty-first century. "You're never quite sure if Anonymous is the hero or anti-hero. The trickster is attracted to change and the need for change, and that's where Anonymous goes. But they are not your personal army—that's Rule 44—yes, there are rules. And when they do something, it never goes quite as planned. The internet has no neat endings.[22]"

What makes Anonymous weighty and complex is that the broader societal response and reaction to them forms its own mirror of chaos and ambiguity. On the one hand, security and software firms secretly applaud Anonymous's exposure of cyber security threats because it

---

[21] There are a few versions of this press release, with the original on a file-sharing site to which the author did not have access. This version is taken from the site Island Info.mu [Mauritius], "Lulzec Hacking Group Announces End to Cyber Attacks," (website), Island Info, accessed May 11, 2018, http://www.islandinfo.mu/mauritius-tomorows-world/lulzsec-hacking-group-announces-end-to-cyber-attacks-846

[22] Quinn Norton, "Anonymous 101: Introduction to the Lulz," *Wired*, November 8, 2011, archived from the original on May 5, 2013.

helps them design better safeguards. Then again, Anonymous has been considered a national security threat by the National Security Agency (NSA), given their assessed potential to take down parts of the power grid. In other ways, they have changed the face of protesting, successfully likening DDoS attacks, for example, to civil disobedience sit-ins. Anonymous is lauded for attacking child porn sites on the one hand but criticized for being vigilantes and taking the law into their own hands, when such sites should be exposed, their hosts arrested, and prosecuted by the proper authorities.

Is the internet a legitimate venue for protest and pranking, for a virtual "sit in" where hackers launch a DDoS attack or otherwise jam a site or take it down? Is this a logical consequence of pioneers like Bill Gates's theft of MS-DOS and Steve Jobs's phone company hacking and going around the law? Perhaps it is in the same way that shoplifting and bank robbing is appropriated as a revolutionary act by those acting on the belief that all property is theft and intellectual property is still property.

Some argue that Anonymous is a censoring organization purporting to be champions of free speech. This irony was writ large during the protests against the Stop Online Piracy Act in 2012. SOPA would expand the ability of U.S. law enforcement to combat online copyright infringement and online trafficking in counterfeit goods. It would allow court orders that bar sites from conducting business with infringing websites and web search engines from linking to such sites. And it would allow court orders requiring internet service providers to block access to infringing websites. SOPA would have expanded existing criminal laws to include unauthorized streaming of copyrighted content, imposing a maximum penalty of five years in prison.

Resistance was huge. More than eight million people contacted their congressional representatives and more than three million emailed them. A hundred and fifteen thousand sites shut themselves down in protest of what they perceived as an infringement on their freedom of speech.

Congress backed down.

Some perceive the actions of Anonymous and many other protesting organizations to be cyber-bullying. Do Anons exercise of their freedom of speech limit someone else's, i.e., when they take a site down? To put it all in perspective, we must note that the actions of Anonymous are tiny in comparison to the practices of the governments of Iran, Russia, and the US.

Trickster "possesses no values, moral or social, is at the mercy of his passions and appetites, yet through his actions, all values come into being."[23] We see this trait played out by a body of folks—can a group of thousands of human beings with a single face BE a trickster god come to life?

When asked if Anonymous had been a force for good, Forbes journalist Parmy Olson replied:

> In some cases, yes, I think it has in terms of some of the stuff they did in the Middle East supporting the pro-democracy demonstrators. But a lot of bad things too, unnecessarily harassing people—I would class that as a bad thing. DDOSing the CIA website, stealing customer data and posting it online just for shits and giggles is not a good thing.[24]

So many questions remain unanswered, and there is some discomfort in speculating how the history of Anonymous, WikiLeaks, and hacktivism will eventually be written.

Anonymous raises questions of morality versus amorality. The Yes Men, a cadre of brilliant twenty-first-century pranksters, are on an

---

[23] Adapted from Paul Radin, *The Trickster*, xxiii-xxiv.

[24] Luke Allnut, "Parmy Olson on Anonymous: 'A Growing Phenomenon That We Don't Yet Understand'," Radio Free Europe/Radio Liberty, June 8, 2012, https://www.rferl.org/a/parmy-olson-on-anonymous-a-growing-phenomenon-that-we-dont-yet-understand/24607895.html.

unabashed moral mission. They enter the fray with a defined political agenda, and while the impact of their pranks can be unpredictable, they're clearly driven by some of the same utopian, pacifist optimism that inspired the dadas and the hippies—they make political hay through absurdity, highlighting the comedy and tragedy of human suffering, political shenanigans and environmental destruction.

## The Yes Men: Back to the Future

The Yes Men and their romp, though kin to the means and ends of Anonymous, differ in many ways, two of them crucial. First, the denizens of Anonymous are characterized as living their lives online. But they come out to the streets when the situation demands action corollary to their activities on the internet playground. The Yes Men made use of websites and online presence to initiate, promote, and sustain their hoaxes, but the internet was a tool to facilitate their main activities, which were in-person actions that in turn attracted significant media attention.

Jacques Servin and Igor Vamos are known by many aliases, but they are Andy Bichlbaum and Mike Bonanno when they are the Yes Men.

The Yes Men follow in dada's footsteps. dada is an obvious link; it came together as an antiwar movement that exposed the horror of World War I. Both movements sought to use absurdity to expose the absurdity of what was being sold as rational. Whenever their hoax was exposed, Bichlbaum would make just exactly that point. And as dada invented the fake news prank as a means of getting to the truth, so follows the Yes Men's motto: "Lies can expose truth." And there is a clear reverence for and inspiration from the disruptive play that Abbie Hoffman and the Yippies and other practitioners of guerilla theater so successfully performed. The movements connect through the use of tactics to embarrass and proclaim the sins of those who would wage unjust wars, destroy the environment, or cause the suffering and death of other people.

The Yes Men demonstrate a fuller completion of the Trickster cycle. They have a sure-footed set of values. To build a mass movement and connect folks who want to continue in their footsteps, they put this notice on one of their websites, yeslab.org: "The Yes Lab is devoted to helping progressive organizations and activists carry out media-getting creative actions around well-considered goals." And while there are stupendous out-loud laughs to be had as we witness and join in their antics, and while the Yes Men raise very provocative questions of morality and ethics, that they operate from a defined moral compass is inarguable.

For Anonymous—whose numbers are far greater than the Yes Men collective—to reach that place of values and a reasonably stable political agenda based on those values, may take longer . . . or maybe forever.

## The Yes Men: Action!

The rise and subsidence of Bichlbaum's and Bonanno's heyday is documented in three films: *The Yes Men* (2003), *The Yes Men Fix the World* (2009), and *The Yes Men Are Revolting* (2014).[25] All the films showcase their theatrical and playful approach to what they call "identity correction," which they achieve by their primary tactic of impersonating entities they have judged to be harmful to the world. The three films trace the arc of a couple of very funny activists who develop their knack for powerful guerilla theater; find their groove and pull off their most dazzling capers; and discover that the work and stress of disruptive play can take its toll, and that they can carry on for only so long.

"What we do is pass ourselves off as representatives of big corporations we don't like. We make fake websites and wait for people to

---

[25] *The Yes Men*, directed by Andy Bichlbaum and Mike Bonanno (Beverly Hills, CA: MGM Studios, 2003), film

*The Yes Men Fix the World*, directed by Andy Bichlbaum and Mike Bonanno (New York: Cinetic Media, 2009), film.

*The Yes Men Are Revolting*, directed by Andy Bichlbaum and Mike Bonanno (New York: The Orchard, 2014), film.

accidentally invite us to conferences."[26] One of the most successful of these ploys was directed at The Dow Chemical Company after their 2001 purchase of the Union Carbide Corporation. In 1984, the negligent operation of a Union Carbide pesticide plant in Bhopal, India, caused an explosion that killed at least 3,800 people immediately, and at least 14,000 more soon thereafter. Half a million people were exposed to the gas, which caused many birth and health defects. The $470 million settlement with the Indian government awarded an average of $2,200 to each family of those killed.

The Yes Men take horrid absurdities like this and present them as art, humor, and crime.

As the twentieth anniversary of the Bhopal disaster approached, the Yes Men put up a fake website purporting to be that of Dow Chemical. While they initially mimicked Dow's disclaimer of any responsibility to do anything further to repair the damages or make amends to the victims (true), they then reversed their tactic and sought to make amends and reparations (false). The fake website had attracted the attention of the planners of a bankers' conference in London, and through the site, fake Dow Chemical was invited to speak.

Posing as a vice president (using the alias of Jude Finisterra), Bichlbaum addressed the conference and announced that they, Dow Chemical, would accept responsibility for the disaster. They would sell off Union Carbide for $12 billion and use the money to clean up the toxic site, provide the people of Bhopal with medical care, and fund research into the hazards of other Dow Chemical products. Shortly thereafter, Bichlbaum/Finisterra did an interview sharing that announcement with BBC News and three hundred million listeners. For the short time that the news media bought the hoax and spread the news, Dow Chemical's stock lost $2 billion in value, dropping over 4 percent in less than a half hour.

---

[26] *The Yes Men Fix the World*, directed by Andy Bichlbaum and Mike Bonanno (New York: Cinetic Media, 2009), film.

Why the big stock sell-off? Investors knew that in a case where a corporation behaves altruistically but not profitably, they will be punished.

Finisterra was near tears as he announced that this was the first time any company of this size had taken responsibility for damages on this scale and channeled their profits to make it right. Of course, he was lying. But it is worth noting that Dow had claimed that they would make reparations for any wrongs that they had inherited in the deal when they acquired Union Carbide.

When confronted in a subsequent BBC Channel 4 interview, Bichlbaum defended their actions, saying, "I wouldn't say it's a hoax. It's an honest representation of what Dow should be doing." For a short while, the Yes Men were on a big hit on Google, famous for a moment.

Aghast at how actuaries factor into what it costs for a corporation to kill people in the path of their version of progress, the Yes Men lied to rescue a bigger truth. In the aftermath of this first hoax, Bichlbaum, still posing as a Dow Chemical executive—this one is named Erastus Hamm—took absurdity to a new level by addressing another conference a few months later with Bonanno and a gold-painted skeleton, Gilda, as a prop. "The only good skeleton is a gold skeleton" he proclaimed. Then the Yes Men demonstrated the Acceptable Risk Calculator. The premise of the calculator was that if people die due to corporate actions, what is the formula by which their deaths can be afforded? A slick PowerPoint presentation demonstrated how an American life is worth more in dollars and cents than one from India.

The media tried to impose shame via *their* version of morality on the Yes Men: *Do you realize that Dow Chemical's stock lost 3 percent in the wake of your hoax? The real problem is that you raised the hopes of these people in Bhopal on the twentieth anniversary of their tragedy, only for them to learn that it was a prank.*

To put it context, the Yes Men gave them two hours of false hope, but Dow had given them twenty years of suffering. And through the hoax, millions learned that Union Carbide and Dow never cleaned up the Bhopal mess.

Over a million people live in Bhopal. So the Yes Men went there to see the effects of their alleged cruelty. In fact, they were hailed as heroes for casting more light on the tragedy. During their visit, they learned that the exposure to the conditions in Bhopal via the hoax, twenty years on, are greatly appreciated by the people there. Thus, on balance, the prank falls on the side of moral good.

And their hoax technique shifted. Posing as a public relations firm, the Yes Men pretended to offer Lee Raymond, the former CEO of ExxonMobil who went on to become the chair of the National Petroleum Council, as a keynote speaker at the 2007 Gas and Oil Exposition (GO-EXPO) in Calgary, Alberta, Canada. The strategy played out that at the last minute, Mr. Raymond was unable to attend, and Bichlbaum, now posing as Shepard Wolff, was another executive from ExxonMobil sent to speak on Raymond's behalf.

Wolff's speech focused on a new biofuel called vivoleum, something we will turn to as petroleum supplies run short. As Bichlbaum/ Wolff was speaking, candles were passed out to the attendees and lit, but they gave off an unsavory odor.

Then Bichlbaum and Bonanno showed a human-interest video they had prepared of a janitor (comedian Reggie Watt posing as such) dying from the effects of climate change and fossil fuels. At the end of the film, with all of the candles in the room lit to memorialize the dead janitor, the audience learned that he had donated his corpse to the research that produced the new biofuel vivoleum, from which the candles are made. Why even though this man died to make the product possible . . . the speech was interrupted, and the Yes Men and their camera crew were thrown off the stage, to scattered applause. Andy was exposed as an imposter and escorted out. The cameras were shut down.

They posed as undersecretaries of the US Department of Housing and Urban Development and went to the Gulf Coast Reconstruction Conference in the aftermath of Hurricane Katrina. Using the same tactic, they promised the HUD Secretary Alphonso Jackson, but then at the last minute, said he couldn't make it. But Ray Nagin, the mayor of New Orleans, when he heard that Secretary Jackson was coming, decided to attend. Likewise, Governor Kathleen Blanco decided that she'd come as well. Their hoax was perhaps working too well, and in the film documenting the event *(The Yes Men Fix the World)*, we see the stress and nervousness of Bichlbaum and Bonanno heighten.

But Bichlbaum got in front of the lectern and announced that HUD is going to work differently. They were no longer going to tear down projects and replace them with mixed-income flats that the original residents cannot afford. They declared that they were going to reopen all of the projects, and they got great applause. They also announced that Exxon and Shell would contribute portions of their $60 billion in profits to restore the wetlands. In fact, Exxon would kick in $8.6 billion.

They invited the audience to a ribbon-cutting at the to-be-reopened Lafitte Projects. People cheer.

The unmasking happened quicker than planned because the governor and mayor were there, and they knew that such a thing would not be announced without their foreknowledge. A reporter doing some quick fact-checking revealed the hoax. The mayor was trying to keep the fake announcement off the news. But the reporter gave Bichlbaum a mic.

*Reporter.* You just pulled off a heck of a hoax.

*Bichlbaum.* I would say that HUD is pulling off the hoax by pretending that tearing down affordable housing is what's going to solve it. I mean that's what they've been doing until now. This is a time when all of these people are clamoring to get back in; they want to get back into their housing, and they deserve to be there. It's crazy.

*Reporter.*   And worth lying to all these people…?

*Bichlbaum.*   Oh absolutely, and actually truth-telling. This is actually truth-telling where normally there would only be lies.

They went through with the ribbon-cutting at the Lafitte Projects and invited contractors to come talk about how to make these projects livable and for people to move back into them. As with the Bhopal escapade, the media played the angle that the Yes Men were giving people false hope, that it was a cruel hoax that preyed upon the displaced tenants' fears and anxieties. But a Lafitte resident spoke up:

> I think what you guys exposed is the fact HUD could do these great things if they wanted to. Secondly, you got the attention of residents, so now they gotta begin to ask "well why AREN'T you doing these things," and number three, you are creating a controversy to feed off, to organize, and to build a struggle to the next level. So in my opinion, everything that you all did was excellent.[27]

Finally, the Yes Men realized that while their messages were reaching millions, the number of messengers was small. In their words, they'd "made a splash, but…hadn't fixed the world. The free market was still destroying New Orleans. Climate change kept getting worse, people were still losing their homes, and in Bhopal, people were still suffering."[28]

So they went for the largest audience in a different medium, the newspaper. They put out a hundred thousand copies of a fake *New York Times* [All the News We Hope to Print]. It was dated six months in the future (published in January 2009 but dated July) with headlines like:

## IRAQ WAR ENDS: TROOPS TO RETURN IMMEDIATELY

---

[27] *The Yes Men Fix the World*, directed by Andy Bichlbaum and Mike Bonanno (New York: Cinetic Media, 2009), film.

[28] *The Yes Men Fix the World*, 2009.

## NATION SETS ITS SIGHTS ON BUILDING SANE ECONOMY: TRUE COST TAX, SALARY CAPS, TRUST-BUSTING

## ALL PUBLIC UNIVERSITIES TO BE FREE

## PENTAGON ENDS SECRET BUDGET

## NATIONALIZED OIL TO FUND CLIMATE CHANGE EFFORTS

## MAXIMUM WAGE LAW SUCCEEDS: SALARY CAPS WILL HELP STABILIZE ECONOMY

## USA PATRIOT ACT REPEALED

## UNITED NATIONS UNANIMOUSLY PASSES WEAPONS BAN

## COURT INDICTS BUSH ON HIGH TREASON CHARGE

Somewhat inspired by the election of Barack Obama, it was distributed as a free special issue of the *New York Times*. Like the dadas, the Yes Men exposed the absurdities of reality and faked a preferable one.

In interviews with "thought leaders" of right-wing think tanks, the Yes Men paint a picture of such leaders' guiding principles: free markets, private property, rule of law, unfettered capitalism, markets unrestricted by government regulation and control, and wealth leads to all good things.

These think tanks work against the demonizing of companies and free market system. At one point, they brag that it is through their efforts that the US did not sign on to the 1997 Kyoto Protocol (to fight global warming) that went into effect in 2005.

That the Bhopal disaster was an unfortunate tragedy on the road to progress, one wonk is quoted as saying "There are always risks of going into the future." That kind of greed dressed up as progress brought us Katrina, the biggest disaster in US history, and countless other tragedies.

Poorly regulated markets and industries made the problem. The Yes Men, playing around as funny tricksters, revealed not so funny consequences of free enterprise run amok. Their position is that the market needs to step up and manage the reconstruction of New Orleans and of Bhopal, and their pranks aim to embarrass publicly the offenders in order to get them to respond.

The Yes Men's escapades include more: exposing the destruction wreaked by subprime mortgages, the coal industry; and global warming. At a conference exhibit hall in the aftermath of Katrina, entrepreneurs featured products like portable bathrooms, bomb detonators, drones, security doors, and fences. The only exhibit with wares meant to help Hurricane Katrina's victims were yurts from Kyrgyzstan, but no one at the conference showed any interest in them.

The Yes Men are inspired by this new layer of idiocy. From the scary (Gilda the gold skeleton) to the gross (Reggie the dead janitor made into candles), the Yes Men peak with the ridiculous. They designed the ultimate disaster technology, something only the richest businessmen could afford: The SurvivaBall!

Posing as executives from Halliburton, the Yes Man attended a catastrophic loss conference and presented the SurvivaBall, something that can save a human being in any catastrophe. It's hard to describe in words, but it's this oversized inflatable suit that protects its wearer. SurvivaBalls can also connect to each other and form a larger organism.

Their presentation attracted interest from a company that is anticipating terrorism. It's all so absurd, yet folks took the ridiculousness seriously.

This piece of theater demonstrated how disaster is exploited by entrepreneurs, with things that before Katrina you couldn't get away with, like privatizing public schools and public housing. But in the aftermath of a disaster like Katrina, you can sell it in the midst of the chaos and confusion. It's free market kool-aid drunk by the government itself, a self-hating government that aids the private sector, not its citizens.

Banksy, the Yes Men, Anonymous . . . subversives, tricksters, and influential disruptive players. In a feat that combines the Yes Men's activism with Banksy's clever subversion, a group of environmental activists painted dotted lines and scissors on dams stopping up the Snake River and other threatened salmon runs.[29]

It's not just happenstance that the Romans, Greeks, and medievals had many festivals, overtly for sacrifice to their gods but also to have a social function of play and a relaxing of rules they intuitively knew were binding human nature. With the advent of Catholicism, we saw Mardis Gras and Rio Carnival as similar times of release. In the next chapter, two more recent expressions of play, release, and celebration—the Fremont Solstice Parade and Burning Man—bring to the present time a more ancient yet less fettered communal expression of play. We explore alongside those disruptive players who envision and build a proactive Play Society. No matter how transient, it's a dream of a Play Society that may yet materialize.

---

[29] DamNation, directed by Ben Knight and Travis Rummel (Patagonia, 2014), film.

# FOURTEEN

# The Fremont Solstice Parade

*At noon of Sunday, July 6th, the fiesta exploded.*
*There is no other way to describe it. . . . It kept up*
*day and night for seven days. The dancing kept up,*
*the drinking kept up, the noise went on. The things*
*that happened could only have happened during a*
*fiesta. Everything became quite unreal finally and it*
*seemed as though nothing could have any conse-*
*quences. It seemed out of place to think of conse-*
*quences during the fiesta. All during the fiesta you*
*had the feeling, even when it was quiet, that you*
*had to shout any remark to make it heard. It was*
*the same feelings about any action. It was a fiesta*
*and it went on for seven days.*

*Ernest Hemingway*[1]

HAVING CONNECTED some dots not previously so joined, we now move from the individual and the subversive to the collective and proactive happenings that foreshadow the Play Society. Such traditions are as old as tribal society,[2] and as contemporary as Burning Man.

Endearing and lovable Trickster characters like Wakdjunkaga, Marcel Duchamp, Raven, Groucho Marx, Andy Kaufman or Bugs

---

[1] Ernest Hemingway, *Fiesta: The Sun Also Rises* (London: Vintage, 1927), 132, 134.

[2] Barbara Ehrenreich, *Dancing in the Streets: A History of Collective Joy* (New York: Metropolitan, 2006).

Bunny . . . are they in any way models for mass movements and whole communities to embrace and express their own trickster characteristics, their own playfulness, to realize the Play Society? Can fantastic individual rascals who challenge power, characters from the fantasies of fairy tales and cartoons, inspire the idea of something "larger than ourselves," a community committed to playfulness and celebration? How do myths, fiction, art, and lone warriors of play affect power, ranking, and fighting when extrapolated to a group experience, a collectively lived sense of playfulness? Could there be such a thing as disruptive play on a mass scale, passionate players storming a mainstream culture intent on protecting its interests in ranking, competition, profit, and order?

The complete takeover of a city by celebration teases out the political possibility, a presentiment of the Play Society. Tracing its origins to the Greek and Roman festival rites of spring, Rio Carnival in Brazil is play's largest Western celebration, rivaled by the New Orleans Mardis Gras, with Catholic Lent rituals immutably grafted onto them both. These are opportunities for the general population to get their playfulness and vices on and out of their systems before entering the deprivations of Lent, or at least getting back to work.

Inching a tad closer to reality than a Sunday night cartoon, the Fremont Solstice Parade is what you get when a community of players carve out a little piece of time and space for collective play en masse. You get a parade; you get a version of Carnival, of Mardis Gras.

Drawing on such inspiration, a solstice parade originated in Santa Barbara, California, and was imported to the Fremont neighborhood of Seattle with great success in the 1980s. Hewing to three basic rules—no words or recognizable logos, no cars, no animals—the Fremont Solstice Parade is an explosion of art and play, a tangible sampling of a functional Play Society. It stands as an island of noncommercial celebration in a sea of branded experiences. While many participants celebrate play, music, art, dance, humor, nudity, and the like, folks like Peter Toms also take the opportunity to denude real estate development, corporatism, profiteering, and the commercialism that bedevil us with a more alienated imitation of authentic play.

The staging of celebration art gradually moves a culture in a playful direction. The Fremont Solstice Parade has had its one day of turning Seattle upside down for over twenty years. It is an institution in terms of its longevity, but anti-institutional in the sense that the communal effort and the art changes with the times. It is play.

## The Fremont Solstice Parade

Everybody loves a parade. It is perhaps the most benign human celebration, It welcomes all comers, and it is, with the exception of military parades, an invitation to play.

But the Fremont Solstice Parade, held every June, is a dangerous affair.

Dangerous because it is so boldly harmless—no damage to the environment, no products marketed or sold, no official politics endorsed, no money exchanged . . . just lots of noise, color, dancing, music, laughter, skin, costume, makeup, singing, and play.

Dangerous because the Fremont Arts Council has sustained, insinuated, and institutionalized durable opportunities for more adults to play, for artists to weave their craft into a playful setting, and for play to gain a greater foothold in a thriving urban community.

Dangerous because how much fun we Westerners are supposed to have in life has never been very clear, and the Fremont Solstice Parade annually tests that limit.

Dangerous because in the Play Society, we get to have a whole lot more fun than we're having now.

About an hour before the 1999 parade is to begin, a bearded man looking like Allen Ginsberg's twin runs down the parade course in his orange kilt, orange and purple scarves, with various percussion instruments fastened to his body. A woman hawks her petition to put the new light rail system underground. A roller-blading videographer cruises by. The soundtrack to all this merriment is a steel drum band playing familiar tunes.

Parade monitors wear felt hats shaped like stars, another woman is in a sunshade umbrella hat. Miming clowns in rainbow wigs are golfing on the asphalt, gushing with the spirit of Wavy Gravy.

The participant-spectator dynamic is called into question. As the energy of this joyful chaos builds, so does a mild anxiety among the crowd of onlookers just a little less secure with their normal patterns. More clowns appear, mocking the tourists who have come to watch the freaks. The whole crowd, local or not, are tourist-like in their observer role. The clowns proffer maps and cameras and ask questions of how to get from here to there. They have their own children-clowns in tow. They photograph the audience.[3]

Bounce, encounter, engage, move on, bounce, encounter, and engage. The rhythms of play, mildly infected by the language of culture and jokes, bubbled up in as close a connection to the child as we are likely to see. And the parade hasn't even begun.

There had been a huge debate that year over the nude bicyclists. Traditionally, they would pedal the course, genitalia flapping and flopping, igniting the crowd's energy before the parade "proper" began. To quote an emailed plea to the Fremont Arts Council members:

> I urge you to return the Solstice Parade and Fair to its original intent and that which has made it successful and set it apart from the ordinary. Keep it free spirited, keep alive the "live and let live" attitude. Trying to prohibit the nude bicycle riders is symbolic of the negative change, of the fact that the Council has strayed from its own mission as a widely inclusive and wildly enthusiastic group. To urge the City Attorney's office to prosecute, to seek people who

---

[3] It hearkens back to the hippie pranks, when Gray Line ran a tourist bus through the Haight-Ashbury, and the hippies would come out with cameras and photograph the gawking straights. We're all playing roles, and it's initially discomfiting, eventually liberating, to be reminded of that.

will testify that they were offended, or to adopt parade rules prohibiting these riders only degrades the organization and community. We have thrived until recently on our diversity of life styles and beliefs in Fremont. The parade, with all its playfulness, audience interaction, and lack of rules was symbolic. Now you want to stifle this. Fremont isn't Fremont.

Clearly, something special and precious was happening for these people, enough that there was debate, that the parameters of fun were consciously arranged. There was a hint of tension and suspense in the air. Would we see the nude bicyclists? Would they get arrested this year, as a couple of them did in '98?

With the parade already over forty minutes late, people started to notice each other and make their own substance. In the hybrid rock concert/family festival/parade atmosphere, little walls begin to crumble as strangers-no-more share conversation, water, food. Maybe we're participants too.

Some war whoops go up as twenty nude, semi-nude and fake-nude (flesh-colored costumes with fake genitals affixed) ride through. Perhaps there will be no arrests—the pre-parade ritual is performed; the event consecrated. One of the seminude bicyclists is plastic-wrapped with all manner of donuts and greasy, cheap pastries hugging his flab. A collective "ugggghhh'" rolls through the crowd.

A parade staffer orders nine people off of a bus stop roof where they'd perched. No anger and confrontation. They protest, but ultimately, five of them dismount. Impatience rustles through the crowd as minutes pass since the last titillation.

This Fremont parade is one of many events staged throughout the year, and it's a *tour de force* of leaderless teamwork (about forty people come to a typical monthly meeting) that comes together "as if" orchestrated by a greater power, or a great Director. Somehow, the team produces details such as cardboard scissors to cut the ribbon; several people to work on one team to make a grove of walking, parading trees; and another team to create a goddess float—all with a minimum of rules and regulations (thus the protest over banning nude bicyclists).

Fifty minutes overdue, the procession finally begins. A mythic bird on stilts and in a rainbow sash—the grand marshal? — struts ahead of the marching band doing a pretty decent version of the Bee Gee's "Stayin' Alive."

And we're off. A troupe of Pez containers—Batman, Tweety Bird, the Hulk, Fred Flintstone, and Charlie Brown. The Alice in Wonderland characters. A grove of about ten trees. Fifteen people dressed up as carrots. Fruits, kids covering their bodies with little balloons to make them look like raspberries and blackberries. A fifteen-foot tall effigy of Washington's Senator Slade Gorton damming a river and holding back the suffering salmon. Wood nymphs protecting a gauze-enclosed float with a holy fire being stoked by studly males inside. Apes with the Monolith from 2001: A Space Odyssey, complete with the movie's shrieking clarion call. Dirty, soiled Teletubbies. Then a pause.

A beauty queen chauffeured by a butler on the front seat of her bicycle for two, Miss Intermission charms us as we await the second act of this grand procession.

The *Vision in Blue*, forty synchronized belly dancers in deep sky-blue outfits. A fake bicycle cop rides by with the ⊘ sign over a nude bicyclist. This is a great signifier of the power of humor, of mockery, of fun, of disruptive play. It is the day's direct example of the imagined world of the parade "players" engaging the real world of laws that could get some of the paraders arrested.

The participants are of all ages. The art—costumes, floats, masks, gadgetry—is all nontraditional. Boundaries are coming down, that's the whole idea . . . in the name of fun and play.

There is a huge goddess float. All topics are game, no exceptions. You can be animate or inanimate, really nude or costumed nude—one woman had a huge fake butt with two ass cracks! Another float was a great replica and mockery of the new baseball stadium, complete with overmuscled players, a retracting roof that didn't work, and a panhandling politician asking the taxpayers for more money to pay for the house of spectacle.

Children in bee costumes cluster around one who has fallen in some kind of skit. "Are they killing the bees or just beating up that kid?" wonders someone in the audience. A TV head. A huge Barney. A troupe playing long corrugated plastic pipes. On the outer margins of the parade, more folks are milling about, eager to make their own scene. A huge bug, the Y2K bug, with compact discs plastered to two computer screens making really scary bug-eyes. Samba bands play right in front of a band of bagpipes. Haunting ghosts carry butterflies, commemorating Tiananmen Square with pale masks that look like elongated marshmallows. And for the finale, we take in gorgeous samba dancers in go-go outfits.

How do you get a large number of people working together without overorganizing the effort and creating hierarchy? If a "community standard," i.e., nude bicycling is being threatened, how does the organization develop a policy that protects the future of the event, the principles of the event, and the freedom of the participants, yet not establish a hierarchical structure? Four hundred and thirty people registered for the parade, but probably over five hundred participated. So over seventy just showed up or were recruited at the last minute. How do you control for the possible provocateurs who could ruin it for everyone?[4]

Commercialism is prohibited from the parade. This is one of the rules that sustains its spirit. In past years, politicians had taken advantage of joining the procession, but this is no longer allowed. It's curious how commercialism nonetheless seeps in; young hawkers distribute free samples of breakfast cereal and sugar-free mints.

---

[4] Yet since its inception in 1989, that has never happened.

One year, I was particularly spellbound and enthralled by the event, but I had a sore throat and had to go into a drug store to pick up some lozenges. The experience was overwhelming in its contrast. My being had fully opened up to the spirit of play, art, and creativity in the parade, not a museum piece to be observed but a vital force, a collective consciousness that permeated, "something in the air." It was in me. When I walked into the drug store, I was overcome by what I can describe only as a perversion of that same creative energy and an intuitive, recoiling revulsion. Blatantly apparent in the packaging of every product, in every display and advertising, was the germ of the same creative impulse bent to the purpose of selling hosiery, deodorant, cigarettes, or aspirin. To be honest, it reminded me of experiences I had had as a teenager on LSD, going into a supermarket after hours high in the forest and looking at packaged bologna and other processed meat, a harrowing experience I do not recommend.

The visceral contrast validates what the Fremont Arts Council collectively understands. When there is play energy astir, we can connect to it. It is free and has fewer boundaries than the normal conduct of our daily life. But in a modern industrialized society, disconnected people who want to reconnect must observe some rules and guidelines in order to cleanse the cultural palate and regain access to that energy. It is not just liberal dogma to say that if it were the Budweiser Solstice Parade, something would be lost. Something would. To wean and nurture that process, the Fremont Arts Council developed a few—as few as possible—principles and goals. It's a stepping stone to a Play Society:

> The Fremont Arts Council's mission is to support, represent, and promote art and artists in Fremont; Fremont is a state of mind and not a zip code.
>
> **What We Do:**
> - We use creativity to build a stronger community.
> - We believe in art as an integral part of everyday life.

- We promote diversity of viewpoints, backgrounds, and art forms.

**The Principles of Our Operation:**
- We accept fiscal responsibility.
- We believe participation and equal access to power is essential.
- We honor integrity.
- We respect our work/play space and environment.
- Recycling is part of our art.
- We support growth that balances our resources, tradition, and intent.
- We communicate effectively both internally and externally.
- We believe in each other's goodwill and working together.

**Goals:**
- To enrich our community, the FAC uses consensus and information sharing
  in order to involve as many people as possible in the creative process.
- The FAC wishes to export the creative process, art, and artists to other communities to enrich their lives.
- The FAC wishes to import other creative processes, art, and artists to bring a new perspective to our stew of creativity.
- The FAC endorses personal responsibility and respectful behavior.
- The FAC empowers individuals in discovering their creative abilities.
- The FAC provides structure that allows for the least amount of bureaucracy and the maximum amount of art making.

And here are excerpts from an interview I conducted with one of the founders of the parade in Seattle, Peter Toms. Toms is a man in his early fifties, owner and operator of his own small business that repairs musical equipment: sound systems, guitar amps and speakers, and public address systems, mainly for bands. With a ready smile, quick wit, long dark hair, and casual postmodern hippie clothing, Toms is a successful businessman and competent key organizer of a major civic event. He hybrids a sense of humor and a solemn commitment to giving people the opportunity to play. We met over lunch in late July of 2000.

Siegel: *Why don't you just tell me about the parade. What's the story? The philosophy, and also maybe the story of how it came together . . . where those things merge.*

Toms: Well, let's see. It's kind of two different stories, really. The reason why it occurred in Seattle, specifically see, is Barbara Luecke and I were both involved with the Solstice Parade in Santa Barbara, and she was executive director of that, and I was an artist-in-residence for that, a volunteer, for a lot of years. And we both separately moved to Seattle in 1987 and 1988. And I went back in 1988 to Santa Barbara to do the Solstice Parade one more time down there. And immediately after I came back, it occurred to both of us, I was talking to her: "Why are we going to Santa Barbara to do the parade when we could just do it here?" So we elected in the fall of 1988 to try to figure out how to get the parade started in Seattle. So nothing much happened for a long time, but that's when we started thinking about it a lot, in early 1988 . . . how's it actually going to happen. And like things in the parade often happen, magic things started to occur as soon as we decided that we were going to do it. A lot of magic things lined up. Amazingly, we got a space, very easily. People started to get hooked in. We had a community of people already that we were involved with.

Siegel: *What's celebration art?*

Toms: Well, it's a broad category of art. It covers, at least in my mind, the definition covers all the soft arts that go towards people celebrating together. That would be costumery, choreography, foil design, but also it includes things like the building of temporary installations for celebrations. It would be altars for the winter feast and various structures that, you know, parade floats would be temporary art forms that revolve around a specific celebration. So we have the maypole, that's a temporary art piece that's erected just for that event. So the idea of celebration art covers a whole broad category of different disciplines.

Siegel: *What I'm hearing is that it's towards the transient celebration. It's not intended to be permanent things, like a statue.*

Toms: It's NOT permanent things, specifically so.

Siegel: *Deliberately temporary, like music in a way.*

Toms: Yeah.

Siegel: *Time bound.*

Toms: You were there. You got it. You witnessed it, and it's gone. That's one of the things I love so much about it. I mean, oddly, like the [Winter Solstice] feast is a great example of celebration art for me, at its peak. Because what happens is we get a space, and then people get in there and work their butts off, for weeks sometimes, to build these installations. And then the whole thing lasts about six hours. People come in, they eat, they enjoy the art, and then they're gone, and we take it down the next day. Kind of like the parade. The parade's even shorter. The parade's only two hours long. But I like that, because then it's place and time dependent. You had to be there. If you weren't, you missed it, you know. And that's just the way it is. I mean I really like that.

Siegel: *It sounds like there's some excitement for you in that.*

Toms: Well, because there's a mode of apperception, is what I think is the word. If you play a piece of music on the stereo, it's one thing. If you go see the musician play it, it's entirely another thing because they may not play it the same way that they recorded it; in fact they rarely do. So when you hear the musician put out their piece of music, you're hearing them do it the way they're feeling, like, at that particular moment, you know, whatever piece of art they're putting out is inflected with what's happening in their lives right now; it's colored in some way. So it's the same with my artwork. When I do a parade float or when I do a mask or something like that, it's colored by what's actually happening in my life right now. So there's a certain sort of real quality to it. It's based in who I am as an artist and a creator, and less in just the object itself. When you go and make a bronze casting, you make a piece of art. You make your statement and then there it sits. And then you go on, and your life goes on, and there it is. And that piece is about, like that particular statement, that particular place and time in your life. And it's sort of kind of dead, in a way. I mean I used to do bronze, and I had a lot of bronze, and what I see when I look at my own bronze pieces is "Oh, that's what I was thinking." And I remember like, whatever was the milieu of my life at the time. It's not relevant now, necessarily. Most of the bronze I did when I was in my early twenties, which was a time of real difficulty for me and ferment. And the artwork is powerful, and I'm not there anymore, you know. So I mean I look at that, and I go "Wow, that's what I was thinking at the time, but I'm not there anymore." So that work was only pertinent then. But the piece itself is permanent. The statement is no longer pertinent…

All I cared about, and all I continue to care about, is what I had to say then, there, and now. So I just built the train, the locomotive float for the parade because I feel really strongly about what's happening with development in Seattle; that's what I'm into right now. So I had to find a way to express that. So what I did was I built this huge fucking train, and it was black and ugly and greasy and smelly and smoky. And loud and nasty and all those things. And it's painted like a big city, 'cause that's what the city is for me. I mean, the city's just, like, rolling over people's lives like a train. Here in Fremont is a perfect example of it. It's all over the place. And I could think of no better metaphor than a big fucking ugly locomotive that's going to come and run over people. Which is exactly what I did. I could be no more bald than that.

Siegel: *Did you do the stadium the year before?*

Toms: I did.

Siegel: *All of a sudden, I have a handle on your style (laughs). How did you get drawn into the Santa Barbara solstice parade? What was the origin of your attraction to this type of event?*

Toms: Well, I was a kid, I mean, I grew up in Santa Barbara, and solstice parade started in 1975, therein or 1974. It depends on who you talk to. And it just, it was evolving, and for the young people in town, it was like the most happening thing around. It was great. The first parade was pretty small, but the second and third parade started to get pretty big. And to the locals at the time, it felt like here was something that was so pure and so much about the locals. It wasn't about the tourists at all. Santa Barbara wasn't even then overrun by tourists on the scale of today. So for the local people, it's like, wow, now here's something that's absolutely about us and our locale, our community, not about external influences at all. It's only really about what we feel like, and we drew everybody. In four years, it went from fifty people to twenty thousand people. I mean, it's like . . . whoa!

Siegel: *And you were in high school?*

Toms: Yeah, I was in high school. I graduated in '79.

Siegel: *So you saw this going on?*

Toms: Yeah, I went every year. Fuck, it was great. It was a great party. Just go down there; it was always something weird. I was into drumming, you know. I wasn't very good or anything like that, but I'd just jump in.

Siegel: *Is it still going on there?*

Toms:  Oh, absolutely. Yeah. They get huge crowds. They get crowds of over a hundred thousand. It's just gigantic.

Siegel: *Is it run with the same parameters?*

Toms:  Yes, we have the same essential rules that they have. Ever since the beginning, they were going for public funding. They've gotten grants, and they've had grant writers, and they've had full-time staff and stuff like that. Well, not quite at the beginning but early on, and they've had some measure of being able to fund people. We've never been successful at public funding really at all.

Siegel: *Is Seattle the only replication? The only "son of Santa Barbara?"*

Toms:  No. It's gone all over the place. Robin Van Lear, who used to be the executive director in Santa Barbara, moved to Cleveland and continued to go for public funding. And now she has a huge organization there, a gigantic parade [Parade the Circle]. Albuquerque, New Mexico, there's another one. Seattle, there's another one. All from Santa Barbara. And now from us has spawned another one in Vancouver.

Siegel: *But it starts in Santa Barbara?*

Toms:  The people who started it, Michael Gonzales and a couple of other people, were interested in . . . well, what did they want to do? They wanted to get people together to celebrate for no reason other than that it was fun to play together. It was great fun to play; that's what they were into. And they wanted to express themselves. They didn't want to have to have any corporate funding. You go to a lot of other cultures around the world, and people will go out and parade all the time for no particular reason other than they do it because it's great. Its only in America, or in Europe maybe, but in America specifically, it's been codified in this particularly bizarre, what I call the Americana parade, which is the huge, corporate-sponsored floats in the floral parade kind of a thing. Incredibly expensive commercial advertising, basically, that's what's evolved. We have the Rose Parade, and we have Chicago parade and New York parade. And it's all these gigantic parades, and they're all about corporations trying to outdo each other and get on television, get television time. It's interesting to me, does Xerox really benefit? I'd like to see their cost-benefit analysis. If they put out $150,000 for a Rose Parade float to get TV time, do they increase their customer base?

Siegel: *You could ask that of all advertising. I guess it's been proven that advertising works.*

Toms: It irritates the shit out of me. So the one thing that makes the Solstice Parade completely different, the essential rule—we have three rules—and one of them is totally essential. And one of them, the one that is totally essential is "No words." No printed words or recognizable logos. And that, like, is so small and so huge simultaneously.

Siegel: *Words and no pictures that are...*

Toms: No recognizable logos. And that, like, completely turns the thing upside down. 'Cause then you get, corporations go, well, what's in it for us? Well, there's nothing in it for you. See ya later. And the politicians go, well, you mean I can't sit in a car? No. Not only that, you can't have a sign that says who you are. Well, I'm gone. Great.

Siegel: *Rules two and three?*

Toms: No motorized vehicles, except for wheelchairs. We want to slow it down. We want to go real slow. We like things to be within people's reach, in the sense of, it's not so big that you can't push it. If you weld a big heavy huge thing together, then you've got to have a motor. So we're sort of partly advancing the temporary quality of everything with that rule. And also, we're simply keeping the cars out. There're plenty of venues for the beauty queens in the convertibles. They have lots of parades to be in, and we're looking for something different. We really are trying to get a whole different array.

That's why the Solstice Parade is totally unique in this area. It looks completely different. These rules are very specific. We didn't craft them. We didn't think of them. Somebody really smart thought of them. They're really simple, and in just a few words, they express this really different paradigm of how to get people out there having fun in front of a big audience. Completely different. And a lot more happening. If you look at the crowd participation level at the Torchlight Parade, it's like watching television. You don't get anything out of it. I've been in the Torchlight twice. People are like, numb. Look at people in the audience at the Solstice Parade; they're all dressed up, and you can throw 'em things. They're laughing and screaming, and you can talk to 'em. They're people. They're just people. Bless 'em, God.

Siegel: *Rule three?*

Toms: It has to do with animals. No live animals. . . . We're trying to get away from nonhuman support images, nonhuman structures that allow us to do maybe more that we would be able to do just by ourselves.

I don't know why it is, but public celebration's been co-opted. More than co-opted, it's been taken away from people. . . . The way we celebrate nowadays in popular culture is football games or the Fourth of July. And the way that that's celebrated, the Fourth of July is a perfect example, is that it's delivered to us via some corporation. All of our celebrations have been removed from us. Supposedly, it's Independence Day, but does anybody pay attention to that? It's kind of amusing to me.

Siegel: *What about a rock concert?*

Toms: That's a good idea. Are we celebrating there? People enjoy music, and they hear the musicians play it. It seems different in character to me. It's about the musicians in the band, it's not about . . . well, what's any celebration about? I mean, yeah, you have a point. What's any celebration about? What's May Day about? What's the Feast about? What's Summer Solstice Parade about? It's about celebrating something. It might as well be a band. It could be a band; it could be a day.

Siegel: *I'd say that some concerts have the ability to turn into celebrations, and others never do. The Feast, Solstice Parade, May Day, Troll-o-ween, those are the main ones?*

Toms: We have a new one, now. Luminata. September 22. It's a lantern walk around Green Lake. The autumnal equinox. Brand new. Never done before. We're not going to do permits or talk to the city in any way. We're simply going to appear there on the twenty-second and, um, do a parade. I think people are going to love it. They're going to dig it. It's going to have that authentic spark that people are looking for, that nonmediated, just straight from people to other people, for free, for no particular reason other than it's great to do.

Siegel: *What if this was accelerated and multiplied, and you woke up tomorrow and the resources and the time and the energy were there to do an event like the Solstice Parade, minimum twelve times a year, once a month . . . what would that be like?*

Toms: My first reaction is . . . Whaaaaaaaaaaaaaaaat!!! No [pleading]!!!

Well, what makes something special? If you do it all the time, it's not special anymore. We all like to have sex; how much sex can you actually have? After a while, I don't want anymore. So the Solstice Parade, I think it's great because it only does happen once a year, and there's a lot of time in between.

Siegel: *On the other hand, and I'm going to push on this a little bit, a football team, that's a huge spectacle every time. They play sixteen games in a season, and baseball, so many. And you yourself were saying there's this dearth of activities where people can come together in a noncommercial authentic event for the sake of its own . . .*

*The Maypole [sic], the Luminata, the Feast, and the Solstice Parade are all qualitatively different, yet there is something that unifies them. What's that thing that unifies them, and what would it be like to have that unifying abstraction in any number of formats occurring more frequently as part of our daily life?*

Toms: It's about personal expression in the context of getting together with people in community. It's a weird one, okay, we have this special blend of people getting together in work groups to build their own personal thing. So they're working side by side on separate things. Everyone's getting to express themselves individually. Say, I want to make this thing; I want to make it purple. They have total freedom to do that, and yet they still get to chat with their neighbor whose working on their thing next door. You get to hang out at the same table and work on this thing all night long, and it's fun, and you get to know people. There's people swirling around. There's lots of single people, and single people get together, and it's a way to meet people. It's a way to simply coexist and communicate in the original sense of the word *community, communicate.* So you still get to express yourself; you still get to scratch that itch inside of needing to be saying something. A lot of things aren't said in words very well, though, a lot of expression isn't. It comes out better other ways, not in words. It's not entirely satisfying to use language. Sometimes we have to use images instead, so what we do is we make things. When you make something, you get to express yourself, but you get to sit next to somebody else who's also expressing themselves. And that's a particularly bizarre, yet very satisfying, state of mind.

It's hard for me being so vehement. We start talking about this, and I get pissed off because there's so little access to this in our society, because it's dangerous. Capitalism and the corporate world doesn't want people to freely express themselves, or if they do, they co-opt it in the sense that they want people to express themselves in terms of buying something. Go buy Levi's because you're expressing your wild side, or whatever. This is bullshit. So they've taken that energy of wanting to creatively express one's self and co-opted it into "buy our stuff 'cause if you buy our stuff, then you are accomplishing that," but it's so unsatisfactory. It's so unsatisfactory. When you go and buy a set of Levi's, it doesn't satisfy the itch to express one's self. It's just an article of clothing.

Siegel: *What makes the Solstice Parade alike or different from Mardis Gras in New Orleans or Carnival in Brazil?*

Toms:  They're similar, mostly. Especially Carnival. There're many, many parades in Brazil. Well, all over the world. Carnival is a Catholic celebration. It comes from Catholic countries. It's a reaction to Lent, or a pre-reaction to Lent is what it is. It's a "get-it-out-of-your-system before Lent happens." It's eons old, and it's all about people in neighborhoods getting out there and getting the juices going before Lent happens. 'Cause Lent of course is the time of sacrifice and . . . so, as it actually exists now, if you go to Rio or some of the cities in Brazil, it's all about neighborhoods competing with each other for prizes, for who's going to be the biggest and the best. So it's like a neighborhood pride kind of thing. So huge parades happen. Neighborhoods all put on their own parades. The parades have big bands, dancers, and all this stuff. And the cooler you are, the hipper your parade's going to be.

So if the Solstice Parade were going to be like that, Fremont would be one parade among many. I mean, we kind of have that in this weird way. We have these Seafair parades, of which we just had one last weekend, this kiddie parade in Wallingford. It was the most godawful excuse for a parade I've ever seen. Seafair, what is it? Kind of a regulating body is what I would say. It sponsors parades all over the city. There's one in West Seattle, there's like twenty-two different Seafair parades. Lake City has one. They're all like quote Seafair Parades. They're really neighborhood events is what they are. But you don't have to live in the neighborhood to be in one.

But it's so sanitized and so . . . there's no conflict of any kind. There's no heat, no politics, no statement, just a couple of high school bands. It's been completely neutered, basically. Any kind of umph they had, any kind of strong feelings of any kind have been excised from those parades.

Siegel:  *So the qualitative distinction between [The Solstice Parade] and the Seafair parades is . . .*

Toms:  They don't want any individual expression in those parades. They specifically exclude it by the regulations. If you want to get a float in the parade, you have to go through this selection process. It's expensive; the floats are expensive. You can't just walk down the street as a community freak. 'Cause that's not what they want. 'Cause those parades are about television and about corporate sponsorship; they're not about community. They say they're about community, but they're not. It's just totally hypocritical. It's not about people at all. It's about corporations. And the Torchlight Parade, being the granddaddy of them all, they specifically exclude political statements. Specifically. 'Cause I was applying to get into the Torchlight Parade this year. And there's a whole list of regulations and rules about how to get your float in the parade, and one of those is "no political statement will be allowed." No statement of any kind will be allowed. They don't want anything definitive about anything. They want nice, nice, nice. 'Cause they don't want to upset anybody on television, and they don't want to upset any of their corporate sponsors. It's all about making money. And it's not about parading; it's just making money in the form of a parade.

Siegel: *Why can't you have both? Why can't you have corporate sponsorship and a community coming together?*

Toms: I suppose you do, like in the sense of a football game. 'Cause those people feel like they're in community. The fans do. It's alien to me, personally, but not to the fans. They think it's great.

Siegel: *What would happen if you allowed it in the Solstice Parade?*

Toms: The money would go up. People would start getting paid. The subject matter would change. We'd be building things for advertising purposes. So I wouldn't build a locomotive; I'd build a big shoe, or a big Microsoft something-or-other. The corporations are spending their money and trying to paint a picture of the world as being very easy, comfortable, or fun. They don't want any conflict. Conflict doesn't sell tennis shoes or software or coffee.

Siegel: *What do you mean when you say they don't want any conflict?*

Toms: Starbucks wants people to buy coffee. And the way to get you to buy coffee is to make them think that when they go have coffee, they'll feel better. Happier, more complete somehow. And if you present conflict, that is not how people feel happier.

Siegel: *So to bring that up, symbolically, through some kind of a float in a parade, is presenting conflict, which the corporate sponsors don't want. But if you say that what we're talking about is play, and that you like to play, how can we be playful and be raising these politically conflicting situations at the same time?*

Toms: I'm gleefully, exuberantly, expressing my opinion. Most happy to have the opportunity to say what I think is true. For me, that's play. I get to design and build fanciful structures based on some statement. I have to say that I'm unusual. Most people that are designing things for the Solstice Parade don't have a political ax to grind. I happen to. I'm unusual. I feel like you can't lose the opportunity. If you've got thirty thousand or fifty thousand people there, coming to see the parade, it's a great opportunity to show 'em something. Why lose the opportunity? Is it effective? I don't care. I just do what I need to do. It feels like play to me.

Siegel: *"Is it effective? I don't care." But it is an issue that you care about. Whether it's the gentrification of Fremont or the light rail system; or it's Safeco Field [the new major league baseball stadium] or development in general. So you must care about being effective somewhere, somehow?*

Toms: Well, it would be great if the political powers that be saw my float and went, "Oh my God, we've got to change our policy." But the chances of that are dismal.

Siegel: *But like you said, thirty thousand people are going to look at it…*

Toms: I think that there are avenues into people's psyches. Different ways to get into people. And you can have more or less penetration through various means. Humor gets in real deep. If you get people laughing, then you can get into their subconscious in a way that you normally wouldn't. There's a certain sort of vulnerability that occurs when you're laughing that I think opens up a whole bunch of gates, and you get your message in there. I think if you're shouting at people and if you're holding signs and braying at them with a bullhorn, all the barriers come up, and you don't get anywhere. Zero penetration. People just shut you off; that's as far as you'll get. I think the Solstice Parade, most people are smiling and laughing because most of the stuff is pretty funny. Even the locomotive is funny. And I was trying to make it funny. And even though it's a dire consequence—what's happening isn't funny at all—to portray it in a funny way is a way to get into people that you normally couldn't. That's what I'm trying for. In that way, the parade is an even better venue for a political statement because people are more vulnerable in a way that they normally aren't.

Can collective play be more than a five-minute prank, a two-hour parade, a four-hour rock and roll show, a day of Mardis Gras? Burning Man extends playtime to a full nine days. Are we slouching towards the Play Society?

# FIFTEEN

# Burning Man

*Hoping and hoping*
*As if by my weak faith*
*The spirit of this world*
*Would heal and rise*

*Joni Mitchell and W.B. Yeats*[1]

AS MUCH TO their chagrin as their amazement, the Grateful
Dead had become the nation's most popular live act in the late 1980s.
In fact, too many people were coming to their shows. The phenomenon of nomads without tickets who followed the band around the
country living a vagabond American adventure à la Kerouac's *On
the Road* was wearing thin. People were dying in the mobs; concerts
were overall more dangerous; fans more ruthless in their quest. But
these were also seekers of something better than what America was
offering them, a different expression than Seattle's Solstice Parade
but of similar kinship.

The Grateful Dead cared about their fans, but their main job was
to show up and play great. It was beyond them to manage the community of Deadheads that was regularly bursting capacity.

On any given Sunday, police and other responders are called into
service to manage the hordes that attend NFL football games. These

---

[1] Joni Mitchell, "Slouching Towards Bethlehem," by J. Mitchell and W.B. Yeats, *Night Ride
Home*. Asylum, 1991, CD.

citywide adaptations are financed by taxpayers who make few complaints. One could just as easily make the case that municipal services wherever the Dead were playing should also have accommodated the Deadheads. Sure, Deadheads presented somewhat different problems, but our society did not step up to solve them the way we do for NFL fans on a regular basis. And Deadheads are just as important as football fans. So instead of the joyful anarchy the Dead hoped to inspire, things went south, leading to a dispiriting trend of vagrancy, unhappy mayhem and violence at concerts, frustration, the death of Jerry Garcia, and the demise of the band.

The vessels, in this case the largest arenas in the nation, had good sound but inadequate control or services. They were not up to the task. The Dead were there to play music with responsive audiences and could not be expected to take on the unticketed 'heads or keep evil from their door, i.e., the Hells Angels. Burning Man, on the other hand, hosted a related vibe and directly engaged the challenge of creating a durable, flexible, evolving, and resilient vessel that **would** work for the ever-changing, ever-expanding, and also wily-anarchic energy of Burners, a direct outgrowth of the San Francisco tradition of playful and fun-loving artists, Beats, hippies, gays, punks, Deadheads . . . and eventually, Burners.

It was time to invent a new mode. And so artists, designers, urban planners, and political visionaries came up with Burning Man, an innovative vessel specifically designed to steward this same kind of hopeful energy with a new approach to art-based community and an evolving capacity to sustain itself. As Allen Ginsberg paraphrased Plato: "When the mode of the music changes, the walls of the city shake."

### Fire

How does one describe the indescribable? Duchamp rejects words. As soon as one begins discussing that most simple of activities, play, it all becomes quite complex and difficult—"Burning Man cannot be described, that its whole is incomprehensible to anyone, even to those who have attended the event."[2]

The annual Burning Man festival, the week leading up to Labor Day in Nevada's Black Rock Desert, is the child and mother of all happenings, rife with opportunities for trickster spirit and play to surface and jump. And maybe, just maybe, Burning Man is a phenomenon that sits still long enough to be recognized as an emerging and evolving model of the Play Society. Its genesis of a wooden effigy—built lovingly and artistically only to be incinerated—is a concept wholly consonant with play: this idea of transient competence—of putting something together with other people with frolic, whimsy, and fun and then tearing it down to start over again—is exactly what we mean when we describe original play. To connect from the animal world to the playpen to the playground to the adult who still plays, and to then do it! To build a great city in the middle of the desert, to share and live a longer glimpse (an entire week!) of what the Play Society might be like. Burners!

Reams have been written about the Burning Man event. More importantly, thousands upon thousands of people have participated. They've grown it and sustained it and spread it beyond the capstone event, spreading its playful ethos globally.

Burning Man and the culture it has spawned relates directly to original play. The odyssey and methods of Burning Man somehow sustain the play element and translate it into a governing principle. And Burning Man's champions speculate about its potential as, firstly, a needed shot of *disruptive play* in society at large and, secondly, as a prototypical model of the Play Society. Burning Man is a vessel for *original play* that breaks through the constraints and hierarchy of *cultural play* and give us bearings, direction, energy, vision, and hope.

---

[2] Samantha Krukowski, ed., *Playa Dust: Collected Stories from Burning Man* (London: Black Dog Publishing, 2014), 8.

What is this radical art that manifests and transports at Burning Man? It's a giant croquet game using wickets made of white PVC pipe and six-foot-diameter rubber balls. It's the *Opulent Temple*, one of the sound camps of the electronic music rave, which camped out near Burning Man in 1992 but played a major part by 1998, featuring many of the planet's greatest DJ's. It's *Critical Tits*, thousands of topless women riding bikes across the desert. *Tantalus*, a 3-D zoetrope that reenacts an American version of the Greek myth, a man's arm trying to get a golden apple that is always just out of reach. *Bummer*, a large wooden Hummer that burned on a Saturday night. *Altered State*, a three-story gazebo replica of the Capitol Dome made from laser-cut, cold rolled steel bearing symbols of Native American peoples. *Spank Bank*, with BDSM, straps, and feathers. It's everyone in costume. It's fantastical sculpture like 2010's *Minaret*. Flaming Lotus Girls and their large-scale kinetic art. The steampunk contraptions of Kinetic Steam Works. The spectacular sound and vision and acrobatics of *The Mutaytor*. It's living art. In books,[3] you can find pictures. In the Black Rock Desert and wherever these artists have continued to spread their creativity, you can have the experience.

---

To burn something is to prove its impermanence. Fire can evoke play, but it's also dangerous.

Cities present an ongoing contrast of the permanent (buildings intended to last a hundred years) and the temporary (from street fairs to the razing of old buildings to make room for new developments). The Metropolis theme of the 2010 Burning Man embraced this dynamic and advanced a liberated approach to urbanism . . . that

---

[3] Brian Doherty, *This Is Burning Man: The Rise of a New American Underground* (Dallas: BenBella Books, 2004); Steven T. Jones, *The Tribes of Burning Man: How an Experimental City in the Desert is Shaping the New American Counterculture* (San Francisco: Consortium of Collective Consciousness, 2011); and Samantha Krukowski, ed., *Playa Dust: Collected Stories from Burning Man* (London: Black Dog, 2014). Detailed accounts and pictures are in these three books and can also be found on the web.

cities can be based upon art instead of commerce, that people know how to take care of themselves, that a city can be playful.

We've seen this quality of transience. Jack Kerouac translating the jazz saxophonist's spontaneous creations into static text; dada art that makes its point and then disappears. Like the impermanence of play, Burning Man is the disposable city.

Parades and carnivals. The problems of managing large crowds for longer periods of time must be solved: safety, transportation, food, child care, latrine, and, in the case of Burning Man, places to sleep. It all gets solved, but just barely, just enough to make it just barely comfortable so that you can stick around and get to the main thing, go out and play.

And the idea of the carnival, of costume and of transgression, is the permission it grants—to go wherever creativity leads you, "to discover the mythic component of life . . . a lot of people are really longing for a sense of the mythic in their lives. And Burning Man gives them the chance."[4] And certainly Trickster is among those mythic components.

## Swirling Fire, Encased in Glass

Here's the quick and gritty story.[5] San Francisco sculptor Mary Grauberger had held solstice bonfire gatherings on Baker Beach for several years. Larry Harvey frequently attended, and in 1986, he added a nine-foot wooden man and a smaller wooden dog to the blaze, calling it a spontaneous act of radical self-expression. From that point on, Harvey took the lead in the event, and the "Man", who would be burned at a culminating event, became the moniker for what morphed into Burning Man, at first a dadaist event cohosted by artists from the Cacophony Society, notably Kevin Evans and John Law.

---

[4] "Scott," quoted in Steven T. Jones, *The Tribes of Burning Man: How an Experimental City in the Desert is Shaping the New American Counterculture* (San Francisco: Consortium of Collective Consciousness, 2011), 190.

[5] For more detailed accounts, check out *This Is Burning Man* by Brian Doherty (2004); *The Tribes of Burning Man* by Steven T. Jones (2011); and *Playa Dust* edited by Samantha Krukowski (2014).

In 1990, they discovered then led folks to the dry lake (playa) in Nevada, the Black Rock Desert. One of the Cacophonists, Michael Mikel, comprehending the risks of people getting lost or dehydrated, created a corps of folks to help out, the Black Rock Rangers. This incipient infrastructure made it possible for the celebration to grow. And grow it did, initially by word of mouth, where people would make the pilgrimage knowing that only the bare minimum accommodations, if that, would be provided.

It was about putting the art first and taking care of your own survival needs. The only rules were "don't interfere with anyone else's immediate experience" and "no guns in the central camp." Sculptors of wood, papier-mâché, metal, and other media, with a flair for the kinetic, the electronically lit, along with fire artists and folks who enjoyed burning things (legally and safely) gave early incarnations of the event its identity, along with the cultivation of a culture that had minimal rules but emergent and passionate principles that were eventually codified.[6]

By 1991, the group was obtaining legal permits through the Bureau of Land Management (Black Rock Desert is federal land). A companion, weeks-long event, "Desert Siteworks," commenced and lasted through 1995. The year 1996 saw the creation of a formal partnerships to own the name "Burning Man" and was that the event opened more widely to the public. And 1996 saw two vehicle-related accidents related to Burning Man. These tragedies gave rise to a five-mile-per-hour speed limit and new safety standards for the art cars and mutant vehicles—an original and essential feature of Burning Man—and priority access for bicyclists and pedestrians. Other new rules included restricting the burning of art to designated burn platforms, a ban on fireworks, and a ban on dogs.

Values emerging from the amoral genesis of Burning Man provoked founder John Law to leave the organization and call for Burning Man's demise, also in 1996. Burning Man had grown from a camping trip

---

[6] In 2006.

of less than one hundred people into a temporary city of about eight thousand. Law eventually sued Burning Man in 2007 over whether keeping some board control over the name and the event prevented it from co-optation, or was *that* a form of co-optation? Law's lawsuit aimed to force Burning Man to enter the public domain, and it disputed whatever those legal structures were protecting: a structured, inclusive gathering based on certain egalitarian and artistic principles or small-scale anarchy? According to Law, "If it's a real fucking movement, they can give up control of the name."[7] This is one of several conflicts that are part and parcel of the Burning Man story.

By 1998, the event more formally integrated urban design with a grid street structure, and architect Rod Garrett, until his death in 2011, became the city designer. Also in 1998, Burning Man added a perimeter fence and made more rules. Burning Man further institutionalized with means of managing money, rights, responsibilities, and governance. How that came about and how Burning Man continues to evolve, and how Burning Man handles conflict, demonstrate a new, iconoclastic, optimistic, and hopefully applicable means of, going forward managing: resistance to institutionalization, control, and suppression; the tension between commerce and art; and the fact that new rules always have their objectors and controversies.

Another transition in the organization from an LLC to a nonprofit was announced in March 2014. The LLC became a subsidiary, and a new LLC, Decommodification LLC, was created. It became the owner and enforcer of all of the intellectual property associated with the Burning Man brand, including logos and trademarks, all under the umbrella of the nonprofit.

Who showed up to the event: punks, avant-garde and outsider and visionary artists, hip-hoppers, antiglobalization activists and Black Bloc anarchists, technoculturalists and hackers, pyrotechnicians, artists who make fantastical art and burn it, people who like to set

---

7  John Law, quoted in Steven T. Jones, *The Tribes of Burning Man*, 140.

off explosives, rappers, psychedelicists, modern primitives, the sexual underground, pagans, postmodern academics, New Agers, riot grrls, slackers, ravers, reggae dreadsters, Zen Buddhists, gnostics, iconoclasts, Deadheads, poetry slammers, goths, tree huggers, libertines and libertarians… counterculturalists all.[8]

Such a wide range of attendees means that Burning Man does not have a single focus. What you're going to experience there is subject to the participants and includes community, artwork, absurdity, decommodification, and revelry. Participation is almost insisted upon; "no spectators" was a watchword of the early days.

The Burning Man event and its affiliated communities are guided by ten principles. According to Larry Harvey, these were already being observed and lived by before he ever wrote them down in 2004, and revised in 2017:

> Radical Inclusion Anyone may be a part of Burning Man. We welcome and respect the stranger. No prerequisites exist for participation in our community.

> Gifting Burning Man is devoted to acts of gift giving. The value of a gift is unconditional. Gifting does not contemplate a return or an exchange for something of equal value.

> Decommodification In order to preserve the spirit of gifting, our community seeks to create social environments that are unmediated by commercial sponsorships, transactions, or advertising. We stand ready to protect our culture from such exploitation. We resist the substitution of consumption for participatory experience.

> Radical Self-reliance Burning Man encourages the individual to discover, exercise and rely on his or her inner resources.

> Radical Self-expression Radical self-expression arises from the unique gifts of the individual. No one other than

---

[8] Adapted from Steven T. Jones, *The Tribes of Burning Man: How an Experimental City in the Desert is Shaping the New American Counterculture* (San Francisco: Consortium of Collective Consciousness, 2011), 17.

the individual or a collaborating group can determine its content. It is offered as a gift to others. In this spirit, the giver should respect the rights and liberties of the recipient.

Communal Effort Our community values creative cooperation and collaboration. We strive to produce, promote and protect social networks, public spaces, works of art, and methods of communication that support such interaction.

Civic Responsibility We value civil society. Community members who organize events should assume responsibility for public welfare and endeavor to communicate civic responsibilities to participants. They must also assume responsibility for conducting events in accordance with local, state and federal laws.

Leaving No Trace Our community respects the environment. We are committed to leaving no physical trace of our activities wherever we gather. We clean up after ourselves and endeavor, whenever possible, to leave such places in a better state than when we found them.

Participation Our community is committed to a radically participatory ethic. We believe that transformative change, whether in the individual or in society, can occur only through the medium of deeply personal participation. We achieve being through doing. Everyone is invited to work. Everyone is invited to play. We make the world real through actions that open the heart.

Immediacy Immediate experience is, in many ways, the most important touchstone of value in our culture. We seek to overcome barriers that stand between us and a recognition of our inner selves, the reality of those around us, participation in society, and contact with a natural world exceeding human powers. No idea can substitute for this experience.[9]

---

[9] "The 10 Principles of Burning Man," burningman.org, accessed April 28, 2018, https://burningman.org/culture/philosophical-center/10-principles/. These revisions from Harvey's original 2004 version are simpler and cleaner, but lack some of the cowboy anarchist feel that characterized the original 10 principles.

In other words, let's be our art and mainly our art, our radical self-expression. This surfaces best if we observe rules of bare minimum. The Black Rock Desert has the bare minimum of what humans need to survive: air. As the need for water, food, sleep, pooping and peeing, shade, and so forth come up, take personal responsibility. Thus, there is decommodification and a new space is created where one's humanity, one's art, one's connection to others, one's radical self-expression, can prevail over consumerism. We free ourselves and our art from commerce. It's dada; it's the Beats; it's the hippies; it's the punks; it's the ravers; construed to be sturdy for one week out of the year. By dissolving commercial mediation—all the things that come between us—people's playful nature can flourish and get out of its box. The gifting economy is consistent with the true gifting nature of art and play and creativity.

Burning Man culture is resilient in part because key Burners ensured creative spaces for artists and participants, but also,

> "It is so durable because they have resisted attempts to force meaning on it. . . . People need a purpose, even San Franciscans leery of paths cut by nationalist, professional, or theological concerns. So we pursue projects—political, social, or artistic—sometimes just to see them done, so our time and passions have an outlet of our choosing, so we can be part of something bigger than ourselves."[10]

And this is why it's so important to consider Burning Man's potential. When people go out looking to be part of something bigger, tragically, they find war, the ultimate form of cultural play, instead of the peace and joy of original play. "War is a force that gives us meaning" intoned Chris Hedges in his book by the same name. Play is another force that gives us meaning, but for some reason, it is more difficult for us to live than war.

---

[10] Jones, *The Tribes of Burning Man*, 55.

## Disney on Acid

As a movement led by and for artists, the Burning Man founders and pioneers did not so much say "let's create a place and time particularly well-suited for play" as they more overtly set out to find space for their art. But by the algebra that likens art to play, it's obvious that Burning Man is a phenomenon that creates excellent conditions and encouragement for a community of play.

We know that culture can contaminate play—that rules, commerce, winners and losers, ranking, militarism, score-keeping, and the maintenance of a historic order all conspire to squelch trickster spirit and original play and replace it with the more competitive cultural play. But out on the desolate Black Rock Desert, the playa, a good number of the artifices of culture are vacuumed off the landscape. This accomplishes two things. First is the erasure of commerce, branding, the familiarity of the matrix that washes over our daily reality—what Burners call the "default world"—all the visual cues of America's cities, towns, and suburbs that tell us where we are and how to behave. Secondly, on an even deeper mental level, the desert removes the perceptual norms of human settlements, and Burners experience the powerful cognitive dissonance of being in an isotropic space (where things appear to look the same in all directions).[11]

> The biggest difference is that all other festivals are on planet Earth. This really sums up both the positive and negative. It's quite the journey to get there and quite the ordeal to stay afloat once inside. But on the other hand, for one week a year, you are truly removed from any forces that propel our everyday society.[12]

Thus, the desert environment heightens the possibilities of original play. Disorientation becomes an opportunity for reorientation.

---

[11] William L. Fox, "Keeping in Strange," in *Playa Dust: Collected Stories from Burning Man,* ed. Samatha Krukowski (London: Black Dog Publishing, 2014), 46.

[12] Scumfrog, quoted in Steven T. Jones, *The Tribes of Burning Man,* 98.

The void initially alarms our senses but then opens us to new universes of possibility. This basic creed of belonging and participation, of living by the ten principles, make Burning Man the biggest playground in the world and an evolving template for the Play Society.

DJ Christopher Lawrence testified: "Then it happened, a moment I will never forget. We rode out of Center Camp and out onto the playa, and my mind exploded with sensory overload like nothing I had experienced before. The music, the noise of explosions, flames shooting into the air, art cars of unimaginable design, neon lights, flares, people in costumes like Disney on acid. There is no way to describe the opening of awareness that accompanies the first impression of the playa. There are no words, no pictures, no videos that do it justice. Now I understood, and in that instant I knew I belonged."[13]

Belonging being an essence of original play, even a definition.

And the purest forms of original play are tactile. There is plenty of touch at Burning Man, and folks are of age and get sexual. But there are opportunities for nonsexual original play as well. One dimension of that is Big Top Burning Man, a sharing of circus arts, something very live and in person, very much in contrast to the internet playground of, for example, Anonymous.

The ten principles are "not an ideology. . . . [They are a] description of a value system . . . of a phenomenon that had already occurred, rather than prescriptive."[14] And Burning Man grew out of the San Francisco's Beats, hippies, gays, and punks, all cultures that had already occurred and were unafraid to be playful in the face of nuclear malaise, war, oppression, and finally a consumerist culture that was killing the planet. As a forging of the more obnoxious pranksterism of punks and the more naive peace-and-love play of the hippies, Burning Man has been able to write the next chapter for both movements, creating a new and even more effectual force.

---

[13] Christopher Lawrence, quoted in Steven T Jones, *The Tribes of Burning Man*, 170-171.

[14] Stewart Harvey, "Black Rock Dawn," in *Playa Dust: Collected Stories from Burning Man*, ed. Samantha Krukowski (London: Black Dog Publishing, 2014), 29.

## From Play to the Play Society

So let's call that force a counterculture. The auspicious and elite Commonwealth Club of San Francisco hosted a panel discussion entitled "Impact of Counterculture" on December 14, 2004, that included Jello Biafra, Larry Harvey, and R. U. Sirius (aka Ken Goffman), who listed the elements of a counterculture: antiauthoritarian, nonconformist, free-thinking, changeable, and often marked by irreverent personalities, pranksters. "The prankster aspect is the special sauce of countercultureness."[15]

And it is no coincidence that Burning Man's origins are in San Francisco:

> "The thing about San Francisco is it tends to attract people who are looking to find themselves, and the ones who do, tend to stay. Well, Burning Man is the same way, a place where people go looking to find a new self, and they try on this and they try on that, and so on and so forth. . . . It has created this culture where people understand they have permission to architect the universe pretty much whichever way they want to. And so San Francisco is this ongoing experiment in mashing people up and seeing what happens."[16]

> The counterculture of the Bay Area resulted in Burning Man, not the other way around. . . . We made Burning Man because we needed it. . . . It was ingrained in our psyche from a young age, in our very genetics."[17]

Burning Man is a little bit dangerous, a hot mess cauldron, and while feeling safe is often a condition for releasing play, the challenges of Burning Man—heat exhaustion, sunburn, dehydration, disorientation, the removal of the default world, etc.—can scare you back to life. Safety cannot be assumed; we live in a dangerous world.

---

[15] Ken Goffman, quoted in Steven T. Jones, *The Tribes of Burning Man*, 49.

[16] Tom Price, quoted in Steven T. Jones, *The Tribes of Burning Man*, 144.

[17] Dan Das, quoted in Steven T. Jones, *The Tribes of Burning Man*, 217.

Burning Man's environment carves out a space that forestalls confrontation with the not-play world, but not with danger. Burning Man invites its participants to playfully cross boundaries. And that's what tricksters do. Thus, it is practice for the disruptive play that recognizes danger, and the disruptive play that will occur if playfulness is going to inform the future of society.

A precept of Burning Man is "no spectators." Come to participate. Dress outrageously, dance madly, make provocative interactive art, embrace it all. Don't just watch! And this is consistent with the play concept of belongingness. Spectators tend not to experience belongingness, participants do. And as Burning Man moved into the twenty-first century, there was a growing sense of community. Ironically, the burning of the Man is a spectator centerpiece. Careful review of Burning Man history suggests that the event was as much the brainchild of the situationist, dada, culture-jamming Cacophony Society—prankster advocates of the Play Society—as it was of Larry Harvey and his sacrificial Man. The Man is more a convenient and recognizable symbol, and his burn more testimony to the transience of everything, not the worshipping of some idol.

And so it is with sculpture to fire art to EDM (electronic dance music) to sex and drugs and circus and project this and project that—these are ALL essential, but also temporary—it's the spirit, **the spirit of noncompetitive play as a first principle of forming a society**—that's the timeless Burner something that defines not just the event but an alternative approach to the social contract.

> The event was really too vast to have a common purpose. . . . [All these groups], they're all there mashed up on top of each other, and they all think it's their place, and they're all right. Because the things that they share in common, which is a decision to express themselves and a decision to tolerate the expression of others, is very rare.
>
> Burning Man, I believe, happened organically as a response to the culture that we've created in this country . . . that cel-

ebrated, even fetishized, consumption for its own sake. And people need an antidote to that. They needed a place where they could be decommodified.[18]

Can something be elaborate; thoughtful; requiring of great planning, discipline, and skilled execution, yet also be part of a celebration of the immediate, of play? This is one of Burning Man's most beautiful paradoxes. Many Burners spend fifty-one weeks out of the year planning for the one in the Black Rock Desert.

In 2000, the building of a temple, that is also eventually burned down, became a main feature of the annual celebration and a city center. From that year on, the temples celebrated unique architecture and invitations to play, to hide out, to climb, to pray, to appreciate: the Mind in 2000, Tears in 2001, Joy (2002), Honor (2003), Stars (etc.), Dreams, Hope, Forgiveness, Sacred Trash, Fire of Fires, Flux, Transition, Juno, Whollyness, Grace, and in 2015, Promise.[19] These temples, plus the city itself, speak to the possibilities of what can be created with minimal regulation but with a shared spiritual, social, and environmental consciousness that preempts such policing. And this shared consciousness is incomplete and rough-hewn at best. These things take time and luck and intention.

You had folks among the originators of the scene saying that people come for art not community; or others saying community's okay, but it's secondary to the art; or yet others saying they come for the art but stay for the community and saying "Art is more than just building the art. It's about community, and this group is really good at taking care of each other."[20]

Larry Harvey describes Burning Man as the first bohemian scene to turn itself into a city.[21] A city built from scratch and leaving no

---

[18] Tom Price, quoted in Steven T. Jones, *The Tribes of Burning Man*, 219.

[19] Of course, their glory needs immediate experience or at least the illuminating pictures this text cannot provide.

[20] Davis Galligan aka Stinky Pirate, quoted in Steven T. Jones, *The Tribes of Burning Man*, 285.

[21] Larry Harvey, quoted in Steven T. Jones, *The Tribes of Burning Man*, 256.

trace, on an annual basis. Burning Man's unique and soulful combination of playful and harm-free but dangerous exploration and survival in an extreme environment was embodied by 2010's Temple of Flux. It was described by one of its creators, Peter "PK" Kimelman, as being about "the beauty in the unsafe, the dangerous and unstable . . . flux: continuous growth, change, and transition."[22]

And out of those conditional parameters, community emerges from the deliberate, muscular, and solid teamwork that builds statues, cars, temples, effigies, altars, gizmos, fire arts, ordnance, and the like—and later from the more fluid and ephemeral relationships found in shared raving to the electronic dance music of the world's top DJs. And in a thousand other ways.

Not having attended Burning Man in the anarchic early years, Gabriel Metcalf has always seen Black Rock City as a city. "In the absence of state-imposed authority and control, you take 50,000 anarchists and put them in the desert and they'll create order out of chaos." And the city they created, he said, is "like being a protagonist in a movie when you arrive in the big city. The Esplanade is one of the great main streets in the world."[23]

> That's the story of Metropolis: The frontier, when Burning Man was all about rugged individuals doing whatever the fuck they wanted, was gone. It was replaced by a city, where free expression still reigns but our collective creations are more important than our individual desire. [We are] creating monuments to nothing more than the art of collective creation.[24]

In a functional anarchy, rules do not need to be written down because our collective and interdependent awareness of each other and an uninhibited flow of compassion and shared consciousness means that we

---

[22] PK, quoted in Steven T. Jones, *The Tribes of Burning Man*, 289.

[23] Jones, *The Tribes of Burning Man*, 251.

[24] Jones, *The Tribes of Burning Man*, 265.

all take care of each other and do no intentional harm . . . but we recognize and live with uncertainty, temporality, and danger. Play.

> It's hard to overstate how the vastness of the playa adds to the mystique of Burning Man. Certainly the demand for a proportion that can compete with this seemingly endless expanse has influenced the construction of huge sculptures and mammoth theme camps, but scale is only part of the equation. Contact with an ancient landscape can activate primal instincts. Existence is vivid and timeless. One can feel at once small and vulnerable, and yet placidly connected to a greater whole. The small miracle of the Black Rock is that despite the exponential growth of the event over the decades that feeling of kinship to our ancient origins is as real today as it was then.[25]

## Swirling Fire, Breaking Glass

The internet allows a stunning range of permutations on online playgrounds like Anonymous and 4chan. Anything from political action to humorous memes, forming of online communities, practical joking, nerd-festing on anime, and the like proliferate and grab one's attention. But when the comparison is made to a live-and-in-person phenomenon of let's touch each other, let's get high together, let's make art, let's dance to a great deejay, let's have kinky sex, let's wear costumes, let's drive around in arty cars, let's install solar panels, let's provide disaster relief and help communities rebuild . . . the live-and-in-person heart of Burning Man reminds us that play is first and foremost a tactile experience, that we started with the play of the infant and speculated on what happens when an adult retains that ability to noncompetitively play. We went through the abstracting process that extrapolated that tactile, original play to art, to political action, to the convergence of the two, and even eventually to the internet,

[25] Stewart Harvey, "Black Rock Dawn," in *Playa Dust: Collected Stories from Burning Man*, ed. Samantha Krukowski (London: Black Dog Publishing, 2014), 29.

which represents the greatest displacement of play from its palpable, animal origins. Burning Man brings us back to that tactile source and provides the most direct answer to this book's original query. And of course, that means that the conflicts, the trickster cycle, the emergence of values, and the cyclic return to amorality, play themselves out in a unique and radically edifying way.

## Burning Man is Disruptive Play: The Establish/Challenge Cycle

Tricksters are typically dismissed because the conventional establishment and maintenance of order does not deal well with such rule-breakers without resorting to systems of punishment or marginalization. At the same time, worthy artists tend to cross boundaries, break rules, and play tricks. Burning Man culture is littered with such characters. So how to design a vessel that contains but does not constrain this energy? How does Burning Man accommodate growth, resolve conflicts, and stay true to its original intentions?

You had Burners of the structural and tactile arts, Burners who design stuff and sew stuff, and Burners who burn stuff and build stuff and drive stuff. But then, in 1992, the music folks, the ravers, began to come, and they were not initially welcomed by all.

What I call the establish/challenge cycle demonstrates how a freer society can emerge and grow while still embracing and digesting disruptive play. And all the while, support more and more people making a living as artists . . . just use that as a metric or as a prime directive. It's a constant churning of the trickster cycle, engaged collectively but populated by many unique individuals.

Burning Man's vitality is regularly replenished by an inalienable right to challenge. Whether or not that challenge is successful is less important than the cycle it propels: continuous improvement, continuous growth, and return to the playground.[26]

---

[26] With the exception of establishing something that would thwart future challenges.

Synonyms for the word *flux* include *fluidity, mutability, change, instability*. How right, then, that the 2010 Temple of Flux was a signature piece. Its construction included a large team of three hundred novices and experts who were taught the basic techniques of whitewashing six-inch strips of plywood then putting together in random angles, subject to each builder's whims and to what "felt right" to them. A dynamic between the improvisations of this team and the CAD-drafted renderings and pencil sketches let this temple be a living work of art that emerged over a four-month period, beautifully, as a materialization of the Burning Man social vision. A temple of caverns and canyons meant to evoke the Burning Man version of Metropolis. So in this example, the establish/challenge cycle worked itself out in the context of art and construction. Here's an idea on paper; here's a technique. We've established them. Go out and build on what we've established, and when the inspiration strikes you, challenge it. And then let's take it from there and see how the temple evolves. And thus, Burning Man creates vessels that can embrace and assimilate the inevitable trickster challenges.

Or does it?

The party started on Baker Beach in San Francisco, but when it grew, when it bled into the nuisance regions of law enforcement,[27] it sought out and established a new vessel in the desert that, away from the default world, had greater potential for allowing challenge, change, flux. The San Francisco iteration was very male-dominated, filled with arguments, rants, and a blow-things-up philosophy. But in the transition to the desert, things fluctuated, and women gained more leadership positions and put more energy into the survival and sustainability of the event.

---

[27] Later on, Burners were instrumental in negotiating with the City of San Francisco when the city wanted to ban fires on Ocean Beach. The Burners installed safe, concrete fire rings that allowed the practice to continue. "If there's any two things we know about, it's fire and not leaving a mess," Tom Price, quoted in Steven T. Jones, *The Tribes of Burning Man*, 143.

Burning Man began as an art festival. But they had to raise money throughout the year to sustain it, and you don't make enough money showing art. So you raise money from the nonmoneyed classes, the supporters of Burning Man, with parties, and parties use music. In this era and with this tribe of supporters, that meant raves and electronic dance music.

And so Burning Man started attracting more than just artists; there were all the freaks who followed the artists out to the desert, all counterculturalists, and a lot of them, mad dancers to amplified and deejayed music. The folks with the sound systems and the beats started setting up sound camps a couple of miles away . . . until 1996, when some folks got run over by a car heading back from the techno ghetto. With that came the realization that if there were going to be sound camps, they needed to be part of the Burning Man city, not apart from it. But there was resistance, feigned or real, from the punks and metalheads, who did not want the music and certainly did not like EDM. The EDM challenge won out, however, and by 1998, spectacular raves were fully a part of Burning Man. Their location and directionality were solved by some simple zoning. Such sound camps became eligible for funding. And within the music makers was a migration from trance to breakbeat, a more energetic group-dancy music, which continues to develop.

Establish art festival. Challenge with raves. Resolve with minimal constraint.

An even greater test of the establish/challenge cycle was that posed by Chicken John, an early artist participant, and the governing body. The artists were getting rankled that Burning Man was starting to be more about a big party in the desert bent on forming community than an opportunity for artists to use the desert as a canvas and make really cool art. In fact, the amount and quality of art was in decline by 2004. And the artists who started Burning Man challenged the governing body of what had become a multimillion-dollar operation. The debate was, is Burning Man about art or is it about community? Is it a civic culture or a revolutionary one? This led to a petition for giving the artists more money and broadening the democracy of the event, in particular the curating of the art. The governing body, affectionately known as the Borg, rejected the petition. That led to a wager, one that established Borg2, predicated on the claim that, given some real estate on the desert and left to their own devices, the more democratic Borg2 could create more and better art. Wager accepted. Borg2 sought to raise $250,000 but could not. Borg2, headquartered in Chicken's Odeon Bar in San Francisco, had a raucous birth, elected its own board, elected a Borg1 board member to its board . . . was farther out on the spectrum of embracing chaos and danger. At a 2005 Borg2 party, the effigies of two pigs were set up to copulate in midair as they burned and shot flames out of various orifices, releasing streams of coins as they immolated.

On one level, the Borg2 challenge failed. They assumed that the Borg had more control of the event than it really does. They could not come up with the money. They couldn't get organized. There wasn't better or more art because of them, and Chicken John lost the bet and had to let himself get dunked. But as a component of the establish/challenge cycle, the Borg2 rebellion was a huge success, reawakening the organizers and the movement to its purpose, to its commitment to freedom and spontaneity, to the importance of the art and lots of it. The year of the challenge, 2005, was one of the best according to many. And Borg2 prompted a substantial increase in the art budget. The amoral and rebellious trickster energy of Borg2 did not topple the order, but because it was embraced instead of expelled, Burning Man experienced a rebirth and an improvement of its evolving order. The trickster rebellion brought the community closer instead of tearing it apart.

Consider an anarchist precept that anything built can and should be eventually toppled. Paul Addis was a Burner who first attended in 1996. But by 1998, Addis had become frustrated with what he and many others saw as a calcification that had set in, the attraction of music over art, of spectators over participants, and he stopped attending. Until 2007. That year, with the support of accomplices who blacked out the lights to conceal his ascent, he sneaked onto the Man and ignited it himself on a Monday (during a full lunar eclipse no less), five days ahead of schedule. Throwing a chaos bomb into the lap of Burning Man. Establish, challenge. There is irony to this challenge, as he represented a conservative voice who wanted to restore his version of the good old days of Burning Man that were more anarchic and dangerous, anything but conservative. Anyway, his prank was controversial and not well-received. He did thirteen months in prison for his act of arson and property destruction. Are characters like Alfred Jarry, Neal Cassady, William Burroughs and Abbie Hoffman role models or better left as fleeting legends? Should folks like Addis be encouraged to adopt such forms of radical self-expression?[28]

The biggest challenge to the establish/challenge cycle is Burning Man's avoidance of commercialism and consumerism, no small feat in the heart of history's glutton, the United States.

On the one hand, there was initiative, particularly strong in 2007-08, to make the event not only more environmentally friendly—managing waste and materials—but for it to be a leader in demonstrating the utility of green energy. Yet the quickest way to move in this direction was to invite the participation of for-profit renewable energy companies. This resulted in a very conventional exhibit space at the 2007 event where companies that made electric cars and other environmentally friendly products were able to display their wares. And there was a movement to create *OK Culture,* a Burning Man "Good Housekeeping Seal" for businesses that observed certain principles.

---

[28] And how could disruptive play be more sweet and mentally healthy? Carrying guns illegally in Seattle and San Francisco got Addis to two more jail terms, (though he never assaulted anyone). And he eventually killed himself in 2012 by jumping in front of a Bay Area Rapid Transit train.

While some felt that Burning Man culture could make this leap to mainstream acceptance and limited commercialism without losing track of where they came from, others reacted against this phase of the cycle, where values (commercial or not) emerge from the amoral stew. And in fact, it's as Burning Man activities spread out around the world that their progressive values seemed to take a lead, whereas the more organic and anarchic processes that underlie this lead still meandered, played, and propagated.

Tom Price commented, "Here in the Bay Area, people talk about creating the next great app, they talk about creating disruptive technology. What we're creating is disruptive culture. We're demonstrating the ability of really anybody to make real substantial, concrete change in the world and do it from a values-based place, do it with a focus on the social, rather than financial, bottom line. And that's destabilizing. And it's empowering."[29]

So the continual issue and intrigue of Burning Man is to contend with and accommodate the human tendency to create rules and institutionalize but to not let such tendencies dominate and kill the spirit, and to never make a rule that cannot be challenged. This principle has worked well on the playa, Burning Man's playground, but what happens when you take Burning Man out to society at large?

## Takin' It to The Streets

For many, Burning Man's implications for society at large is what it's all about. Here are some examples.

Two Burners, Chicken John and Reverend Billy of the Church of Stop Shopping have run for mayor of San Francisco. These are folks who have taken the noncommercialism of Burning Man and sought to apply it to mainstream politics. Other Burners worked with the city government of San Francisco to import and export Burning

---

[29] Tom Price, quoted in Steven T. Jones, *The Tribes of Burning Man*, 177.

Man art onto the streets of the city as public art. "Why couldn't San Francisco become one great rotating gallery of art?"[30]

When Hurricane Katrina hit New Orleans and the Gulf Coast in 2005, during the Burning Man celebration, a number of Burners immediately left Black Rock City for the Gulf Coast, and the skills Burners excel in—building temporary structures, surviving in harsh environments, and being joyful in the midst of chaos[31] created special relationships and a revelation of what Burners could offer the world at large. Out of these efforts—in particular in Pearlington, Mississippi—Burners Without Borders was founded, and Burning Man skills were directed to aid in disasters around the world: natural, like hurricanes on the Gulf Coast and earthquakes in Haiti, and man-made, like refugee crises in Syria and Greece. In these instances, the overall morality debate is moot . . . and the danger is a given. Few argue with the rightness of helping those displaced and victimized by natural disaster and war. Burners Without Borders delivers not only labor and technical skills but also Burning Man's innovative approaches to solving problems of human survival and its leaderless approach to building teams and working together.

Every Burning Man has a theme, from concepts like Nebulous Entity, Wheel of Time, Seven Ages, and The Vault of Heaven in the 1996–2005 era to the more political Hope and Fear [The Future], Green Man, American Dream, and Metropolis [Life of Cities] between 2005 and 2010. Themes since have seemingly retreated from the overtly political. Carnival of Mirrors, Da Vinci's Workshop, and Radical Ritual are the themes of 2015–17. But the event has grown into a phenomenon that begs speculation about how a quasi-utopian community might have broader impact. What are the prospects of the countercultural becoming cultural? Not to oppose but to become the mainstream.

---

[30] Larry Harvey, quoted in Steven T. Jones, *The Tribes of Burning Man*, 257. .

[31] "The encampment they created in Pearlington had a sense of play and whimsy that the other do-gooders there lacked." Jones, *The Tribes of Burning Man*, 117.

And from the apolitical, anarchist, or even libertarian origins emerge a powerful influencer of the US progressive movement, in perhaps the most heterogeneous bundling of causes since the sixties.

In less overtly political overtones, the Burning Man spirit has spread to EDM fundraising raves, particularly in San Francisco; to regional branches of Burning Man in Calgary, Texas, Colorado, Delaware, New England, New Zealand, Australia, North Carolina, South Africa, Spain, Israel, and many other locales.

Can Burning Man become the Play Society? How would a society that is based on play get things done? Would the Play Society be possible when we need roads and doctors and construction and smartphones and grocery stores and all the things that require a disciplined order and process? Burning Man energetically answers this calling every year for a week when it becomes one of the largest cities in Nevada, where the necessities of a city to function are met, but met sparingly. Yes, it's libertarian, but it's also utopian, interdependent, and joyful, and it successfully lets art . . . and play . . . rule, without neglecting human necessity, without making war, without class exploitation. It's not about play eliminating order; it's about letting play and art flourish, and thus optimizing order by minimizing it.

There is the serendipity and beauty of a program initiated by wildly creative sculptors and fire artists, attracting a larger and larger crowd, one that eventually adds cohesion through the introduction of dance music and becoming a carnival of human dimensions, variations, and activities. As it becomes less of a festival and more of a society, we get a living experiment: a society where the art comes first. This is human destiny. This is what the purpose of human progress is and must be. A species that is fed, clothed, cured, sheltered, and sustained...has no purpose if it cannot be even more. Thus, achieve peace. Achieve environmental balance. But base new societies on the priority of art, of *homo ludens*, [hu]man the player. If there is magic in play and in art, society should be built in a way that encourages the release of such.

So is what is good for Burning Man good for society? "Since creativity is the engine that drives it, once it stops being creative, the motivation to participate becomes diminished, and you get a city full of tourists coming to experience a thing that has already stopped happening."[32] Noted comic artist Robert Crumb made a similar comment about the utopian flash of Haight-Ashbury, that by the time folks found out about it, it was over. Burning Man learned from history and has figured out some means for durability. Starting with material artists instead of musicians may have been key.

Burning Man's sturdiness is unprecedented based on our examples to date, but it makes sense in a way, if this is the consequence of the inspiration of Trickster gods, of dada, of the sixties, that some folks would apply themselves to the idea of sustaining and communalizing this playful sensibility . . . even starting with the modest notion of keeping it going for one week *every year* . . . smart!

But Burning Man is better defined as less of a political movement and intentional utopia model and more as an unintentional one, focused first on folks building the city they've always wanted. Are the artists of Burning Man a metaphor of their own making or a societal slow explosion that spreads its ways and means throughout the world?

---

[32] Tom Price, quoted in Steven T. Jones, *The Tribes of Burning Man*, 214-215..

# SIXTEEN

# The Road Ahead

*Far beyond the reaches of the universe, infinity is trying to communicate with us.*

*Yayoi Kusama[1]*

*Play is voluntary, an end unto itself. Its goals are self-imposed. Organized games that have prede-termined rules, winners and losers, have left the domain of play. In play, there is more attention to process than on a goal or outcome.*

*O. Fred Donaldson[2]*

BUGS BUNNY had been romping through the American psyche for decades, but by 1969, the golden age of animation was coming to a close and the mainstream popularity of this Trickster icon was waning. The entertainment machine was metastasizing and gearing up for new characters and the fify-seven-channel[3] cable reality that was to take over in the 1980s.

---

[1] From a taped interview regarding her exhibition, *Infinity Mirrors,* shown June 30-September 10, 2017 at the Seattle Art Museum.

[2] O. Fred Donaldson, *Playing by Heart: The Vision and Practice of Belonging* (Nevada City, CA: Touch the Future, 1993).

[3] Bruce Springsteen, "57 Channels (And Nothin' On)," by Bruce Springsteen, *Human Touch,* Columbia, 1992, vinyl recording.

But in 1974, Mel Brooks released his masterful satire of the Hollywood western, *Blazing Saddles.* The film is, in essence, a ninety-minute Bugs Bunny cartoon that launches the Trickster myth anew into politics. The plot twists and wanders like a Wakdjunkaga story cycle, evoking the cartoon irrationality of the archetype. Now the Bugs figure is a black man (Cleavon Little as Bart) who ends up as sheriff in a blatantly racist Wild West, where he is demeaned and called nigger in almost every scene. Yet as Trickster, he wins battles and sustains the appropriate slapstick mockery that makes for powerful antiracist satire. The film endures as a signpost for how Americans have yet to come to terms with their most tenacious malignancy.

Trickster mythology pops up everywhere in *Blazing Saddles.* First and probably the most famous is the fart joke, where the bad guy cowpokes are sitting around a campfire eating beans. In another, Bart invents the candygram, disguises himself as a Western Union courier, and has the candy box explode in bad guy Mongo's face . . . they even appropriate the Looney Tunes music when the prank is set and Bart makes his speedy exit.

Madeline Kahn as Lili von Shtupp is the German temptress modeled after Marlene Dietrich . . . except she talks with a lisp and even has the line "I'm not a wabbit."

The movie takes place in 1874, yet it has elements of trickster time travel, like a medieval executioner in the middle of an Old West town and World War I German soldiers as von Shtupp's backup dancers in the saloon. Eventually, the whole movie breaks the fourth wall, and in oblique homage to Looney Tunes' *Duck Amuck,*[4] the action bleeds onto the various Warner Brothers sets, including a crew of gay dancers being directed by a fey Dom DeLuise.

The film uses the old gag where our heroes, Bart and the Waco Kid (Gene Wilder), subdue a couple of the enemies, in this case

---

[4] Duck Amuck, directed by Chuck Jones (Burbank, CA: Warner Brothers, 1953), short film, cartoon.

two members of the Ku Klux Klan, stealing and donning their costumes. When their disguises are easily discovered (get it, black guy in a KKK robe?), Bart quips "And now, for my next impression . . . Jesse Owens!'" as he skedaddles, just as you would expect in a cartoon.[5] Or, for example, in the Winnebago tale where Wakdjunkaga must elude an angry brother or duped tribe.

Bugs Bunny and *Blazing Saddles* are both released and distributed by Warner Brothers. Brooks was inspired; this was the only movie he made for the House of Bugs. This is significant because *Blazing Saddles* takes risks that, for example, Disney Studios would have never abided, like the frequent use of the word *nigger*, and it's very ribald and R-rated. Even the Warner Brothers folks almost refused to release it, taking the loss rather than risking condemnation. And many reviewers did not like it, reacting to its low-brow approach.

Yet it is number six on the American Film Institute's 100 Funniest American Movies of All Time, and it was a huge box office hit, making more money than any other for Warner Brothers that summer. And Madeline Kahn received a Best Supporting Actress Academy Award nomination.

Thus, the trickster elements of a winning and powerful prankster-ism, mockery of our follies (in this case racism), hero in disguise, time travel, fart jokes, and references to the hare strike a timeless chord with a broad audience. Carl Jung would nod in satisfaction at how this ancient archetype emerged on the modern stage. And *Blazing Saddles* is relevant, clearly pointing out that we are still plagued by racism. Yet the film—thanks to screenplay writers Richard Pryor[6] and Mel Brooks—graces us with playfulness about something that more commonly inspires solemnity and testaments of suffering and

---

[5] You can watch the film clip on YouTube. https://youtu.be/TJkHykGRXrw

[6] Richard Pryor was originally cast in the Bart role, but his contract and reputation as a racy comedian kept him off the screen. As part of the writing team, however, his humor is evident throughout. There were also three other writers: Norman Stenberg, Andrew Bergman, and Alan Uger.

oppression. Disruptive play strikes again from Bugs Bunny, from the trickster demigod. He munches on his eternal carrot and asks us, "Eh, what's up, doc?" And the best of Western culture nudges us to incorporate Bugs as our own inner director, bringing us closer to the Play Society.

Oh, come on. How could something as silly as elevating the status of Bugs Bunny, of proposing what essentially amounts to carnival as social model, even be worth consideration?

In fact, contemporary dramas like the British television series *Black Mirror* suggest much more probable scenarios where mediated pleasures and corrupted play amplify the brink of dystopia.

In one of its more humorous episodes, "Nosedive,"[7] human interaction has been fully commercialized, and one's status is based upon immediate ratings—one to five stars—texted into a social media site strikingly similar to Facebook, Yelp, or Uber. Your barista, Uber driver, friends close and distant, Facebook "friends" all get to take a shot at you, in person or online . . . you are continually rated and averaged on a scale of one to five stars. The result is a transactional society akin to high school cliques, but the implications of this dystopia—institutionalized phoniness—are terrifying and all too plausible. Greed migrates from the marketplace to our relationships. While fertile grist for humor and satire, the scenario foretells a distressingly atomized, isolated, and mediated life, one devoid of play or authentic relationship.

Then there is "The Waldo Moment."[8] Waldo is an animated TV show meme who brings in higher ratings by harassing a political candidate, projecting his cartoon bear on a truck-mounted mobile screen and casting insults, bad jokes, and humiliations. He also enters the

---

[7] *Black Mirror*, Season 3, episode 1, "Nosedive," directed by Joe Wright, written by Rashida Jones, Michael Schur, based on a story by Charlie Brooker, October 21, 2016, Channel 4. Viewed on Netflix.

[8] *Black Mirror*, Season 2, episode 3, "The Waldo Moment," directed by Bryn Higgins, written by Charlie Brooker and Christopher Morris, February 25, 2013, Channel 4. Viewed on Netflix.

race for a seat in Parliament. Waldo is a mean-spirited trickster type, like a 4chan troll come to life. He taps popular frustration with the status quo, but he delivers no hope, just attacks the establishment . . . which sells well. Eventually, the CIA gets wind of Waldo's effectiveness, and he is adopted worldwide and used to win elections and represent the agenda of those in power. This is a modern binding of Trickster, not a liberation.

Bugs Bunny and other tricksters are in it for the fun of it, fun that is authentically liberating. Dark facsimiles like Waldo employ the potency of the archetype's ancient powers to strike a similar chord that also resonates. Such twisted Tricksters convince us that we're crossing boundaries and getting free, when in fact such trolls are vehicles for propaganda that binds us to an oppressive status quo. Waldo, who is a co-opted character from the outset, tricks folks into thinking they've upset the status quo when in fact they've accepted its full takeover. And "The Waldo Moment" has been cited as one of the more lucid explanations of the 2016 presidential election.

Charles Brooker penned all of the *Black Mirror* episodes of dystopia and twenty-first-century technology going only slightly more amok than it already has. In "Hated in the Nation,"[9] a mastermind hacker takes social media pile-on hating to its logical next step, assassinating whoever is voted by the online masses as the most hated of the day. He then doles out vigilante justice by turning the same murder machine—GPS-controlled electronic bees—on the haters. It's the meanness of trolls taken to another level. Nothing playful here, but Brooker paints dramatic and visceral pictures of the risk of venturing onto amoral ground.

These (a)morality plays of the twenty-first century sensitize us to the life-or-death stakes of social media havoc. Brooker joins the

---

[9] *Black Mirror*, Season 3, episode 6, "Hated in the Nation," directed by James Hawes, written by Charlie Brooker, October 21, 2016, Channel 4. Viewed on Netflix.

mounting tidal wave of cynicism that harbingers the dystopian inverse of the Play Society. Yet I still hope that such dramas serve as warnings and not prophecies. Besides an endless list of movies and books that feed our obsession with our demise and dire and deadened futures: *The Hunger Games*, 1984, *The Terminator*, *Brave New World*, *Invasion of the Body Snatchers*, *Children of Men*, *Gattaca*, *The Matrix*, *Minority Report*, *Snowpiercer*, *The Trial*, *Metropolis*—this list is a mere fraction—*Black Mirror* represents, in episode after episode, all too realistic near-future bummers.

We began this exploration with the idea of play and playfulness in the infant child, animals, and all life forms. And also with the Trickster archetype, the inevitable accomplice of the adult who yet retains original playfulness. We witnessed the power and magic of the Trickster in cultures outside the Western world, and his/her binding within it.

Reaction to the enormity of World War I's horrors busted the Trickster out of jail, and the West has been contending with disruptive play ever since. Through art and antiwar activism, the road has been littered with the hilarity and painful awareness provoked by dada's absurdist response to that war. In the shadow of nuclear terror, the Beats detonated a rucksack revolution that brought an even more powerful and even more playful response to yet another miserable conflict, Vietnam. And art, music, comedy, graffiti, pranksterism, guerilla theater, online freedom fighting, countercultural participation, and collective and prolonged celebration continue to wage war on war[10] and other things that are not fun: exploitative commerce, rampant consumerism, environmental disaster, hate.

We have fought the war to end all wars. We have joined religions that preach peace and have clear directives based on their understanding of good and evil. We have developed governmental structures mission-bound to serve all citizens and create the conditions for a universally just and happy and healthy life. Because such efforts have

---

[10] Wilco, "War on War," by Jeff Tweedy and Jay Bennett, *Yankee Hotel Foxtrot*, Nonesuch, 2002, CD.

so tremendously failed, because we have not been able to avoid war, we must consider Trickster unbound coupled with collective play-fulness as an antidote. To propose carnival as social model, a poetic synonym for utopian anarchism and the Play Society, is the only thing that makes sense in any culture so sickened by war, commerce, and consumerism.

---

A functioning anarchist society that starts and restarts itself can muster the resources to feed, clothe, cure, shelter, and love but is less likely to aspire to or succeed in war. Commerce and consumption are not absolute evils; they are just out of control, and a Play Society could bring them into a proportion that does not disconnect us from a real life or lead us into more war.

We have seen at least glimmers of the path illumined by disrup-tive players who poked the bear and brought their original playful-ness face to face with the orderly power structures built on cultural play. So in the mode of Jarry, Duchamp, Abbie, Andy, the Yes Men, Banksy, Lisa Simpson, Bugs, Burning Man, and Anonymous, just stay true to these simple concepts:

- The most effective way to fight power is to not take it seri-ously.

- To emerge, a Play Society means tearing things down and rebuilding a society based on art and play instead of com-merce.

- Rules are indeed made to be broken . . . when we get to the "right" rules, most everyone will realize/feel the rightness of them and follow them . . . we will at that time be recon-necting with nature, with the divine, with that which both precedes and follows history, the 'order' of play, of an under-stood and felt irrationality.

To the skeptics, I repeat that commerce and competition have their place, but have bloviated, and it is by putting art and play first, and **then** 'organizing' a society, that we avoid the missteps of the past. For example, Burning Man.

If we are to trust the diligence of Barbara Ehrenreich's research in *Dancing in the Streets*[11] and of Peter Stallybrass and Allon White in *The Politics and Poetics of Transgression*[12]—and based on the extent of their reviews of numerous anthropological studies, we likely should—we learn that rituals, rites, religions, celebrations, dances, incantations, prayers, trances, and all modes of experiencing ecstasy were prevalent among the indigenous peoples of the Americas, Australia, Africa, Europe, and Polynesia, as well as in Asia (though much further in the past there). But we also learn that in their haste to "civilize the savages" and impose a religion, enslave, exploit, and rule, imperial powers routinely condemned and dismissed, and eventually repressed such customs. Thus, our current knowledge of the substance of such experiences is limited. We like to believe that through music and the melding of such spirit traditions with Christianity, i.e., vodun, the phenomenon survives, but in-depth knowledge of communal ecstasy is limited.

Based on what we do know, I should like to propose that the playfulness of the Trickster flourishes and is nurtured in such ecstatic environments, influencing and leading but also replenishing that playful spirit. And for those personalities whose trickster traits are more prominent, they "change gears" from the disruptive play mien that kicks in when confronted with a repressive power structure to the mode of original play that it is safe to adopt in the absence of such power.

Have we at least been stumbling in that direction? Themes that have dominated the cultural landscape might include: a slapdash ide-

---

[11] Barbara Ehrenreich, *Dancing in the Streets: A History of Collective Joy* (New York: Metropolitan, 2006).

[12] Peter Stallybrass and Allon White, *The Politics and Poetics of Transgression* (Ithaca, NY: Cornell University Press, 1986), 1-44.

alistic vision (the sixties and its aftermath) a world of high competence and materialism (the eighties and its aftermath) that hopefully led to some new visions;[13] and a social media/technological troll version of the primordial amoral soup (the twenty-first century to date). In other words, we went from an avid exploration of play to a renewed suppression of it in the interest of high achievement to atomized and technologized numbing pleasures, only to beckon play's reemergence.

Play that is mediated through a consumer relationship is probably not play. Authentic play doesn't cost anything, and no one seems to have time for anything that doesn't cost anything.[14]

So it's about developing an economic system that features, protects, and benefits from more and greater opportunities to stay clear of order, ranking, and commerce, *play zones* if you will. When democratic control of the economic world is achieved, people will be able to create the time, energy, and resources for such zones. A good start would be a twenty-four-hour workweek and twelve weeks of vacation. As we move towards these new proportions, the value of competence and ranking will be reconsidered; the Play Society, which is what the Impressionists, dadas, Beats and hippies were proposing, would take shape.

How are we going to get there? Using popular music as a reflection of the zeitgeist of its times: sixties rock claimed utopian visions with a magnificent reach that clearly exceeded its grasp. The punk music of the late seventies was a dark reflection—sixties optimism turned upside-down—and wailed on about a promise undelivered. Subsequent punk aesthetics canceled sexiness as we had come to know it, wiping the slate clean for a new vision of sex and sexuality that was foreshadowed by glam and is emerging now.

---

[13] Witness all the recent books on play besides this one: *Beyond Love and Work* (by Lenore Terr); *Deep Play* (by Diane Ackerman); *Play: How It Shapes the Brain* (by Stuart Brown and Christopher Vaughan); *Serious Play* (by Michael Schrage); *The Reinvention of Work* (by Matthew Fox); *Rejuvenile* (by Christopher Noxon); etc.

[14] Jeremy Rifkin, *The Age of Access* (New York: Tarcher/Putnam, 2000).

In the aughts, rebel creativity moved smoothly into the machine, and a core of millennial technologists have taken charge and will be the dominant artistic force for the next twenty years. Whether they represent a ghost in the machine who holds on to visions of a liberated society or are merely tools who want to run the confidence game, take our money, and leave our souls thirsty . . . we don't know yet. That is the question, and the answer lies in whether we resign ourselves to the opiate of mediated pleasures or we come to understand play and embrace it as a way to become conscious tools of the universe. In an optimum scenario, our technological power would be put to the latter purpose.

---

Shaya Mercer's film *Trade Off* documents the 1999 "Battle in Seattle," where protesters effectively shut down a meeting of the World Trade Organization and educated millions on what is at stake as this group of unelected officials govern international trade through the setting of rules and sanctions. In one scene, a protester is having a reasonably intelligent debate with a manager from the Niketown superstore in downtown Seattle. They are discussing, quite seriously, the issues surrounding the need to make a profit versus the ethics of taking advantage of cheap foreign labor. There's nothing funny about it, but it's impossible to keep a straight face because the protester is dressed as some kind of electric fly, complete with fine-mesh tea strainers for bug-eyes, microcircuitry taped to his gut, felt antennae, and diaphanous wings. Have the playsters and the pranksters returned?

What the WTO demonstrations revealed was the first effective recombination of the highly effective and broad coalition of the '60s that splintered into monochromatic single-issue groups in the '70s and '80s. Though only a first step, organized labor, socialists, artists, environmentalists, anarchists, politicos from around the world, and human rights activists formed a unified movement that was varied and deep. It was not like a one-night stand, though; it felt more like folks had been woodshedding and sticking to their key issues, practicing for the opportunity to make a difference that they knew would come. The purpose of the demonstrations was to compel the WTO to reassess the basis of its membership, its mission, and how it conducts business. Demonstrations since, especially those of Occupy, Black Lives Matter, ever-broadening Pride parades, and the Women's March of 2017, have furthered such emerging coalitions.

What happens when you get such a broad group working together, when ironworkers, radical feminists, street puppeteers, environmentalists, and anarchists are actually playing *together*, is that there is room for that most elusive but key element of humor and play to show its face. Michael Dolan of Public Citizen was a key spokesperson during the demonstrations, and he's a smartass organizer who doesn't miss an opportunity to make a wisecrack. Han Shan is an assertive, well-dressed anarchist who knows how to talk about the serious points but has a sense of humor and a sense of the absurd. Perhaps more important are the thousands of artists who take an active interest in political affairs, see its connection to their creative output, and make statements like the WTO demonstrations colorful, entertaining education.

For example, in protest of the WTO rulings that wiped out protections for sea turtles caught in shrimp nets, over fifty demonstrators dressed up as turtles. Other demonstrators threw a wine and cheese party on the street, featuring French cheese that had been made illegal by the WTO's punishment of France for not accepting dairy products with bovine hormones. And we really don't know why this other guy was dressed up like an electric fly, but he was pretty funny.

Times of unrest, where the existing order is upset and people taste the chaos underneath, can be frightening for many. Others feel excitement and a chance to express hope and make a move towards better times. But such times—be they revolutions, rebellions, riots, demon-

strations, nonviolent protests, new communities, elections, legisla-
tion, spontaneous carnival, raves, concerts, or something we've never
seen before—have as many interpretations as they do participants.
A lot of different agendas spurt out once the lid is off normal daily
life. Witness this dispatch I sent out from those very WTO demonstrations in Seattle, November 1999, which could have easily come
from the front lines of the sixties:

> Many of you have been reading the news: cops everywhere;
> tear gas; rubber bullets; labor, environmental, human rights,
> and anarchist demonstrations. The fabric of our man-
> ufactured daily lives is ripped asunder, and the demons
> and seeds, the unfulfilled wants and unsalved pains that
> seethed just beneath the veneer, as diverse as humans are,
> are released. That's why it gets so confusing so quickly. It's
> about the WTO. No, it's about all injustice and private
> property. No, it's the right to peaceably assemble, to have
> legal representation, to be able to walk unmolested through
> your own neighborhood, to have a voice at the international
> trade table, to do away with the international trade table,
> keep China out, let China in, no more Gap, no more Star-
> bucks.

> People are generally only seeing the peaceful and legal labor
> march of 20,000-40,000 on Tuesday in contrast with the
> "anarchists" who destroyed property, but there was a third
> group who peacefully pulled off a mass and well-planned
> civil disobedience that essentially prevented the first day
> of the WTO from happening, and probably ensured that
> Clinton and Moore and others acknowledged the validity
> of their claims and put child labor, health, representation,
> and the environment on the top of the agenda.

> It is as if society's own unconscious, the collection of all its
> dreams, are released to run rampant.

The demonstration in Washington, DC, five months later at a meeting
of the International Monetary Fund featured street puppets as well.
And San Francisco has a long tradition of "arting up" their political

demonstrations, with a degree of outrageousness always added to the mix by its strong and colorful gay community. What was promising about the Seattle demonstrations was its multigenerational composition. One expects the adolescents seeking adventure, whom these demonstrations depend upon for energy, volunteerism, and numbers. The other members of this emerging community saw participation in the WTO action as a natural extension of political commitments and personal disciplines they had been nurturing for the past five to fifty years. Force had found form, and one sensed that the ability to mount this action, to publicly express a political position as part of collective groups, would recur. If it can again as a diverse communal action, then play stands a chance of reemerging, not just out in the Nevada desert, not just for a few hours, but smack dab in the middle and oftener and oftener. Perhaps we can find a form that can begin to sustain play as a cultural practice.

A Play Society would challenge the hegemony where we rank people's worth according to their competence, but it would also engender certain risks. This is why the lessons of twentieth-century rebels—from dada to WTO to James Dean to the antiwar movements—are so critical. Viewed as a time when we got a peek of what a Play Society might look like, the sixties also witnessed a collapse of discipline, and veterans of that time came to realize that some baby got thrown out with the bathwater when the establishment's walls came down. By adopting antiestablishment lifestyles and rejecting American establishment culture, the values of ritual and discipline also suffered. Thus, the search of the past fifty years for new spiritual grounding continues today.

A solution to this problem is found in the distinctions between original play and cultural play. Fred Donaldson is a devotee of *original play*, which he defines as a substance of the universe that occurs in all life; it is the behavior by which love and belonging are expressed, given, and received. Whenever play moves into contest, sex, age, or other roles and rules, it becomes what is comprehensively defined by Huizinga as *cultural play*. Issues of maturity and narcissism are issues only for cultural play, not for original play. *Disruptive play* occurs in the rare times when the rhythms of original play suddenly appear in a cultural setting.

What was the original and elemental divinity of play first delivered to so-called primitive people? And were their lives in fact so harsh and difficult that there was no time for play? Or was play less a relief from hardship and more the goal and reason for enduring it? Abraham Joshua Heschel explains that "The Sabbath is not for the sake of the weekdays; the weekdays are for the sake of Sabbath."[15]

And what was the nature of the journey from the stuff of folks' daily life to the deification of playfulness into Trickster characters and gods? Does the adoption of these qualities by solitary warriors of play like Abbie and Andy and rascals like Bugs and Bart and Lisa bring this divine light into our very real lives? Would collective expressions of play like the Fremont Solstice Parade, Burning Man, and Rio Carnival represent the consolidation of this energy and its push into society at large?

Play is a very physical activity that includes a specific kind of touch[16] that, for lack of better terms, looks like frolic and wrasslin'. But play also successfully makes the transition to less touch-dependent forms found in the antics of Tricksters, comedians, fictional characters, parades, online shenanigans, and the like. I admit to trepidation when one attempts to call video gaming or augmented realities play, yet this is part of the journey, and it has its champions.[17]

---

[15] Abraham Joshua Heschel, *The Sabbath* (New York: Meridian Books, 1963), 14, wherein he quotes *Zohar*, I, 75.

[16] Nonsexual, no pinching, tickling, or clutching.

[17] Jane McGonigal, *Reality Is Broken: Why Games Make Us Better and How They Can Change the World* (London: Vintage, 2012); Jane McGonigal, *Superbetter: How a Gameful Life Can Make You Stronger, Happier, Braver and More Resilient* (London: HarperThorsons, 2016).

But the bottom line is this: Play set free and embraced by society at large makes for a new spiritual grounding and a more perfect political reality.

One way of expressing this is the possibility that art could be fully integrated into daily life. Rather than pointing the way to a higher ideal, we become that ideal, and so it is not the end of art, but the end of its distinction from ordinary life, the dada vision. Rather than a world without injustice or conflict as subject matter for art, our lives could become art, and we thus realize that improved world.

This excerpt from an interview with *Harper's* Editor Emeritus Lewis Lapham grounds the case for the Play Society in political reality. During the commemoration of the 150th anniversary of *Harper's Magazine,* Lapham gave an interview to an alternative weekly paper and broached the topic:

> I think of humor as implying a sense of wisdom, imply-
> ing some sense of proportion, implying a proper attitude
> towards the absurdity of the human predicament . . . [but]
> it's a coping mechanism. I don't think it has a political. . . . I
> wouldn't claim that kind of role for it; I think it just helps me
> get through the day. Seriously, I don't think it brings down
> governments or makes political movements. The people who
> tend to change the world politically, they're very humorless.
> You don't think of Lenin or Hitler or Ralph Nader as being
> wits . . . people that have too much of a sense of humor are
> not likely to end up with political power.[18]

And in point of fact, trickster disruptive players can be fully engaged in the politics of their times but do not run for office or try to accumulate power.

But if you always do what you've always done—let men lacking humor rule—you'll get what you've always got, men lacking what Lapham acknowledges humor [play] brings: a "sense of wisdom, implying

---

[18] Lewis Lapham, "Things as They Might Become," interview by Eric Fredericksen, *The Stranger,* June 29, 2000.

some sense of proportion, implying a proper attitude towards the absurdity of the human predicament." Lapham inadvertently provides the answer and the dilemma.

## What About Now?

In *The History of Childhood,* Lloyd deMause offers his psychoanalytic theories of childhood's role in historical change. He states: "Specific childhood experiences must occur to sustain specific cultural traits, and once these experiences no longer occur the trait disappears."[19]

Thus, in the vulnerable state that US secularism places itself, the sixties were truly revolutionary in that numerous cultural traits—college fraternities and sororities, Boy Scouts and Girl Scouts, military service, family structures, sexual identities, prejudicial college admissions policies, agonistic values—were temporarily beaten back or diminished in their social import. Estrangement between fathers and sons, mothers and daughters of that generation is the most striking and painful, but also most opportune. It left us with a rare vacuum of rites of passage and other traits and with the ongoing problem of trying to explain what has happened since.

Since then, many have worked to create new rituals and a relevant spirituality—be it pagan wicca, Buddhism, gender liberation, cosplay, polyamory, a new wave of Islam devotees or a renewal of Christian and Jewish faiths—that will somehow bring community to the most diverse nation in history. The rich resources of our culture, our broad palette of entertainment activities, our sense of social justice, the enormous force of technological advance, and our collective determination comprise our toolbox for fashioning a new culture that somehow moves the human condition forward. This is the preeminent task of our time.

And it's where fun comes in. As the baby boomers die off, the millennials could redefine American culture as a place for play. The

---

[19] Lloyd deMause, ed., *The History of Childhood* (London: Jason Aronson, 1995), 3.

maturing of authentic play into adult daily life—making the world safe for play—will bring on an opportunity to transcend, where we can "stop making sense" and start living lives of interconnected meaning and joy. The idea is to create, as Abbie said, "an experience so intense that you actualize your full potential. You become LIFE. LIFE IS FUN."[20] Plato concurred:

> God alone is worthy of supreme seriousness, but man is made God's plaything, and that is the best part of him. Therefore every man and woman should live life accordingly, and play the noblest games and be of another mind from what they are at present. . . . For they deem war a serious thing, though in war there is neither play nor culture worthy of the name, which are the things we deem most serious. Hence all must live in peace as well as they possibly can. What, then is the right way of living? Life must be lived as play."[21]

Twenty-four hundred years later, we are on the threshold of being able to take Plato's ideas out for a spin. As (and if) our society achieves economic, environmental, and social balance, the search for a meaningful life will take on greater importance and become more complex. Viktor Frankl identified the urgency of this quest. His school of logotherapy was inspired by the need to address existential boredom, to help people who have lost track of their own search for meaningfulness.[22]

If there are historical lessons that can help solve this modern crisis, we must not ignore them. Stories of disruptive play are filled with such lessons. Play has meaning but not purpose; thus, it is the perfect anti-

---

[20] Abbie Hoffman, *The Best of Abbie Hoffman: Selections from Revolution for the Hell of It, Woodstock Nation, Steal This Book and New Writings* (New York: Four Walls Eight Windows, 1989), 19.

[21] A quote from Plato, *Laws*, vii, 796. Quoted in Johann Huizinga, *Homo Ludens: A Study of the Play Element in Culture* (Boston: Beacon Press, 1955), 18-19.

[22] Viktor E. Frankl, *Man's Search for Meaning* (Boston: Beacon Press, 1955), 129.

dote for existential crisis in a world of questionable purposes. Only by entering a state that discards purpose—that plays—might our true purpose be discovered.

The increase of play in daily life will signify that we are meeting the existential challenge, hopefully in a society that is also mature and spiritually grounded. Like the highly disciplined artist who, after years of toil on a masterpiece, recaptures in art, architecture, music, or athletics the innocent spontaneity of a child's play, we could achieve a commonly experienced sense of flow, communities and a society attuned to more primal growth patterns.

The stories in this book are the story of how we can promote original play but also develop a strong sense of how we can shepherd and steward its spirit to transform cultural play. Adherents of a play ethos are finding ways to personally survive and to create spheres of play around them. Players continue to emerge through the arts, and the potential and challenges of cyberspace as playground lies before us. African-Americans and minorities have consistently debunked the rationality of the dominant culture and never hesitate to play with our assumptions. And we can always make the effort to connect better with our children and listen to what their lives are telling us.

Optimum playing in the third millennium will depend upon our ability to fully connect with the wisdom of our elders. Ironically, it is their perspective that will remind us of what we had as children and forgot. They've been through the wringer of a life yoked to *cultural play* and the enlightened among them recall *original play's* true value. It is our elders who will endow us with the means of playing in a way that is genuine, that allows play—as understood by children and other beings—to lead us forward. We can then build a culture of rich lives that, by our loving acts of play, truly honor and connect to the Source of life.

# Selected Bibliography

Ackerman, Diane. *Deep Play*. New York: Random House, 1999.

Banksy. *Wall and Piece*. London: Century, 2005.

Beck, Julian. *The Life of the Theatre: Notes Toward a Statement on Anarchism and Theatre*. San Francisco: City Lights, 1972.

Becker, Ernest. *The Birth and Death of Meaning*. New York: The Free Press, 1973.

Bloom, Harold. *Shakespeare: The Invention of the Human*. New York: Riverhead, 1998.

Breton, André. *Surrealism and Painting*. Translated by Simon Watson Taylor. London: Macdonald and Co., 1972.

Brooks, David. *Bobos in Paradise: The New Upper Class and How They Got There*. New York: Simon & Schuster, 2000.

Cassady, Neal. *The First Third*. San Francisco: City Lights, 1971.

Casteneda, Carlos. *The Teachings of Don Juan: A Yaqui Way of Knowledge*. New York: Washington Square Press, 1968.

Charters, Ann, ed. *The Portable Beat Reader*. New York: Penguin Books, 1992.

Coleman, Gabriella. *Hacker, Hoaxer, Whistleblower, Spy: The Many Faces of Anonymous*. New York: Verso, 2015.

Csikszentmihalyi, Mihaly. *Flow*. New York: Harper Perennial, 1991.

Darnton, Robert. *The Great Cat Massacre and Other Episodes in French Cultural History*. New York: Vintage, 1985.

deMause, Lloyd, ed. *The History of Childhood*. London: Jason Aronson, 1995.

Doctorow, E.L. *The Book of Daniel*. New York: Random House, 1971.

Doherty, Brian. *This is Burning Man: The Rise of a New American Underground*. Dallas: BenBella Books, 2004.

Donaldson, O. Fred. *Playing by Heart: The Vision and Practice of Belonging*. Nevada City, CA: Touch the Future, 1993.

Ehrenreich, Barbara. *Dancing in the Streets: A History of Collective Joy.* New York: Metropolitan, 2006.

Forster, E.M. *Aspects of the Novel.* London: Hodder and Stoughton, 2012.

Franck, Dan. *Bohemian Paris: Picasso, Modigliani, Matisse, and the Birth of Modern Art.* New York: Grove Press, 2007.

Frankl, Viktor E. *Man's Search for Meaning.* Boston: Beacon Press, 1959.

Gaiman, Neil. *Norse Mythology.* New York: W.W. Norton, 2017.

Garcia, Jerry. *Garcia: Interview with Charles Reich and Jann Wenner.* Boston: Little, Brown, 1995.

Gardner, Howard. *Creating Minds: An Anatomy of Creativity Seen through the Lives of Freud, Einstein, Picasso, Stravinsky, Eliot, Graham, and Gandhi.* New York: Basic, 1993.

Gitlin, Todd. *The Sixties: Years of Hope, Days of Rage.* Toronto: Bantam Books, 1987.

Goodchild, Peter. *Raven Tales: Traditional Stories of Native Peoples.* Chicago: Chicago Review Press, 1991.

Gottlieb, Annie. *Do You Believe in Magic: Bringing the 60s Back Home.* New York: Simon & Schuster, 1987.

Hall, Sir Peter. *Cities in Civilization.* New York: Pantheon, 1998.

Harrison, Hank. *The Dead Book: A Social History of the Grateful Dead.* New York: Links Books, 1973.

Hemingway, Ernest. *Fiesta: The Sun Also Rises.* London: Vintage, 1927.

Heschel, Abraham Joshua. *The Sabbath.* New York: Meridian Books, 1963.

Hoffman, Abbie. *The Best of Abbie Hoffman: Selections from Revolution for the Hell of It, Woodstock Nation, Steal This Book and New Writings.* New York: Four Walls Eight Windows, 1989.

Hoffman, Abbie. *Revolution for the Hell of It.* New York: Dial, 1968.

Huizinga, Johan. *Homo Ludens: A Study of the Play Element in Culture.* Boston: Beacon Press, 1955.

Hyde, Lewis. *Trickster Makes This World.* New York: Farrar, Straus and Giroux, 1998.

Jezer, Marty. *Abbie Hoffman: American Rebel.* New Brunswick, NJ: Rutgers, 1992.

Jones, Steven T. *The Tribes of Burning Man: How an Experimental City in the Desert Is Shaping the New American Counterculture.* San Francisco: Consortium of Collective Consciousness, 2011.

Kerouac, Jack. *On the Road.* New York: Penguin, 1957.

Kerouac, Jack. *The Dharma Bums,* New York: Viking Penguin, 1958.

Krukowski, Samantha, ed. *Playa Dust: Collected Stories from Burning Man.* London: Black Dog, 2014.

Leland, J. *Hip: The History.* New York: Harper Perennial, 2005.

Lennon, John, and Jann Wenner. *Lennon Remembers.* New York: Popular Library, 1971.

Marcuse, Herbert. *One-Dimensional Man: Studies in the Ideology of Advanced Industrial Society.* Boston: Beacon Press, 1964.

Margulies, Lynn, and Bob Zmuda. *Dear Andy Kaufman, I Hate Your Guts!* Los Angeles: Process Publishing, 2009.

Maslow, Abraham H. *Toward a Psychology of Being.* 2nd ed. New York: Van Nostrand Reinhold, 1968.

McGonigal, Jane. *Reality Is Broken: Why Games Make Us Better and How They Can Change the World.* London: Vintage, 2012.

McGonigal, Jane. *Superbetter: How a Gameful Life Can Make You Stronger, Happier, Braver and More Resilient.* London: HarperThorsons, 2016.

Moore, Christopher. *Fool.* New York: Harper, 2009.

Motherwell, R.B. *The Dada Painters and Poets.* New York: Wittenborn, 1951.

N. *A Pleasant Vintage of Till Eulenspiegel.* Translated by Paul Oppenheimer from the edition of 1515. Middletown, CT: Wesleyan University Press, 1972.

Pearce, Joseph Chilton. *Magical Child.* New York: Plume, 1977.

Pearl, Arthur, Douglas Grant, and Ernst Wenk, eds. *The Value of Youth.* Davis, CA: International Dialogue, 1978.

Pine, Joe, and Jim Gilmore. *The Experience Economy.* Cambridge: Harvard, 2000.

Quinn, Edward, and Paul J. Dolan, eds. *The Sense of the 60's.* New York: The Free Press, 1968.

Radin, Paul. *The Trickster: A Study in American Indian Mythology.* New York: Schocken, 1956.

Raskin, Jonah. *For the Hell of It: The Life and Times of Abbie Hoffman*. Berkeley: University of California Press, 1998.

Richter, Hans. *dada: art and anti-art*. London: Thames and Hudson, 1997.

Riesman, David, Nathan Glazer, and Reuel Denney. *The Lonely Crowd: A Study of the Changing American Character*. Abridged edition. New Haven, CT: Yale, (revised edition, 2000).

Rifkin, Jeremy. *The Age of Access*. New York: Tarcher/Putnam, 2000.

Rilke, Rainer Maria. *Selected Poems of Rainer Maria Rilke, A Translation from the German*. Translated by Robert Bly. New York: Harper & Row, 1981.

Rousseau, Jean-Jacques. *Emile or On Education*. Translated by Allan Bloom. New York: Basic Books, 1762, 1979.

Sartre, Jean-Paul. *Essays in Existentialism*. New York: Citadel, 1993.

Shakespeare, William. *King Lear*. Mineola, NY: Dover, 2011.

Shattuck, Roger. *The Banquet Years*. New York: Vintage, 1968.

Shattuck, Roger. *The Innocent Eye: On Modern Literature and the Arts*. New York: Farrar, Straus and Giroux, 1984.

Short, Robert. *Dada and Surrealism*. Secaucus, NJ: Chartwell Books, 1980.

Stallybrass, Peter, and Allon White. *The Politics and Poetics of Transgression*. Ithaca, NY: Cornell University Press, 1986.

Susman, Warren I. *Culture as History: The Transformation of American Society in the Twentieth Century*. New York: Pantheon, 1984.

Thompson, Robert Farris. *Flash of the Spirit: African & Afro-American Art & Philosophy*. New York: Vintage, 1983.

Tomkins, Calvin. *Duchamp: A Biography*. New York: Owl, 1997.

Tytell, John. *Paradise Outlaws: Remembering the Beats*. New York: William Morrow, 1999.

Witcover, Jules. *The Year the Dream Died: Revisiting 1968 in America*. New York: Warner Books, 1997.

Wolfe, Tom. *The Painted Word*. New York: Farrar, Straus and Giroux, 1975.

Wyndham, John. *The Chrysalids*. London: Penguin Books, 1977.